D1206033

The Mathematics of Derivatives
Securities with Applications
in MATLAB

The Mathematics of Derivatives
Securities with Applications
in MATLAB

Mario Cerrato

A John Wiley & Sons, Ltd., Publication

This edition first published 2012
© John Wiley & Sons, Ltd

Registered office
John Wiley & Sons Ltd, The Atrium, Southern Gate, Chichester, West Sussex, PO19 8SQ, United
Kingdom

Editorial office
John Wiley & Sons Ltd, The Atrium, Southern Gate, Chichester, West Sussex, PO19 8SQ, United
Kingdom

For details of our global editorial offices, for customer services and for information about how to
apply for permission to reuse the copyright material in this book please see our website at
www.wiley.com.

Wiley also publishes its books in a variety of electronic formats and by print-on-demand. Some
content that appears in standard print versions may not be available in other formats. For more
information about Wiley products, visit us at www.wiley.com.

Designations used by companies to distinguish their products are often claimed as trademarks.
All brand names and product names used in this book are trade names, service marks, trademarks
or registered trademarks of their respective owners. The publisher is not associated with any
product or vendor mentioned in this book. This publication is designed to provide accurate and
authoritative information in regard to the subject matter covered. It is sold on the understanding
that the publisher is not engaged in rendering professional services. If professional advice or other
expert assistance is required, the services of a competent professional should be sought.

Library of Congress Cataloging-in-Publication Data

Cerrato, Mario.
   The mathematics of derivatives securities with applications in MATLAB / Mario Cerrato.
      pages cm. – (The Wiley finance series ; 585)
   Includes bibliographical references and index.
   ISBN 978-0470-68369-9
   1. Derivative securities–Statistical methods.   2. Finance–Statistical methods.
3. Probabilities.   4. MATLAB.   I. Title.
   HG6024.A3C3665 2012
   332.64′57015195–dc23

A catalogue record for this book is available from the British Library.

ISBN 9780470683699 (hbk); ISBN 9781119973409 (ebk);
ISBN 9781119973416 (ebk); ISBN 9781119973423 (ebk)

Set in 10/12pt Times by Aptara Inc., New Delhi, India

Printed in Great Britain by TJ International Ltd, Padstow, Cornwall

Contents

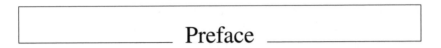

Preface

This book is entirely dedicated to the Lord. 'Love the Lord your God with all your passion and prayer and intelligence. Love others as well as you love yourself.'

Jesus Christ

I was persuaded to write this book because, in my view, the majority of books available in this area are extremely advanced for students who do not possess an excellent mathematical understanding of probability theory and stochastic calculus.

Quantitative finance has become a very popular topic in which an increasing number of students are becoming interested. However, a large number of students are ill-equipped with respect to the mathematical skills required to study this subject. This book is aimed at these students. It also assumes a sufficient understanding of general mathematics and finance, and the objective is to teach students the *fundamentals* of probability theory and stochastic calculus required to study quantitative finance.

The topics covered in this book are presented using both an academic approach (i.e. critically discussing the latest research in the area) and a practitioner's approach (i.e. discussing ways to implement the models practically). Thus, in my view, although the book was initially conceived for MSc/PhD students pursuing quantitative finance programmes, it is now also of use to practitioners.

The book does not attempt to cover in detail proofs of theorems and lemmas unless explicitly considered necessary, as this is not the intended goal. The objective is to use a 'less formal', sometimes 'less rigorous', approach to explain theorems, while focusing on their link with the financial models.

The book is divided into two sections. The first part is a review of the essential concepts in probability theory and stochastic calculus. It therefore does not add to this area but, unlike other books, tries to cover some topics in probability in a way that should be more accessible to those students who do not possess a strong understanding of this area. This part is also instrumental in appreciating the second part of the book. The book starts with key concepts of probability theory, such as the sigma field, and discusses different laws of convergences, using, where possible, an informal but rigorous approach.

The second part of the book discusses financial models. It does not attempt to cover every conceivable model but focuses on the main financial models and discusses ways to implement them practically. It starts discussing the Black and Scholes model and its practical limitations. It then moves on to more advanced models, such as stochastic volatility and interest rate models. These models are always critically discussed, citing the latest research in the area as well as different ways of implementing them in practice.

Generally, the chapters in this book contain MATLAB codes, which will help readers to understand the models better and tailor them to their specific cases. Computer codes are written in a simple way and with plenty of explanations. The idea is to show students and practitioners how financial models can be implemented in MATLAB.

It is still likely that this book will contain errors. I will appreciate comments from readers, which can be sent to mario.cerrato@glasgow.ac.uk.

It is necessary at this point to clarify some of the mathematical notations presented in the book. Generally, if we deal with a random variable Y indexed on, say, $N = 1, 2, \ldots, n$, the random variable is written as Y_n. The same random variable, at time t, indexed on N is written as $Y(t)_n$. Also, in the first part of the book, a Brownian motion process has been denoted by B_n. However, to avoid confusion with the numeraire B_n appearing in the second part of the book, the Brownian motion process will be denoted by W_n.

Finally, I wish to thank my students who have provided feedback on the material covered in this book. Also, I wish to thank John Crosby for his comments and support, Kostantinos Skindilias and Steve Lo for their help on Chapter 13 and Chapter 14 and my family for their love. A special thank you to D'Aponte Giuseppina (my mother).

Mario Cerrato

1
An Introduction to Probability Theory

1.1 THE NOTION OF A SET AND A SAMPLE SPACE

To set up an experiment we, generally, need to define the so-called outcome(s) of the experiment. We expect the outcomes to be distinct and, after collecting them, we obtain what is known as a set. Suppose that ω is a possible outcome from a random experiment, and Ω is a set. We say that $\omega \in \Omega$, in the sense that the outcome belongs to a particular set. To clarify this, consider an example where we have two possible outcomes from a random experiment. Assume we toss a coin. There are now two possible outcomes: heads (ω_1) or tails (ω_2) so that $\{\omega_1, \omega_2\} \in \Omega$.

This set is the sample space. Thus, a set Ω that includes all possible distinct outcomes of an experiment is called a sample set. The inclusion of distinct possible outcomes forces us to introduce the notion of an event. Indeed, since a random experiment can generate several possible outcomes, we may want to consider not just the individual outcome but also combinations of outcomes.[1]

Remark 1.1

If A and Ω are sets, we say that A is a subset of Ω, where every element of A is also contained in Ω. More formally, what we call events are subsets of Ω. Consider two subsets: A and B.

(1) Union $A \cup B$: means A or B, a set of outcomes that are either in A, B or both.
(2) Intersection $A \cap B$: means A and B, a set of outcomes that are in both A and B.
(3) A*: means not A, a set of outcomes in the universal set Ω that are not in A.

---

[1] It therefore follows that an event is a subset of the sample space. We can specify an event by listing all the outcomes that make it up.

1.2   SIGMA ALGEBRAS OR FIELD

An experiment generates a series of outcomes and they all belong to the same universal set Ω. The next step is to assign a probability to each single outcome. However, given the potentially very large dimension of Ω, we are forced to first give it a certain structure. For example, consider a random experiment that can generate values anywhere on the real line. In this case, the probability that any single real number will be realized is zero. Therefore, a structure is needed that can identify which subsets of the outcome space can have probabilities assigned to them. This structure is called sigma algebra. A sigma algebra or field on Ω is a collection of subsets of Ω, say F, satisfying the following conditions:

Proposition 1.1

(1) $\Omega \in$ F.
(2) If $A_i \in$ F for $i = 1, 2, \ldots, n$, the set $\cup A_n \in$ F.
(3) If $A \in$ F then $A^* \in$ F.

Remark 1.2

A sigma field is a nonempty set (1) (i.e. is a field) and is closed under countable unions and intersections.[2] A sigma field provides the most general mathematical notion to formalize an event space.

Sigma algebra can also be interpreted as a 'measure of information'. To understand this, consider certain 'states of the world' all contained in Ω. We do not know which state of the world is the true one, but we do know that the true one is contained in Ω. If we suppose the information we possess is contained in F and use proposition (1), we can reasonably assume that the true state of the world is contained in F.

1.3   PROBABILITY MEASURE AND PROBABILITY SPACE

A function $f(.) : W \to Z$ is a relation where for each element, say $x \in W$, there exists one unique element, say $y \in Z$, such that $(x, y) \in f$. Consider now the (probabilistic) function $P(.)$ satisfying a set of assumptions. Suppose, for simplicity, that it is defined between the real numbers 0 and 1. A probability measure P, on $\{\Omega, F\}$, is a function $P : F \to [0, 1]$ satisfying:[3]

---

[2] Countable means that the set A has the same cardinality as N (the natural numbers). A set that is not countable, for example, is the real numbers R, since this set is more numerous than N.

[3] In other words, what we are doing here is to attach to each element of the subset F a real number from the interval [0,1].

(1) For any event A, $P(A) = 0$ and $P(\Omega) = 1$.

(2) If for a countable sequence of mutually exclusive events $A_1, A_2 \ldots$, then

$$P(\cup_{i=1}^{\infty} A_i) = \sum_{i=1}^{\infty} P(A_i)$$

Remark 1.3

The first assumption (1) is just a matter of convention. According to Kolmogorov,[4] we choose to measure the probability of an event with a number between 0 and 1. Equation (2) is important since we can now attach probabilities to events by using mutually exclusive events. Generally this can be split into two parts: the case, as above, of infinitely many events and the case of finitely many events.

The triple $\{\Omega, F, P\}$ given by a set Ω, a field F of subsets of Ω and a probability measure P on $\{\Omega, F\}$ is called a probability space. The probability space represents the basic mathematical structure used in probability theory to build a model.

Definition 1.1

An event A is called null if $P(A) = 0$. If $P(A) = 1$ we say that A almost certainly occurs.

1.4 MEASURABLE MAPPING

Proposition 1.2

Let us consider a nondecreasing sequence. Let $A_1, A_2 \ldots$ be a nondecreasing sequence of events such that $A_1 \subset A_2 \subset \ldots$; for such a sequence in the limit $\lim_{n \to \infty} A_n = \cup_{n=1}^{\infty} A_n$, and therefore $P(A) = \lim_{n \to \infty} P(A_n)$. Also, consider a nonincreasing sequence. Let $B_1, B_2 \ldots$ be a nonincreasing sequence of events such that $B_3 \subset B_2 \subset \ldots$; for such a sequence in limit we have $\lim_{n \to \infty} B_n = \cap_{n=1}^{\infty} B_n$, and therefore $P(B) = \lim_{n \to \infty} P(B_n)$.

Theorem 1.1

Consider a sequence of events $A_1, A_2 \ldots$ in the event space of interest. For $\{A_n\}_{n=1}^{\infty} \in F$, if $\lim_{n \to \infty} A_n = A \in F$, then $\lim_{n \to \infty} P(A_n) = P(A)$.

---

[4] These axioms were derived by the Russian mathematician A. N. Kolmogorov. One can use these axioms to calculate probabilities.

Remark 1.4

The result is known as continuity properties of a sequence of events. It states that the limit of the probability of a sequence of events converges to that event. Therefore, according to this theorem, we conclude that the limit of a sequence of events is itself an event. How can we justify this?

Proof of Theorem 1.1

We provide a partial proof of Theorem 1.1 where we only consider nondecreasing events.

Let $\{A_n\}_{n=1}^{\infty}$ be nondecreasing, that is $A_1 \subset A_2 \subset A_3 \subset \ldots A_n \subset A_{n+1} \subset A_{n+2} \ldots$ and consider mutually exclusive events

$$(A_{s+1} - A_s) \cap (A_{t+1} - A_t) = 0 \quad \text{for} \quad s \neq t$$
$$P(A_{s+1} - A_s) = P(A_{s+1}) - P(A_s)$$

For simplicity, set $A_0 = 0$ and consider A_n:

$$\lim_{n \to \infty} A_n = \bigcup_{n=1}^{\infty} A_n = A_1 + A_2 + A_3 + \ldots + A_{s+1}$$

Since these are mutually exclusive events and using Proposition 1.2

$$P(\lim_{n \to \infty} A_n) = P(A_1) + P(A_2) + P(A_3) \ldots$$
$$P(\lim_{n \to \infty} A_n) = \lim_{n \to \infty} P(A_n) = P(A)$$

Therefore a sequence of events converges to the event itself (although we have proved convergence from below only, convergence from above, that is assuming nonincreasing sequence, is also needed).

1.5 CUMULATIVE DISTRIBUTION FUNCTIONS

Consider the following sequence of real numbers $\{X_n\}_{n=1}^{\infty}$ each indexed on the natural numbers $N = (1, 2 \ldots n \ldots)$ and, for simplicity, assume that $\{X_n\}$ is nonstochastic. The simplest definition of convergence implies that $\{X_n\}$ will converge to a variable, say X, if, for any arbitrary number, say $\varepsilon > 0$, $|X_n - X| < \varepsilon$ for all $n > N(\varepsilon)$, so that $\lim_{n \to \infty} X_n = X$. Suppose now that $\{X_n\}$ is stochastic and defined on (Ω, F, P), if $P(\lim_{n \to \infty} X_n = X) = 1$, we say that X_n converges almost certainly to X. This is the type of convergence involved in Borel's strong law of large numbers (LLN), and it implies strong convergence. This is often substituted by a weaker form of convergence. This type of convergence is, instead, associated with Bernoulli's result of a weak law of large numbers.[5] In this case X_n converge in probability to X if, for any $\varepsilon > 0$, $\lim_{n \to \infty} P(|X_n - X| < \varepsilon) = 1$.

Remark 1.5

The former form of convergence requires $|X_n - X| \to 0$ as $n \to \infty$. This condition implies that it is virtually guaranteed that the values of X_n approach the value of X as $n \to \infty$. The latter states that if you select a tolerance epsilon and choose an n that is large enough, then the value of X_n will be guaranteed to be within the tolerance of the values of X. Thus, the values that the variable can take (which are not close to X_n) become increasingly restricted as n increases. However, it should be noted that X_n may converge in probability to X, but not with probability one.[6]

1.6   CONVERGENCE IN DISTRIBUTION

Consider a sequence of random variables $\{X_n\}_{n=1}^{\infty}$ and its distribution function[7] $\{\Phi\}$. We say that $X_n \overset{D}{\to} X$ converges in distribution if $\Phi_n(x) \to \Phi(x)$ as $n \to \infty$ for all x for which $\Phi(x)$ is continuous. This means that

$$\lim_{n \to \infty} \Phi_n(x) = \Phi(x) \tag{1.1}$$

The following relationship between different models of convergence (convergence in distribution D, in probability P and almost surely as) and different rates can be established:

$$|X_n \overset{as}{\to} X| \Rightarrow |X_n \overset{P}{\to} X| \Rightarrow |X_n \overset{D}{\to} X|$$

Convergence in distribution (D) is the weakest form of convergence. In fact, this type of convergence is entirely defined in terms of convergence of the distribution but nothing is said about the underlying random variable. As a consequence, one can use this model of convergence even when the random variables are defined on different probability spaces. This would be impossible in the case of convergence in probability P and as.

1.7   RANDOM VARIABLES

As previously discussed, an experiment generates an outcome (for example ω, with $\omega \in \Omega$). The outcome takes the form of a numerical value defined over

---

[5] See Appendix A1.1 for a discussion of Bernoulli's LLN and Borel's result.

[6] The reverse is true, that is if $X_n \overset{as}{\to} X$ then $X_n \overset{P}{\to} X$.

[7] Distribution functions will be discussed in more detail in the following sections.

R such that $X : \Omega \to R$ and we assign a probability to every single outcome.[8] The main problem with this approach is that the outcome set will have so many elements that it would be impossible to arrange them in a sequence so that we can count them. We can overcome this problem by using a sequence of intervals (i.e. a subset of R), for example $\{(-\infty, x)\}$ for any $x \in R$. The set made of all possible subsets of the real numbers R is $B(R)$.[9] Hence the pre-image of the random variable $X(.)$ forms a mapping from the Borel field back to F such that

$$X^{-1}(.) : B(R) \to F$$

This will ensure that the random variable will preserve the structure of F. We can finally assign probabilities to $\{(-\infty, x)\}$ for $x \in R$. Suppose that B_x are elements of $B(R)$; we have

$$P X^{-1}(B_x) = P_x(B)_x \text{ for each } B_x \in B(R)$$

and, assuming that $P(.) : F \to [0, 1]; X^{-1}(.) : B(R) \to F$,

$$P_x(.) = P X^{-1}(.) : B(R) \to [0.1] \tag{1.2}$$

1.8   DISCRETE RANDOM VARIABLES

A random variable X is called discrete if it can take on, at most, a countable infinite number of values $x_1, x_2 \ldots$ of R, and its distribution is specified by assigning probabilities to each one such that $P(x_i) = P_r(X = x_i) > 0$, with $i = 1, 2 \ldots$ and[10] $\sum_i P_r(x_i) = 1$.

For example, consider the number of telephone calls arriving at a corporation's switchboard (say X_i). In this example the random variable has discontinuity at the values $x_1, x_2 \ldots$, and it is constant in between. Such a distribution is called atomic.

1.9   EXAMPLE OF DISCRETE RANDOM VARIABLES: THE BINOMIAL DISTRIBUTION

Suppose that we toss a coin N times, with n being the number of heads, and assume that in each trial the probability of success is P_r and the probability of

---

[8] For example, if we toss a coin we can get two possible outcomes, heads or tails. However, we often want to represent outcomes as numbers. A random variable is a function that associates an outcome to a unique numerical value. The value of this variable will change from one trial to another. Its value can be anything. However, for us it will always be a number.

[9] This is the Borel field.

[10] The probability mass of a random variable. It is the function or formula that gives the value $P_r(X = x_i)$ for each element of x.

failure $1 - P_r$. Using a binomial distribution we have

$$f(n|N) = \binom{N}{n} P_r^n (1 - P_r)^{N-n} \quad \text{with} \quad n = 0, 1, 2, \ldots, N$$

$$\text{where} \binom{N}{n} \text{ is a binomial coefficient } \frac{N!}{(N-n)N!}$$

(1.3)

In this example the random variable X has a binomial distribution that is defined as $X \sim B(N, p)$.

Example 1.1

MATLAB can be used to generate binomial random numbers. Consider a vector of length n: $c = [01011]'$. Generate a matrix (z) whose rows represent all the possible combinations of the elements of c taken $N = 3$ at the time. The MATLAB function nchoosek, $z = \text{nchoosek}(c,N)$; Specify c = [8,10,9,11]; N = 3; $z = \text{nchoosek}(c,N)$. The matrix z contains $N!/(N-n)N!$ rows and N columns of the possible outcomes.

1.10 HYPERGEOMETRIC DISTRIBUTION

In a binomial distribution, we assume that the probability of success (i.e. tossing a coin and getting heads) is constant. This is a consequence of considering independent events (i.e. in each trial, the probability of heads and tails is independent and equal to $1/2$). Suppose instead that we have a finite population of N balls in a box. M balls are red and $N - M$ black. Assume we draw n balls randomly (but no replacement is considered) from the population. What is the probability that p of the n balls are red?

The size of the sample M that we can draw from the population N is $\binom{N}{n}$. Since we want exactly p balls (among n) to be red,[11] we have $\binom{M}{p}$, leaving $\binom{N-M}{n-p}$ ways in which our sample $n - p$ balls are black. If we assume that X is the number of red balls in the sample, then X can be described by a hypergeometric distribution:

$$f(X = p) = \frac{\binom{M}{p}\binom{N-M}{n-p}}{\binom{N}{n}}$$

(1.4)

Example 1.2

Consider, for example, the scenario where there are $N = 1000$ possible clients visiting a bank branch each day. Suppose that $M = 100$ visit the local branch to

---

[11] Remember that M (of the N) balls are red.

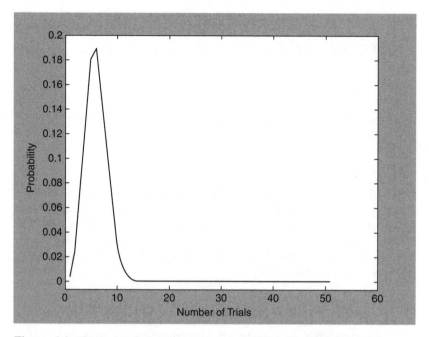

Figure 1.1   Example of a hypergeometric probability distribution function

open a bank account (or any other sort of operation that produces revenue) and 900 $(N - M)$ visit the branch for general enquiries. Suppose we randomly select $n = 50$ clients. What is the distribution of the number of clients visiting the branch in order to open a bank account? The distribution ranges from 0 to 50. Using MATLAB we can calculate the hypergeometric probability distribution function (pdf) for the given scenario. The hypergeometric pdf is obtained using the MATLAB function hygepdf. Thus, using hygepdf(p,N,M,n) given by hygepdf(0:50,1000,100,50) we obtain the distribution shown in Figure 1.1.

1.11   POISSON DISTRIBUTION

There are some events that are 'rare', that is they do not occur often – for example a car accident or the default of senior bond. When the event has a small probability of occurring, we can model it using a Poisson distribution. Suppose that μ is the mean value of X. The Poisson distribution is defined by

$$P(X = x) = \frac{e^{-\mu}\mu^{\lambda}}{\lambda!} \tag{1.5}$$

where λ is called the intensity parameter.

1.12 CONTINUOUS RANDOM VARIABLES

A continuous random variable can take on any real value. The distribution function can be expressed as follows:

$$\Im_x(x) = \int\limits_{-\infty}^{x} f(x)\mathrm{d}x \quad \text{for all } x \in R$$

1.13 UNIFORM DISTRIBUTION

The uniform distribution function is a continuous distribution. Its probability density function takes on a constant probability within a certain interval, say (a, b), and zero otherwise:

$$f(x) = \begin{cases} 1/b - a \\ 0 \end{cases}$$

and the cumulative distribution function (cdf) $\Im_x$ is

$$\Im_x(x) = 0 \quad x < a$$
$$\Im_x(x) = \frac{x - a}{b - a} \quad a < x < b$$
$$\Im_x(x) = 1 \quad b < x$$

Example 1.3

Generate an integer between 1 and n, say 1000, with each of these integers having the same probability. Using the MATLAB function randint(1,n,n)+1, we have obtained the cdf plot shown in Figure 1.2.

1.14 THE NORMAL DISTRIBUTION

The normal distribution is the most widely used distribution in statistics. Its simplicity of treatment makes it very appealing. Assume that X is a continuous random variable with mean μ and variance σ^2. The probability density function (pdf) is given by the following:

$$f(x) = \frac{e^{-(x-\mu)^2/(2\sigma^2)}}{\sigma\sqrt{2\pi}} \tag{1.6}$$

We say that it follows a normal distribution. A special case of the normal distribution arises when we set $\mu = 0$ and $\sigma = 1$. In this special case

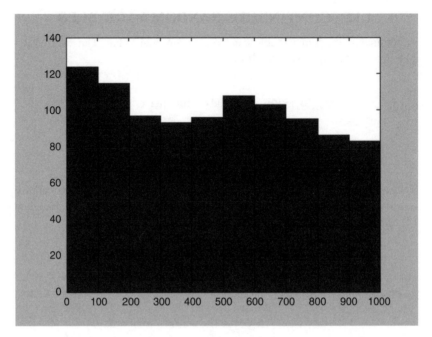

Figure 1.2   Example of the cdf of a uniform random variable

Equation (1.6) becomes

$$f(z) = \frac{e^{-1/2z^2}}{\sqrt{2\pi}} \tag{1.7}$$

We say that the random variable Z follows a standard normal distribution. Therefore, the standard normal distribution is a special case of the normal distribution. Note that an arbitrary normal variable X can be easily transformed into a standard normal variable Z by changing the variable to $Z \equiv (X - \mu)/\sigma$ with $dZ = dX/\sigma$.

Example 1.4

Using MATLAB we generate two stock price sequences. In the first case we assume the stock price to be normally distributed with mean (i.e. expected value) 20% and variance (risk) 70.7%. In the second scenario, we assume the distribution of the stock price process to be standard normal. The MATLAB routines for these two pdfs shown in Figure 1.3 are given by the following:

x=0.2+sqrt(0.707)*randn(100000,1),
with x having mean 0.2 and variance 0.707

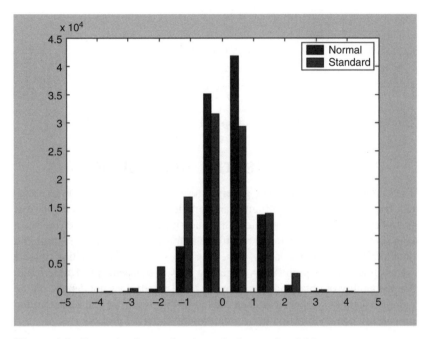

Figure 1.3   Example of normal and standard normal variables

and

x=randn(10000,1), with x being a standard normal variable

1.15   CHANGE OF VARIABLE

Suppose you are interested in the pdf of a random variable after being subject to a transformation. Consider the random variable $Z \sim N(0, 1)$. We know its pdf. However, suppose we want to find the pdf of $\log(Z)$ instead. In this case, we use the so-called change of variable. If $f(z)$ is the pdf of Z, we say that the pdf of $Y = \log(Z)$ is given by

$$f(y) = f(g^{-1}(y))\frac{dz}{dy}$$

The expression in the parentheses is the pdf of Z in terms of Y. To understand the method, consider the following practical example. Consider the random variable $Z \sim N(0, 1)$, with the pdf given by Equation (1.7), and assume we are interested in the pdf of $Y = e^{Z}$. Using log transformations find Z and dZ/dY. Indeed, $Z = \log(Y)$ and $dZ/dY = 1/Y$. Thus, after this transformation, we obtain

$$f(y) = f(\log(y))\frac{1}{y}$$
$$= \frac{1}{\sqrt{2\pi}}e^{-1/2(\log(y))^2}$$

This result shows that the distribution of Y is a lognormal distribution.

1.16   EXPONENTIAL DISTRIBUTION

The exponential distribution is generally used to model the time until a certain event occurs. One important characteristic of this distribution is that it is 'memoryless'. To see this, consider the following example. Suppose you toss a coin starting at time $t_0 = 0$ and record the number of times $t_1, t_2, \ldots$ until you obtain tails. Assume that $x_i = t_i - t_{i-1}$ for $i = 1, 2, \ldots$ is the waiting time. If we assume that the probability of getting tails is independent of time t (i.e. the probability of obtaining tails between t and $t + dt$ does not depend on the number of times we have obtained tails until that time) we can represent the probability density function of the continuous stochastic process x as

$$f(x) = \frac{1}{\beta}e^{-(x-\mu)/\beta} \quad \text{with } x \geq \mu \text{ and } \beta > 0 \tag{1.8}$$

where μ is the location parameter and β is the scale parameter (often set to $\lambda = 1/\beta$). The cumulative distribution function of the exponential distribution is given by

$$\Im(x) = 1 - e^{-x/\beta} \quad \text{with } x \geq 0; \beta > 0$$

1.17   GAMMA DISTRIBUTION

The gamma distribution is a special case of the exponential distribution. If exponential distributions are based on exponential functions, gamma distributions are based on gamma functions. These functions are known to have smaller variances than exponential functions since they have two shape parameters that give greater control over the shape of the distribution.

Suppose that X follows a gamma distribution with parameters r and λ; then the pdf is

$$f(x) = \frac{1}{\Gamma(r)}\lambda^r x^{r-1}e^{-\lambda x} \quad \text{if } x \geq 0, r > 0, \lambda > 0$$
$$f(x) = 0 \qquad\qquad\qquad \text{otherwise} \tag{1.9}$$

Equation (1.9) shows that the gamma distribution is a special case of the exponential distribution when $r = 1$. The scale parameter λ affects the spread of the distribution while r affects the overall shape.[12]

Example 1.5

The MATLAB code for plotting the pdf of a gamma distribution is shown below:

```
%gamma (xmin,xmax,λ,r)
%pdf of a gamma distribution with parameters λ and r > 0,
in the interval (xmin,xmax)

function y=gamma(xmin,xmax,λ,r)
x=[xmin:.1:xmax];
const1=r^λ; const2=gamma(λ);
for i=1:length(x)
y(i)=const1/const2*x(i)^(λ-1)*exp(-x(i)*r);
```

The pdf (on the interval (0:50)) is shown in Figure 1.4 and is constructed for three different values of λ ($\lambda = 1, 2, 3$) using a constant r. It is clear that for $\lambda = 1$ the gamma distribution drops to an exponential distribution.

1.18   MEASURABLE FUNCTION

Generally, we are not interested in random variables but only in certain functions of them. We would also like the function to retain the original structure of the random variable from which it originated. A function f is a rule that associates each element $f(x) \in R$ with each $x \in R$. R is known as the domain of the function

$$f(.) : R \rightarrow [0.1]$$

1.19   CUMULATIVE DISTRIBUTION FUNCTION AND PROBABILITY DENSITY FUNCTION

We have defined a random variable as a probability experiment whose outcomes are numerical values. All the probability information about a certain random variable is captured in the cumulative distribution function (cdf) $\Im_x(x)$. The cdf

---

[12] Note, if X and Y are two gamma functions with a common scale parameter λ then $Z = X + Y$ is also a gamma function with the same scale parameter. Otherwise the shape parameter of Z will be given by the sum of the scale parameters of X and Y.

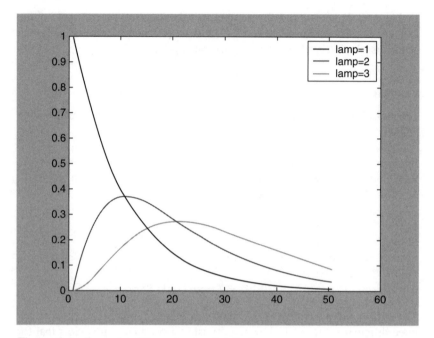

Figure 1.4   Example of three gamma distributions

gives the probability that the random variable X is less than or equal to[13] x. For a continuous random variable, its cdf is given by

$$cdf \equiv P_r(-\infty < X < x) = \int_{-\infty}^{x} f_x(X)dx \equiv \Im_x(x) \tag{1.10}$$

Remark 1.6

A random variable X with a given distribution function is said to have two tails, given by

$$P_r(X > x) = 1 - \Im_x(x) \text{ and } P_r(X < x) = \Im_x(-x)$$

where $x \to \infty$.

---

[13] If X is a discrete random variable and x_i are the values taken by this variable, and if we arrange x_i in ascending order such that $x_1 < x_2 < \ldots x_n$, then the cdf is given by

$$\Im_x(x_i) = P_r(X \leq x_i)$$

or

$$P_r(X > x_i) \equiv 1 - \Im_x(x_i) \quad \text{and} \quad P_r(x_{i-1} < X < x_i) \equiv \Im_{x_1}(x_i) - \Im_{x_{i-1}}(x_{i-1})$$

We can recover the cdf from the pdf.

Example 1.6

Consider this simple example with the discrete random variable X having the following probability distribution $P_r(x_i)$:

x_i	0	1	2	3	4	5
$P_r(x_i)$	1/32	5/32	10/32	10/32	5/32	1/32

The cumulative distribution function is given by

x_i	0	1	2	3	4	5
$P_r(x_l)$	1/32	6/32	16/32	26/32	31/32	32/32

Remark 1.7

Therefore the cdf is zero at the beginning of the sample and one at the end. It is an increasing (right-hand-side) function (see Proposition 1.3). However, why is the cdf so important? Firstly, it is very easy to find the probability of a random variable given its cdf. In this case, we can avoid solving integrals. Secondly, probability density functions (pdfs) are easy to create given cdfs. Indeed, we only need to differentiate the cdf.

Proposition 1.3

If $\Im_x(x)$ is the cumulative distribution function of X, it follows that:

(1) $\lim_{x \to -\infty} \Im_x(x) = 0$, $\lim_{x \to \infty} \Im_x(x) = 1$.
(2) $\Im_x$ is right continuous, i.e. $\Im_x(x + dx) \to \Im_x(x)$ as $dx \to 0$.
(3) if $x < y$ then $\Im_x(x) \leq \Im_y(y)$ for any x, y real numbers.

Remark 1.8

Proposition 1.3 shows that the cumulative distribution function integrates to 1. Condition (2) ensures that the cumulative distribution function is continuous (increasing) and differentiable. This condition ensures the existence of a density.[14] Condition (3) is relevant when considering discrete random variables (see also footnote 16).

A different way to look at the probability information contained in a random variable is to use the probability density function (pdf). A pdf shows the probability that a continuous random variable X takes on a value between $\{(-\infty, x)\}$. In a more formal way, if $\Im_x(x)$ is a cumulative distribution

---

[14] After all, as we shall see, a density function can be obtained by differentiating the cdf. Proposition (1.3 (2)) ensures that the cdf is differentiable.

function, then

$$\Im_x(x) = \int_{-\infty}^{x} f_x(x)dx \quad \text{where } f_x(x) \geq 0$$

Thus $f_x(x) \geq 0$ means that a probability density does not always exist. In general, a probability distribution has a density if its cumulative distribution function is absolutely continuous. In this case it is differentiable everywhere and its derivative can be used as a probability density. In this case $f_x(.)$ is the pdf that corresponds to $\Im_x(.)$

Proposition 1.4

If $\Im_x(x)$ is the cumulative distribution function of X and $\Im_x(x) = \int_{-\infty}^{x} f_x(x)dx$, then the density function of X is such that

(1) $f_x(x) \geq 0$ for all $x \in R$.
(2) $\int_{-\infty}^{x} f_x(x)dx = 1$.
(3) $\Im_x(b) - \Im_x(a) = \int_{a}^{b} f_x(x)dx$.

Remark 1.9

Proposition 1.4 (1) and 1.4 (2) are the same as for the cdf. Proposition 1.4 (3) states that we can always calculate the probability that a random variable is between the real numbers a, b by simply calculating the area under the probability density function.

Example 1.7

Suppose that X is a random variable with the cdf given by

$$\Im_x(x) = 0, x < 0$$
$$\Im_x(x) = \frac{x^3}{8}, 0 \leq x \leq 2$$
$$\Im_x(x) = 1, x \geq 2$$

Use the cdf to create $f_x(x)$. If we differentiate the cdf we obtain

$$f_x(x) = \frac{d\Im_x(x)}{dx} = \frac{3x^2}{8}$$

Thus, using the result above gives

$$f_x(x) = \frac{3x^2}{8}, 0 \leq x \leq 2 \quad \text{and} \quad f_x(x) = 0, \text{ otherwise.}$$

Assume now that we are interested in the probability, P_r, such that $P_r(1 \leq X \leq 3)$. Using the cdf, we solve $\Im(3) - \Im(1)$, rather than solving

$$\int_{1}^{3} \frac{3x^2}{8} dx$$

Thus, we get

$$P_r(1 \leq X \leq 3) = \Im(3) - \Im(1) = \frac{27}{8} - \frac{1}{8} = \frac{26}{8}$$

1.20   JOINT, CONDITIONAL AND MARGINAL DISTRIBUTIONS

Suppose that X and Y are two random variables from an experiment and that X takes the value x and Y takes the value y. We can consider (X, Y) as a random variable taking on values $(x \times y)$.[15] There exists a relation between the distribution of (X, Y) and the distribution of X and Y. The former is called joint distribution, the latter is the marginal distribution.

Consider the joint density function of X and Y, $f(X, Y)$. We say that (X, Y) has a bivariate distribution. Its joint cumulative distribution is

$$\Im(x, y) = \int_{c}^{d} \int_{a}^{b} f(x, y) dx dy \qquad (1.11)$$

Remark 1.10

With discrete random variables, we can specify $\Im(x, y) = P_r(X \leq x, Y \leq y)$ and the joint cumulative distribution shows the probability that X generates a number smaller than x and Y a number smaller than y.

Proposition 1.5 states the main properties of cdfs for joint random variables.

Proposition 1.5

If X and Y are random variables defined on the same probability space (Ω, F, P), then the cumulative joint distribution $\Im(x, y)$ has the following properties:

(a) $0 \leq \Im(x, y) \leq 1$ for all x, y;
(b) if $x > c \rightarrow \Im(x, y) \geq \Im(c, y)$ and if $y > c \rightarrow \Im(x, y) \geq \Im(x, c)$;

---

[15] Note that you can also consider X as being defined over the interval $[a, b]$ and Y on $[c, d]$, provided that the pair (x, y) is inside the rectangle $a \leq x \leq b$ and $c \leq y \leq d$.

(c) $\Im(\infty, \infty) = 1$;

(d) $\Im(-\infty, -\infty) = 0$.

Remark 1.11

Proposition 1.5 (a) states that probabilities are between 0 and 1. Proposition 1.5 (b) states that the cdf cannot decrease if we increase the value of a variable.[16] The intuition behind 1.5 (c) is very simple. The probability that $x \leq \infty$ and $y \leq \infty$ is 1. Proposition 1.5 (d) is a consequence of 1.5 (c), i.e. the probability that $x \leq -\infty$ and $y \leq -\infty$ is zero.

As in the case of a single random variable, we can also construct pdfs for joint random variables:

$$f(x, y) = \frac{d\Im(x, y)}{dxdy} \tag{1.12}$$

The marginal density function is

$$f(.) = \int_{-\infty}^{x} f(x, y)dx \tag{1.13}$$

Assume that we are interested in the conditional density of X given $Y = y$. In this case, using (1.13), we have

$$f(x|Y = y) = \int_{-\infty}^{x} f(x|Y = y)f(y)dy \tag{1.14}$$

Remark 1.12

$f(x, y)$ contains all the information needed on X and Y. However, sometimes we need the pdf of one variable given the joint pdf. In this case we are interested in the so-called conditional density, given the marginal density (i.e. pdf) of one of them.

Example 1.8

Consider two continuous random variables x and y having joint pdf $f(x, y) = 1$, for $0 \leq x \leq 1$ and $0 \leq y \leq 1$. Calculate the marginal pdf of x and y. Using

---

[16] To understand this, consider the case of discrete random variables and assume the following cdfs: $\Im(10, 10) \geq \Im(5, 10)$. From the first cdf we conclude that $x, y \geq 10$ but from the second we have that $y \geq 10$ while $x < 10$.

(1.13), we have

$$f(x) = \int_{y=0}^{1} dy \text{ and } f(y) = \int_{x=0}^{1} dx$$

Thus, the marginal pdf of x and y is equal to 1.

1.21   EXPECTED VALUES OF RANDOM VARIABLES AND MOMENTS OF A DISTRIBUTION

For random variables, in general, moments completely specify their distributions. These, in fact, provide all the information needed in a random variable. For example, if x is a continuous random variable, the mean of x can be defined by $\mu_x = E(x)$. However, this expression does not always exist. In fact, it can be shown that it does not exist if $E(x) = \int_{-\infty}^{\infty} x f(x) dx$ is not convergent.

Example 1.9

Show that, if the distribution of the random variable Z is a standard normal distribution, its mean is equal to zero and its variance is equal to one.

From Equation (1.7), we know that the pdf for a standard normal variable is given by

$$f(z) = \frac{e^{-1/2z^2}}{\sqrt{2\pi}}$$

As for the case of discrete random variables, the mean is given by

$$E(z) = \frac{1}{\sqrt{2\pi}} \int_{-\infty}^{\infty} z e^{-1/2z^2} dz$$

or

$$E(z) = \frac{1}{\sqrt{2\pi}} \int_{a}^{b} z e^{-1/2z^2} dz$$

If the integral above is convergent, its solution is the process. For convergence we expect

$$\lim_{\substack{a \to -\infty \\ b \to \infty}} \frac{1}{\sqrt{2\pi}} \int_{a}^{b} z e^{-1/2z^2} dz < \infty$$

In this particular case, the mean is very simple since we are dealing with an odd function[17] spacing on a symmetric interval and having an odd symmetry. Therefore, since $(a, b) \equiv (-a, a)$, the above limit can be rewritten as

$$\lim_{a \to -\infty} \frac{1}{\sqrt{2\pi}} \int_{-a}^{a} z e^{-1/2z^2} dz = 0$$

The variance can be obtained by extending the results above. Remember that the variance is, broadly speaking, a measure of the dispersion of a certain value of z from its mean $E(Z)$, given by

$$\text{Var}(Z) = \int_{-\infty}^{\infty} [z - E(Z)]^2 f(z) dz$$

Thus, it follows that

$$\text{Var}(Z) = \frac{1}{\sqrt{2\pi}} \int_{-\infty}^{\infty} z^2 e^{-z^2/2} dz - [E(Z)]^2$$

We now integrate by parts.[18] If we set $v = z \to dv = dz$ and $u = -e^{-z^2/2}$, it follows that

$$\text{Var}(Z) = \frac{1}{\sqrt{2\pi}} e^{-z^2/2} z]_{-\infty}^{\infty} + \frac{1}{\sqrt{2\pi}} \int_{-\infty}^{\infty} e^{-z^2/2} dz$$

The second part of the equation above is simply $\int_{-\infty}^{\infty} f(z) dz$, which integrates to one. The first term is zero. In fact, this is an odd function on a symmetric interval.

APPENDIX A1.1   THE BERNOULLI LAW OF LARGE NUMBERS

Bernoulli's law of large numbers (LLN) is one of the most important results in probability theory. To understand it, suppose you toss a coin seven times and consider the following sequence of heads (H) and tails (T): {T,H,T,H,H,H,H}. What is the probability that in the next toss we get tails (T)? Looking at the sequence of events one would say that the probability is greater for heads (H). The intuition is that after many tosses the number of tails and heads will be more or less equal. However, the problem with this intuition is that we are

---

[17] If $A(x)$ is a function such that $A(-x) = -A(x)$, we say that $A(x)$ is an odd function.

[18] Note you can either apply the integration by part rule twice or simply assume $z^2 = z^* z$.

assuming that coins have a memory while this is not the case. This example introduces the idea behind Bernoulli's LLN.

In a more formal way, consider a sequence of n independently distributed random variables:

$$\{X_n = 1\} = \{H\}, \{X_n = 0\} = \{T\}, P_r\{X_n = 1\} = P_r\{X_k = 0\} = \frac{1}{2}$$

$$\text{for } n = 1, 2 \ldots$$

The Bernoulli LLN states that

$$\lim_{n \to \infty} P_r \left(\left| \frac{1}{n} \sum_{i=1}^{n} X_i - \frac{1}{2} \right| < \varepsilon \right) = 1 \text{ for any } \varepsilon > 0 \tag{A1.1}$$

Proof

We provide a simple proof of the Bernoulli LLN. The proof requires the assumption that Chebyshev's inequality is satisfied. Assume that $\{X_n\}$ is a sequence of independent identically distributed random variables having finite expectation, that is $E[X_n] = X$. It follows that

$$P_r \left\{ \left(\frac{X_1 + X_2 + \ldots + X_n}{n} \right) - X > \varepsilon \right\} \to 0 \text{ as } n \to \infty \text{ for any } \varepsilon > 0$$

Suppose that $S_n = X_1 + X_2 + \ldots + X_n$ and the variance is $\text{Var}(X)$. It follows that, using partial sums and Chebyshev's inequality, we obtain

$$\lim_{n \to \infty} [P_r(S_n) > z] \leq \frac{n \, \text{Var}(X)}{z^2} \quad \text{for} \quad z = n\varepsilon \tag{A1.2}$$

since as $n \to \infty$ the right-hand side of (A1.2) approaches zero. It follows that

$$\lim_{n \to \infty} P_r[S(n) > n\varepsilon] \to 0$$

$$\lim_{n \to \infty} P_r \left[\frac{S(n)}{n} - X \right] > \varepsilon \to 0$$

Equation (A1.1) is satisfied.

Another important law in probability theory is the so-called Borel LLN. Assume that S_n is the partial sum of the process. We say that the Borel LLN is satisfied if

$$P_r \left(\lim_{n \to \infty} \left[\frac{1}{n} \sum_{i=1}^{n} X_i(s) \right] = \frac{1}{2} \right) = 1 \tag{A1.3}$$

where we attach a probability to the set of elements $s \in S$ such that

$$\sum_{i=1}^{n} X_i(s) \to \frac{1}{2} \text{ as } n \to \infty$$

Note the difference in convergence in (A1.2) and (A1.3). In (A1.2) we have a convergence in terms of probabilities, while (A1.3) involves convergence of $\sum_{i=1}^{n} X_i(s)$. Therefore if we repeat the experiment (i.e. toss a coin), the proportion (i.e. s) of times that any events occur is approximately equal to the probability of the event's occurrence on any particular trial (i.e. $^1/_2$); the larger the number of repetitions, the better the approximation tends to be.

APPENDIX A1.2   CONDITIONAL EXPECTATIONS

Consider the continuous random variable Y and its sigma algebra, say $\sigma(Y)$, and suppose that

$$E(X|Y) = E(X|\sigma(Y)) \tag{A1.4}$$

We call (A1.4) the conditional expectation of X given the information on the random variable Y. It is obvious that, in this case, $\sigma(Y)$ does not carry more information than Y.

Remark A1.1

Simply, we can say that $E(X) = E(E(X|\sigma(Y))) = X$. This result will be clear later after discussing the rules for conditional expectations. Now you should note that by this definition, in effect, the random variable X seems to be a kind of average value of the conditional expectation $E(X|\sigma(Y))$.

Some important rules of conditional expectations are given below.

Rule A1.1

If $E|X| < \infty$, then the conditional expectation $E(X|Y)$ exists and it is unique.

Remark A1.2

Rule A1.1 states that if you consider a random variable X and its sigma algebra $\sigma(X)$ and suppose that $\sigma \in \sigma_1$, and if it is the case that $E|X| < \infty$, then it must be true that $prob(Z \neq Z') = 0$. Here the random variable Z' generates the sigma algebra σ_1.

Rule A1.2

The conditional expectation is linear. Therefore, if a_1, a_2 are positive constants then $E[(a_1 X_1 + a_2 X_2)|\sigma(Y)] = a_1 E(X_1|\sigma(Y)) + a_2 E(X_2|\sigma(Y))$.

Remark A1.3

This property is self-explanatory.

Rule A1.3

The expectation $E(X)$ and $E(E(X|Y))$ are the same.

Remark A1.4

Rule A1.3 requires independence of X and Y. This is not difficult to obtain since a conditional expectation must be true if X does not carry more information than Y or, in other words, $\sigma(X) \in \sigma(Y)$.

Rule A1.4

If $X \in \sigma$ and $\sigma(Y)$ generates X, then $E(X|Y) = X$.

Remark A1.5

This is a direct consequence of Rule A1.3. If $\sigma(Y)$ contains all the information on the variable X, then we may consider the latter as a constant. The best example to clarify that would be $E(1|\sigma(Y)) = 1$.

Rule A1.5

If $\sigma_1 \in \sigma_2$, then $E(X|\sigma_1) = E(E(X|\sigma_2))|\sigma_1)$ and also we have that

$$E(X|\sigma_1) = E(E(X|\sigma_1))|\sigma_2).$$

Remark A1.6

Rule A1.5 is self-explanatory and is a consequence of Rule A1.4.

2
Stochastic Processes

2.1 STOCHASTIC PROCESSES

Stochastic processes arise naturally in many applications in finance, for example when dealing with asset prices.

Definition 2.1

Let (Ω, F, P) be a probability triple, and assume that t is an interval on the real line such that $t = [0, T]$. We say that a family z of stochastic processes is a mapping process X, such that $X_t : \omega \to X(\omega, t) : \Omega \to R^z$.

Remark 2.1

Note the analogy with the definition of a random variable. These are both mapping processes! Indeed, a stochastic process, broadly speaking, is a sequence of random variables.

Definition 2.2

A process $(X = \{X_n : n \in Z\}, Z^+ := \{0, 1, 2, 3 \ldots\})$ defined over (Ω, F, P) is said to be adapted if, for each $n \in Z$, the random variable X_n is measurable with respect to F_n.

Remark 2.2

From Definition 2.2 we define a filtration as a family of sigma algebras. A stochastic process is a sequence of random variables. We know (see Chapter 1) that a random variable is a mapping process from the Borel field back to F such that it preserves the structure of F. In this case the process F_n is an increasing and independent sequence of sigma algebras containing all the information on X_n up to time t_n.

This result is very useful in many practical applications. For example, in finance we generally assume that past and present values of asset prices are known to investors and that they use this information to formulate their expectations when trading.

2.2 MARTINGALES PROCESSES

Definition 2.3

Suppose that (Ω, F, P) is a probability space with filtration $\{F_n\}_{n\geq 0}$ under F and let X_n be a stochastic process under (Ω, F, P). This process is said to be martingale if:

(a) X_n is adapted to the filtration $\{F_n\}_{n\geq 0}$;
(b) $E|X| < \infty$;
(c) $E[X_n|F_{n-1}] = X_{n-1}$.

Remark 2.3

The assumption in (c) is typical of martingale processes. It states that given the whole history of X up to $n-1$, the best predictor of X_n is X_{n-1}. The assumption in (b) (integrability assumption) is a technical assumption. One interesting issue about this assumption is that, although a martingale process has an unbounded variance, nevertheless the integrability condition is imposed. We shall clarify this issue in Lemma 2.1.

A supermartingale process is such that $E[X_n|F_{n-1}] \leq X_{n-1}$ and the submartingale process is $E[X_n|F_{n-1}] \geq X_{n-1}$. Thus, a supermartingale resembles a martingale except that the conditional expectations of future values can now be less than the current value. It therefore follows that all martingales are also supermartingales, but the opposite is not true. Submartingales are processes where $-X$ is a supermartingale.

Note that if X_n is a martingale then each component is a martingale and we can write:

(i) $E(X_0) = E(X_1) = \ldots = E(X_n)$
(ii) The sum of two martingales is a martingale.

Theorem 2.1   The optional stopping theorem

If X is a martingale and Γ is a stopping time, then X is a martingale and $E(X_{\Gamma \wedge n}) = E(X_0)$. If X is a supermartingale and Γ is a stopping time, then $E(X_{\Gamma \wedge n}) \leq E(X_0)$.

Lemma 2.1

Suppose that X is a martingale process and Γ a stopping time; it follows that:

(a) $\Pr(\Gamma < \infty) = 1$;
(b) $E[X_{\Gamma \wedge n}] < \infty$;
(c) there exists a positive constant $k < \infty$ such that $|X_n(\omega) - X_{n-1}(\omega)| \leq k$.

Remark 2.4

Conditions (a) and (b) simply remind us that a gambler has a finite lifetime, and therefore the amount of money he or she can make is itself finite. These two conditions are important for Theorem 2.1 to hold. In fact, if $T = \infty$, it follows that, for each n, although $E(X_{\Gamma \wedge n}) = E(X_0)$ in the limit, $E(X_{\Gamma \wedge n}) \neq E(X_0) = 0$. Condition (c) suggests that the 'winning process' is bounded upwards.

Remark 2.5

A simple example may help to further clarify Remark 2.4. Suppose you are a gambler and you have available an infinite amount of money to play a game. Suppose that the game consists in tossing a coin and winning £1 if the outcome is heads, otherwise you lose £1. Suppose also that you have an infinite lifetime. If the coin is fair, it follows that the winning process is a martingale. However, the process has an unbounded variance in this case, and therefore the integrability condition will not hold. Suppose now that your lifetime is finite. You can introduce this by introducing stopping times. In this case the winning process is still a martingale but now the integrability condition will hold.

Example 2.1   The optional stopping theorem

This section follows Rogers and William (2000). The optional stopping theorem and Lemma 2.1 play an important part in the context of martingale theory. To understand the implications of this theorem consider the following example. Assume that X is a martingale and Γ is a stopping time. Suppose that your initial stake is X_0. Also suppose that you bet \$1 on each game n and that $X_n - X_{n-1}$ is your fortune between one game and the other. Suppose that you keep betting \$1 in each game and you stop your game at Γ. Define by $C^{\Gamma}(\omega)$ the realization of your process (given the state of the world ω). It follows that

$$C_n^{\Gamma}(\omega) = I_{(n \leq \Gamma)} \quad \text{with } C_n^{\Gamma}(\omega) = 1 \text{ if } n \leq \Gamma(\omega) \quad \text{and} \quad C_n^{\Gamma}(\omega) = 0$$

Thus, for each n, your state is given by $(C^{\Gamma *}X)_n = X_{\Gamma \wedge n} - X_0$.

This should be intuitive since the state of the process (in each game) is the difference between your fortune in that particular game and your initial fortune. By specifying $X_{\Gamma \wedge n}$ we are simply posing a limit upon our game (note that the lifetime of our gambler can be as large as ∞). Indeed, in our case, our gambler has to have a finite lifetime.

If X^{Γ} is the process X stopped at Γ, defined by $X_n^{\Gamma}(\omega) = X_{\Gamma(\omega) \wedge n}(\omega)$, then we have

$$C^{\Gamma *}X = X^{\Gamma} - X_0 \tag{2.1}$$

Taking the expectations we have $E(X_{\Gamma \wedge n}) = E(X_0)$.

This shows that the realization of the process C^Γ is bounded (i.e. it is equal to 1) and nonnegative, and it is perfectly predictable since C_n^Γ can only be zero or one. Secondly, it does not matter how good your strategy for stopping the game is, the martingale strategy remains the best strategy (under reasonable hypothesis) since the process $X^\Gamma(\omega)$ is a martingale process. It follows that the amount of money a gambler with a finite life would expect to have when he or she decides to stop the game is (on average) the same amount as the initial one.

Lemma 2.2

If X is a supermartingale on (Ω, F, P) and Θ_n is a predictable nondecreasing process such that $\Theta_0 = 0$, since Θ_n is unique, $\{X_n + \Theta_n\}_{n>0}$ is a supermartingale.

   If X is a submartingale on (Ω, F, P) and Θ_n is a predictable nondecreasing process and that $\Theta_0 = 0$, then, since Θ_n is unique, $\{X_n - \Theta_n\}_{n>0}$ is a submartingale.

Remark 2.6

Lemma 2.2 plays an important role in finance. Suppose that the value of a contingent claim (a stock option), say Z_n, is such that $Z_n = \max(X_n - K)e^{-rdt}$, where r is the risk-free rate of interest, X_n the stock price process and K the strike price. We know that this process is a martingale (we shall show this in the chapters to follow). Suppose that Θ_n is a predictable nondecreasing process and that $\Theta_0 = 0$ (this might be, for example, cash). Suppose that V_n is the value of a portfolio consisting of a long-position on Z_n and a short-position on Θ, that is $V_n = Z_n - \Theta_n$. This portfolio can be perfectly hedged (since V_n turns out to be a martingale) in each period by trading stocks and bonds.

Definition 2.4   Local martingale

A process Y is said to be a local martingale if Y_0 is F_0 measurable and there exists an increasing sequence of stopping times Γ_n such that at each stopped point the process $Y_{\Gamma_{n \wedge t}} - Y_0 : t \geq 0$ is a martingale.

Remark 2.7

Local martingales are very important as these are martingales at each stopping time and therefore satisfy all the conditions in Definition 2.3 including the integrability condition.

Definition 2.5   Semi-martingale

Suppose that X is a martingale and (Ω, F, P) a probability space. We say that the process X is a semi-martingale if it can be written as

$$X = X_0 + Y + A \tag{2.2}$$

where Y is a local martingale and A is a process with finite variance.

Remark 2.8

We shall discuss these processes further in Chapter 3 when we introduce Ito's calculus. At this stage it is sufficient to know that a semi-martingale process is a sum of a martingale and a path of finite variation.

2.3   BROWNIAN MOTIONS

Definition 2.6

A real-valued stochastic process $B(t)$ is a Brownian motion if:

(a) $B(0) = 0$, $\forall \omega$;
(b) it is a continuous process;
(c) for $0 \leq t_0 \leq t_1 \leq \ldots \leq t_n$, $B(t_1) - B(t_0), \ldots B(t_n) - B(t_{n-1})$ are independent;
(d) for every t, s with $t \neq s$, $B(t) - B(s)$ is independent and normally distributed with zero mean and variance $t - s$.

Remark 2.9

Definition 2.6 above completely specifies a Brownian motion process. It follows that a Brownian motion process is a Markov process, in the sense that the probability distribution of the future values of the process only depends on the current value of the process. A Brownian motion is characterized by independent increments. It follows that the probability distribution of changes in the process in a time interval is independent from that in a different time interval (nonoverlapping). Finally, each increment of a Brownian motion process is normally distributed with mean zero and variance $t - s$. Thus, the variance increases linearly with time. It is important to stress again that, from the definition above, by construction a Brownian motion process has no memory. In Example 2.2 below we provide a proof of (d) and (c) given in Definition 2.6.

Example 2.2

We build our proof of (d) and (c) on Nielsen (1999). Suppose that $B(t)$ is a Brownian motion. It follows that the process

$$B^*(t) = t B(1/t) \quad \text{if } t > 0$$

with

$$B^*(t) = 0 \quad \text{if } t = 0$$

is also a Brownian motion with variance $t - s$ (d), with $0 < s < t$, and uncorrelated consecutive increments (c).

We can write the increments of the process as

$$B^*(t) - B^*(s) = t B(1/t) - s B(1/s)$$

Thus, it follows that

$$B^*(t) - B^*(s) = (t)^2(1/t) - (s)^2(1/s)$$
$$B^*(t) - B^*(s) = t - s$$

Consider now nonoverlapping consecutive increments $0 \le t_1 \le t_2 < t_3$. Using the result above, we have

$$t_3 - t_1 = \text{var}(B^*(t_3) - (B^*(t_2)) + \text{var}(B^*(t_2) - (B^*(t_1)) + 2\text{Cov}(.)$$
$$t_3 - t_1 = (t_3) - (t_2) + ((t_2) - (t_1)) + 2\text{Cov}(.) = 0$$

Example 2.3

As an example of Brownian motion, Figure 2.1 shows three different paths of Brownian motion with drift. These have been generated using the MATLAB routine in Appendix A2.1.

Proposition 2.1   Brownian motions as random walks processes

Let $B(t)$ be a Brownian motion process and define by $M_n = \sum_{j=1}^{n} X_j$ a sequence of independent random walk processes, with steps $X_j(\omega) = 1$ if the state of the world is, for example, heads and $X_j(\omega) = -1$ if it is tails; then

$$B^j(t) = \frac{1}{\sqrt{n}} M_n$$

Remark 2.10

Proposition 2.1 states that a Brownian motion process can also be viewed as the limit of random walks processes.

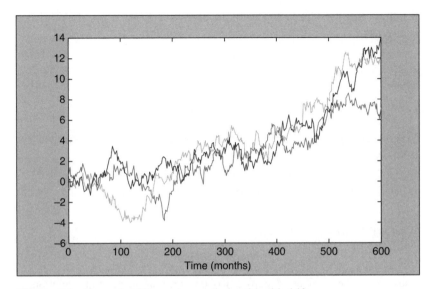

Figure 2.1 Example of Brownian motion paths with drift

Theorem 2.2   The central limit theorem

To understand fully the construction of a Brownian motion process, we first need to introduce an important theorem, the central limit theorem.

Let $X_1, X_2 \ldots, X_n$ be a sequence of independent identically distributed random variables with mean μ and variance σ^2 and let $M_n = X_1 + X_2 + \ldots + X_n$. It follows that

$$\frac{M_n - n\mu}{\sqrt{n\sigma^2}} \tag{2.3}$$

The process in (2.3) converges in distribution to a normal variable $N(.,.)$ as $n \to \infty$, with $M_0 = 0$. If $\mu = 0$ and $\sigma^2 = 1$, then

$$\frac{M_n}{\sqrt{n}} \tag{2.4}$$

and the process in (2.4) converges in distribution to a standard normal variable $N(0,1)$ as $n \to \infty$, with $M_0 = 0$.

Example 2.4

Consider tossing a coin and suppose that

$$X(\omega) = 1 \text{ if } \omega \text{ is heads with probability } p$$
$$X(\omega) = 0 \text{ if } \omega \text{ is tails with probability } q = 1 - p$$

It follows that the expected value of the process is $E(X) = p$ and its variance is given by

$$\text{Var}(X) = E(X)^2 - [E(X)]^2 = pq$$

where

$$E(X)^2 = p$$

Now, suppose you toss the coin n times, assuming that each toss is independent from the other, what is the expected value of this fair game?

$$E(M_n) = \sum_{j=1}^{n} np \tag{2.5}$$

What is the variance in this case?

$$\text{Var}(M_n) = npq \tag{2.6}$$

Thus, since the number of steps (n) is proportional to the time duration, it follows that the variance increases linearly with the time. Suppose now that we split the time interval t into n subintervals each of equal length $dt = 1/n$ with $\lim_{n \to \infty} 1/n = 0$. Assume that the process M_n has stationary, independent increments[1] and $p = q$. If $B_n(t)$ is the state of your fortune at t, it follows that

$$B_n(t) = \frac{M_n}{\sqrt{n}} \to N(.,.) \text{ as } n \to \infty \tag{2.7}$$

Thus, after many plays the probability distribution of the event will resemble a Gaussian distribution. Note that here we rescaled the time interval by a factor n and the stake by a factor $\sqrt{n}$. The process above satisfies Definition 2.3 and therefore $B(t)$ is a Brownian motion process.

2.4   BROWNIAN MOTION AND THE REFLECTION PRINCIPLE

Proposition 2.2

Consider a Brownian motion $B(t)$. $B(t)$ is continuous with probability one, but it is nowhere differentiable.

Remark 2.11

The proof is in Rogers and Williams (2000).

---

[1] This condition is necessary to characterize the process M_n as a symmetric random walk.

Proposition 2.3

Consider a Brownian motion $B(t)$ that starts at $B(0) = 0$ and define a stopping time Γ_a, with $a > 0$, as the first time the Brownian motion hits a. The hitting time is defined as

$$\Gamma_a = \inf t > 0 : B(t) = a$$

Therefore, if Γ_a is a stopping time by continuity of paths we have

$$\Gamma_a \le t = \{B(s) = a \text{ for some } s, 0 \le s \le t\} \tag{2.8}$$

Remark 2.12

Preposition 2.3 states that the value $B(t)$ assumes at Γ_a is exactly equal to a.

Lemma 2.3   Reflection principle

Let $B(t)$ be a Brownian motion process with stopping time Γ_a, with $a > 0$. Define

$$B(t) = B(t) \qquad \text{if } t < \Gamma_a$$
$$B(t) = 2a - B(t) \quad \text{if } t \ge \Gamma_a$$

It follows that $B(t)$ is also a Brownian motion.

Remark 2.13

The reflection principle states that Brownian motions reflected after they hit a barrier preserve the same motion (distribution) as the original Brownian motion. For example, the probability distribution of $B(t)$ when $\Gamma_a < t$ can be calculated as

$$\Pr(B(t) < a | \Gamma_a \le t) = \Pr(B(t) > a)$$
$$= \Pr(B(t) < a | \Gamma_a \le t) + \Pr(B(t) > a | \Gamma_a \le t)$$

and using the symmetry and continuity principle for Brownian motions we have

$$= \Pr(B(t) > a | \Gamma_a \le t) + P(B(t) > a | \Gamma_a \le t)$$

Thus, it follows that

$$\Pr(B(t) < a | \Gamma_a \le t) = 2P_r(B(t) > a)$$

We can use the reflection principle as an argument to derive the cdf of the hitting time as a random variable:

$$\Pr(\Gamma_a \le t) = \frac{2}{\sqrt{2\pi t}} \int_{a/\sqrt{t}}^{\infty} \exp(-y^2/2)dy \tag{2.9}$$

where we have used the change of variable $y = a/\sqrt{t}$.

One can now differentiate the cdf to obtain the pdf as

$$f_{T_a}(t) = \frac{a}{\sqrt{2\pi}} t^{-3/2} \exp(-a^2/(2t)) \tag{2.10}$$

This result finds application in different areas of finance. For example, barrier options can be modelled using generalizations of this lemma.[2]

Remark 2.14

In the next chapters we shall be using the reflection principle to obtain the price of a barrier option. Thus, it is convenient to introduce briefly the concept of joint distribution of Brownian motions and their maximum. Consider the Brownian motion process defined above and define its maximum as $M(t) = \max_{0 \le s \le t} B(s)$. Suppose that $a \ge 0$ and $a \ge z$. We are interested in the distribution of the joint process $P_r(M(t) \ge a, B(t) \le z)$. We can write it as

$$P_r(M(t) \ge a, B(t) \le z) = P_r(\Gamma_a \le t, 2B(\Gamma_a) - B(t) \le z)$$
$$= P_r(\Gamma_a \le t, B(t) \ge 2a - z)$$

The above result is correct since $M(t) \ge a$ implies $\Gamma_a \ge t$. The second expression follows instead from Lemma 2.3. Furthermore, note that $P_r(M(t) \ge a, B(t) \ge a) = 0$. Thus, it follows that

$$P_r(M(t) \ge a, B(t) \le z) = P_r(B(t) \ge 2a - z)$$
$$= 1 - N\left(\frac{2a - z}{\sqrt{t}}\right)$$

where N is the cumulative normal distribution and the explicit result follows when considering $B(t) \sim N(0, t)$.

---

[2] Other important applications of Lemma 2.3 concern modelling default times and events.

Theorem 2.3   *Martingale representation theorem of Brownian motions*

If $B(t)$ is a Brownian motion process adapted to a filtration $F(t)$ and $X(t)$ is a martingale under $F(t)$, then there exists an $F(t)$ measurable process $\varphi(t)$ such that

$$X(t) - X(0) = \int_0^t \varphi(s)\mathrm{d}B(s) \text{ or } X(t) = X(0) + \int_0^t \varphi(s)\mathrm{d}B(s) \quad 0 \le t \le T$$

Remark 2.15

See Rogers and Williams (2000) or Etheridge (2002) for a proof. The importance of this theorem will become clear in the next chapter when we introduce Ito's processes. Here, we only stress the importance of this theorem in finance.

Note that as a consequence of this theorem the two processes above are adapted to the same filtration. Thus, the path of $X(t)$ is continuous and indistinguishable from that of $B(t)$. In the next chapter we show that we can also write the process for $X(t)$ as $\mathrm{d}X(t) = \varphi(t)\mathrm{d}B(t)$.

Suppose now that the price of a stock (IBM, for example) follows the process described by $B(t)$. If $B(t)$ is the motion for the stock price and $X(t)$ the one for a European option on IBM, then, according to the theorem, we can use IBM stocks to replicate the option. In this case φ will be the units of the IBM shares that we need to trade in order to replicate the option.[3]

2.5   GEOMETRIC BROWNIAN MOTIONS

Proposition 2.4

Suppose that $B(t)$ is a one-dimensional Brownian motion having the form $\exp(B(t))$ and an initial value $B(0)$; then we say that $\exp(B(t))$ is a geometric Brownian motion.

Remark 2.16

We shall see the importance of geometric Brownian motions in the next chapters when we model asset prices.

---

[3] In this example we have been very general. In the next chapter we will formally address this point.

APPENDIX A2.1   AN APPLICATION
OF BROWNIAN MOTIONS

A simple MATLAB code to generate paths of Brownian motions is the following:

```
function b=brownian(T,NSteps,Rep)% generate an
individual path of a BM
dt=T/NSteps; %Replications,NSteps, Time.
e=randn(1,Rep);
b=zeros(1,NSteps);
b0=0; b(1)=b0; %initialize the process
for i=2:NSteps
b(i)=b(i-1)+sqrt(dt)*e(i); %simulated path
end
```

The function is called *Brownian*. The output *b* generates Brownian motions paths. The inputs are time (T), the number of steps in which the time interval is divided (NSteps) and finally the number of Monte Carlo replications (Rep).

The first line of the code splits the time (T) into a given number of intervals (NSteps). The second line uses the MATLAB code randn to generate a random number from a normal distribution. The final line is a vector of zeros, which will contain all the simulated data.

3

Ito Calculus and Ito Integral

3.1 TOTAL VARIATION AND QUADRATIC VARIATION OF DIFFERENTIABLE FUNCTIONS

Suppose that $f(x)$ is a continuous function defined over the interval $[0, T]$ and let $H = \{t_0, t_1, \ldots, t_n\}$ be the partition of the interval, such that

$$0 = t_0 < t_1 < \ldots < t_n = T$$

Define the mesh of the partition:

$$\|H\| = \max_{k=0,1,\ldots,n-1}(t_{k+1} - t_k)$$

The total variation $[V]_T$ on $[0, T]$ is defined by

$$V_T = \lim_{\|H\| \to 0} \sum_{k=0}^{k-1} |f(t_{k+1}) - f(t_k)| \qquad (3.1)$$

Since $f(x)$ is continuous and differentiable the mean value theorem ensures that there is a point $f(t_k^*)$ within $f(t_{k+1}) - f(t_k)$ such that

$$f'(t_k^*)\Delta f(t_k) = f(t_{k+1}) - f(t_k)$$

Thus, it follows that

$$V_T = \lim_{\|H\| \to 0} \sum_{k=0}^{k-1} |f(t_{k+1}) - f(t_k)| f'(t_k^*)$$

$$= \int_0^T f'(t_k^*)dt \qquad (3.2)$$

The total variation of a differentiable continuous function is hence given by

$$V_T = \lim_{dt \to 0} \int_0^T f'(t_k^*)dt = 0$$

Following the same approach the quadratic variation $[V]_T^2$ of $f(.)$ is

$$[V]_T^2 = \lim_{\|H\|\to 0} \sum_{k=0}^{k-1} [f(t_{k=1}) - f(t_k)]^2$$

$$= \int_0^T f'(t_k^*)^2 dt$$

$$[V_T^2] = \lim_{dt\to 0} \int_0^T f'(t_k^*)^2 dt = 0$$

The conclusion is that with differentiable functions total and quadratic variations are zero.

Remark 3.1

The quadratic variation measures the number of up/down movement of the process $f(.)$ within the interval $[0, T]$. Sometimes, it is also called the realized variance. When there is only one local maximum/minimum (i.e. in the example above) the quadratic variation is zero. Is the quadratic variation also zero when $f(.)$ is a Brownian motion?

So far we have assumed that the function $f(.)$ is continuous and differentiable, which means its graph is smooth. We can still think about this type of function. However, try to think of a function that is nowhere differentiable. It is very difficult to imagine this function.

Consider, for simplicity, a Brownian motion path, $B(t, \omega), t \geq 0$, and consider that $f(B(t)).f'(B(t))$ does not exist. Indeed,

$$\lim_{dt\to 0} \text{Var}\left(\frac{B_{t_0+dt} - B_{t_0}}{dt}\right)$$

does not exist. Furthermore, we now have that

$$\lim_{\|H\|\to 0} \sum_{k=0}^{k-1} |f(B_{k+1}) - f(B_k)| = \infty$$

Definition 3.1

A function $f(x)$ is said to have bounded p-variation for some $p > 0$, if:

$$V_T = \lim_{\|H\|\to 0} \sum_{k=0}^{k-1} |f(t_{k+1}) - f(t_k)|^p < \infty \tag{3.3}$$

In general, we indicate the p variation by $[V_T]^p$.

Definition 3.2

The function $f(B(t))$ satisfies Definition 3.1 above for $p > 2$ but not for $p \leq 2$.

Suppose now that we are interested in $\int_t^T f(t) dB(t)$. Paths of $B(t)$ have no derivative, and we also know that

$$B(T) = \lim_{\|H\| \to 0} \sum_{k=0}^{k-1} f(t)[B(t_{k+1}) - B(t_k)] \neq \lim_{dt \to 0} \int_t^T f(t) dB(t) = 0$$

Indeed, convergence of the partial sum to the integral requires f to be differentiable. Furthermore, it also requires the Brownian motion process to have bounded total variation (which we know is not the case). What can we do here?

3.2 QUADRATIC VARIATION OF BROWNIAN MOTIONS

Let us consider the quadratic variation process:

$$[B(T)]^2 = p\lim_{\|H\| \to 0} \sum_{k=0}^{k-1} [B(t_{k+1}) - B(t_k)]^2$$

Firstly, recall that increments of Brownian motions are independent with variance equal to $[B(t_{k+1}) - B(t_k)]^2 = t_{k+1} - t_k$. Also note that $E[B(T)]^2 = T$. Therefore, the limit of the process will converge in the mean square sense to dt. This result implies that the quadratic variation of a Brownian motion can be made equal to zero by a simple adjustment using a time factor:

$$E[B(t_{k+1}) - B(t_k)]^2 - t_{k+1} - t_k = 0$$
$$E([B(T)]^2) - T = 0$$

or, in differential form:

$$dB^2(t) = dt$$

The result above can also be generalized to any bounded continuous martingale.[1] It follows that in the case of Brownian motions, although the total variation is still not zero, the quadratic variation can be made zero by scaling the process by a time factor. This result justifies the application of Ito calculus to Brownian motion processes.[2] The construction of the Ito integral follows from this result. The next sections consider these issues in greater detail.

---

[1] We shall look at this in the following sections.

[2] Note that this represents the limit result of the partial sum in (..).

3.3   THE CONSTRUCTION OF THE ITO INTEGRAL

Suppose that $B(t)$ is a Brownian motion process adapted to the filtration $F(t)$ and $\varphi_n(t)_{i=1}^n$ is measurable in $F(t)$ with $\varphi(t)$ being square integrable in the sense that $\int_0^t \varphi_n^2(t)dt < \infty$. We assume that $\varphi_n(t) = \sum_{i=1}^n \varphi_i 1_{I_i}(\omega, t)$. Thus, the indicator function can be conveniently defined as follows. Suppose that s, T, with $s \le T$, are stopping times with $1(\omega, t) = 1$, if $s < t \le T$ and $1(\omega, t) = 0$, otherwise.

Remark 3.2

Note that although we have assumed $t < \infty$, we may well have the case where $T = \infty$. Therefore, we also need the following assumption:

$$\int_0^t 1_s dB_s \equiv H(B_{T \wedge t} - B_{s \wedge t})$$

where $H = 1(s, T)$.

Remark 3.3

We shall discuss applications of the Ito integral in finance in the following sections.

The Ito integral can now be defined as

$$I_n(T) = \int_0^T \varphi_i(t)dB(t) = \sum_{i=0}^n \varphi_i(B(t_{i+1}) - B(t_i)) \qquad (3.4)$$

Remark 3.4

Thus, an Ito integral is defined by a suitable pre-visible stochastic process[3] as an integrand and by the integrator that is a martingale (we shall also see that we can define Ito integrals with respect to semi-martingale integrators).

Remark 3.5

The Ito integral has a very important interpretation in pricing financial derivatives. We shall discuss it further in the next chapters.

---

[3] A pre-visible stochastic process only depends on the information up to the current time but not on any future information.

3.4   PROPERTIES OF THE ITO INTEGRAL

(a) Linearity property

If

$$I_{1n}(T) = \int_0^T \varphi_{1n}(t)dB(t) \quad \text{and} \quad I_{2n}(T) = \int_0^T \varphi_{2n}(t)dB(t)$$

it follows that

$$I_{1n}(T) \pm I_{2n}(T) = \int_0^T (\varphi_{1n} + \varphi_{2n})dB(t)$$

(b) Continuity property

The Ito integral $I(T)$ is continuous with the upper limit T.

(c) Ito isometry

$$I_n^2(T) = E \int_0^T \varphi^2(t)dt$$

(d) Martingale property

$$E I_n(t)/F(s) = E \sum_{i=0}^n \varphi_i (B_{t_{i+1}} - B_{t_i})|F(s) = I_n(s)$$

Lemma 3.1

Proof of the martingale property

Let us first consider the case where $s < t_i < t < t_{i+1}$:

$$E(\varphi_{t_i}(B_{t_{i+1}} - B_{t_i}))|F(s) = E(\varphi_{t_i} E(B_{t_{i+1}} - B_{t_i})|F_{t_i})|F(s) = 0$$

The result is a consequence of the fact that increments of Brownian motion $B_{t_{i+1}} - B_{t_i}$ are independent of F_{t_i}.

Let us now consider the case when $t_i < s < t_{i+1}, s \wedge t$:

$$E(\varphi_{t_i}(B_{t_{i+1}} - B_{t_i}))|F(s) = \varphi_{t_i}(B_s - B_{t_i})$$

Therefore in general, when $s < t$,

$$E I_n(t)|F(s) = \sum_{i=0}^n \varphi_i (B_s - B_{t_i}) = I_n(s)$$

3.5   THE GENERAL ITO STOCHASTIC INTEGRAL

We now consider the case where the integrand $\varphi(t)$ may not be an elementary process but we still assume that it is square integrable and measurable in $F(t)$. It follows that, for any process $\varphi_n(t)$,

$$\lim_{n \to \infty} E \int_0^T |\varphi_n(t) - \varphi(t)|^2 dt = 0 \tag{3.5}$$

and also that

$$\lim_{n \to \infty} \int_0^T \varphi_n(t) dB(t) = \int_0^T \varphi(t) dB(t) \tag{3.6}$$

To prove (3.6) we need to introduce an important inequality, the Doob squared maximal inequality.

Theorem 3.1

Suppose that $X(t)$ is a continuous martingale process;[4] then

$$E[\sup_{0 \le t \le T} X^p(t)] \le 4E[X^p(T)]$$

and, for $p = 2$,

$$E[\sup_{0 \le t \le T} X^2(t)] \le 4E[X^2(T)]$$

(The proof is in Rogers and Williams, 2000.)

Remark 3.6

Theorem 3.1 provides an upper bound (the right-hand-side part) for the expected maximal variation that the process can reach over an interval. Note that the theorem holds for $p > 1$.

We can now state a proof for Equation (3.6). We assume that

$$\lim_{n \to \infty} E \int_0^T |\varphi_n(t) - \varphi(t)|^2 dt = 0$$

---

[4] This process will be properly defined in the next section.

Rewrite the stochastic integral for simple processes as

$$I(\varphi_n)_T = \int_0^T \varphi_n(t) dB(t)$$

First we check that $\lim_{n \to \infty} \int_0^T \varphi_n(t) dB(t)$ exists.

Consider two simple functions, say $\varphi_n(t)$ and $\varphi_m(t)$, and use Doob's maximal inequality to write

$$E[\sup_{0 \le t \le T} I(\varphi_n)_t - I(\varphi_m)_t]^2 \le 4[E \int_0^T [\varphi_n(t) - \varphi_m(t)]^2 dt \qquad (3.7)$$

where the right-hand side of (3.7) is a consequence of the Ito isometry.

Since $\varphi_n(t)$ and $\varphi_m(t)$ are simple functions, it follows that as $(n, m) \to \infty$, the right-hand side of (3.7) will tend to zero. Thus, the limit exists. Now define the limit:

$$I(\varphi_n)_T = \lim_{n \to \infty} \int_0^T \varphi_n(t) dB(t) = \int_0^T \varphi(t) dB(t) = I(\varphi)_T \qquad (3.8)$$

The result in (3.8) implies that the limit (see the right-hand side of (3.8)) does not depend on the simple approximant process used. As a consequence of (3.8) we have

$$\lim_{n \to \infty} E[I(\varphi_n)]_T^2 = E[I(\varphi)_T^2] \qquad (3.9)$$

The martingale property of the limit above is also preserved. (This proof is left as an exercise.)

3.6 PROPERTIES OF THE GENERAL ITO INTEGRAL

(a) Linearity property

If

$$I_1(T) = \int_0^T \varphi_1(t) dB(t) \quad \text{and} \quad I_2(T) = \int_0^T \varphi_2(t) dB(t)$$

it follows that

$$I_1(T) \pm I_2(T) = \int_0^T (\varphi_1 + \varphi_2) dB(t)$$

(b) Continuity property

The Ito integral $I(T)$ is continuous with the upper limit T.

(c) Ito isometry

$$I^2(T) = E \int_0^T \varphi^2(t) \, dt$$

(d) Martingale property

3.7 CONSTRUCTION OF THE ITO INTEGRAL WITH RESPECT TO SEMI-MARTINGALE INTEGRATORS

Define by μ^c the space of continuous local martingales such that $X \in \mu^c$. Suppose that $S(n), T(n)$, with $S \le T$, are stopping times, with $n \in N$ $\{S_i : i = 1, 2, \ldots, n\}$ and $\{T_i : i = 1, 2, \ldots, n\}$. We consider the case where $T(n) = \inf\{t : [X] > n\}$. Under this assumption $X^{T(n)}$ is a martingale and in particular we have that $\mu_c = \mu_c^2$,[5] where μ_c^2 denotes the space of continuous L^2 martingales.

Remark 3.7

Note that in this case we obtain a martingale with bounded variation. We shall now define a semi-martingale process using the canonical decomposition of continuous semi-martingales.[6]

Consider the continuous martingale process defined above and suppose that the process $M(t)$ can be written as

$$M(t) = M(0) + X(t) + A(t) \tag{3.10}$$

where $A(t)$ is a process with paths of finite variation and $M(0)$ is a martingale vanishing at zero.

The process $M(t)$ is called a semi-martingale process. A semi-martingale can be decomposed into a martingale process and a process of finite variation. Suppose now that $H(t)$ is a general integrand, such that $\int_0^t H^2(s) \, ds < \infty$. We can then rewrite Equation (3.10) as

$$H(t)M(t) = H(t)X(t) + H(t)A(t)$$

---

[5] See Rogers and Williams (2000) for more details.

[6] Note that since the semi-martingale process we are considering is continuous it has a unique decomposition.

or in integral form as

$$\int\limits_0^t H(s)dM(s) = \int\limits_0^t H(s)dX(s) + \int\limits_0^t H(s)dA(s) \qquad (3.11)$$

The first term on the right-hand side of the equation is the Ito integral. The second term is the Stieltjes integral, and this is well defined. Thus, we can prove the existence of $\int_0^t H(s)dM(s)$ if we prove the existence of $\int_0^t H(s)dX(s)$.

Remark 3.8

At this point, intuitively there should be no problem to admit the existence of the integral in (3.11) since X has finite variation. However, Theorem 3.2 below should contribute to clarification of the issue in a more rigorous manner.

Theorem 3.2

Let $X(t)$ be a continuous martingale, such that $X \in \mu^c$, and $H(t)$ a pre-visible process. It follows that

$$E \int\limits_0^t (H^2(s))d[X]_s < \infty \qquad (3.12)$$

Note that $[X]$ is the quadratic variation process associated with X.[7]

Proof

We know that $X(t)$ is a continuous martingale process, with finite variation. Consider the stopping times $s(n)$ and $T(n)$, with $s \leq T$. For any two stopping times we have

$$E[(X_{T(n)} - X_{s(n)})^2]|F_{S(n)} = E[(X_{T(n)}^2 - X_{s(n)}^2)]|F_{s(n)}$$
$$= E[([X]_{T(n)} - [X]_{s(n)})]|F_{s(n)}$$
$$d[X]_{s(n)} < \infty$$

Since H is a pre-visible process, it follows that

$$E[(H^*X)_s^2] = \int\limits_0^t H^2(s)d[X]_s < \infty$$

---

[7] This is necessary to avoid confusion with the previous notations we have used.

Thus, $\int_0^t H(s)dM(s)$ is an integrable function and is a local martingale itself. This result also shows another important aspect of the Ito integral.

Definition 3.3

Let μ_c^2 be the space of L^2 bounded martingales X such that $X \in \mu_c^2$; then the Ito integral $\int_0^t H(s)dM(s)$ is the image of H under the extension of the isometry condition to the $L^2(X)$ space:

$$E(H^*M)^2 = E \int\limits_0^t H^2(s)d[M]_s$$

Remark 3.9

This result is the consequence of the structure imposed on the integrand and integrator. Indeed, we have been less stringent on the martingale integrability condition by imposing a local integrability.

3.8 QUADRATIC VARIATION OF A GENERAL BOUNDED MARTINGALE

We now consider again the quadratic variation and assume a generalization of the previous case when we have two semi-martingales, M_1 and M_2. Write the Ito integral as

$$I(s) = \int\limits_0^t M_1(s)dM_2(s)$$

Remark 3.10

Note that now the integrand and the integrator are semi-martingales.

Let us consider, for simplicity, its discrete version:

$$I_s = \sum M_{1k-1}(M_{2k} - M_{2k-1}) \tag{3.13}$$

Applying the summation by parts to (3.13), we obtain

$$M_{1s}M_{2s} - M_{10}M_{20} = \sum_{k=1}^s M_{1k-1}(M_{2k} - M_{2k-1}) + \sum_{k=1}^s M_{2k-1}(M_{1k} - M_{1k-1})$$

$$+ \sum_{k=1}^s (M_{1k} - M_{1k-1})(M_{2k} - M_{2k-1}) \tag{3.14}$$

Thus, in a similar way as with (3.14), we obtain the so-called integration by parts formula for semi-martingales. We state this result below.

Definition 3.4

Suppose that X, Y are two semi-martingale processes. The integration by parts formula is given by

$$X(t)Y(t) - X(0)Y(0) = \int_0^t X(s)\mathrm{d}Y(s) + \int_0^t Y(s)\mathrm{d}X(s) + \int_0^t \mathrm{d}X(s)\mathrm{d}Y(s)$$

$$(3.15)$$

As it stands, Equation (3.15) does not tell us much. It is therefore convenient to rewrite it in a slightly different way:[8]

$$M_{1s}M_{2s} - M_{10}M_{20} = \sum_{k=1}^{s} M_{1k-1}(M_{2k} - M_{2k-1}) + \sum_{k=1}^{s} M_{2k-1}(M_{1k} - M_{1k-1})$$

$$+ \sum_{k=1}^{s} \Delta M_{1k} \Delta M_{2k} \qquad (3.16)$$

The terms in the parentheses on the right-hand side are martingales differences. It follows that Equation (3.16) reduces to

$$M_{1s}M_{2s} - M_{10}M_{20} = \sum_{k=1}^{s} \Delta M_{1s} \Delta M_{2s}$$

Set

$$\sum_{k=1}^{s} \Delta M_{1s} \Delta M_{2s} = [M_1, M_2]_s$$
$$M_{1s}M_{2s} - M_{10}M_{20} = [M_1, M_2]_s$$

We now obtain the following martingale process:

$$I_s = (M_{1s}M_{2s} - [M_1, M_2]_s) - M_{10}M_{20} \qquad (3.17)$$

Remark 3.11

Note that the quantity in the brackets above is the co-variation of a continuous martingale process defined as $[M_1, M_2] \equiv 1/4[M_1 + M_2] - [M_1 - M_2]$.

At this point it would be interesting to consider the case where the martingales M_1 and M_2 are standard Brownian motions (i.e. $M_1 = M_2 = B$).

---

[8] Again for simplicity we consider its discrete version.

3.8.1 Quadratic variation of a general bounded martingale

Suppose now that $M_1 = M_2 = B$. Thus, Equation (3.17) becomes

$$I(s) = \sum B_{k-1}(B_k - B_{k-1})$$

Using the integration by parts, in exactly the same way as we did above, we obtain

$$B^2(s) - B^2(0) = \sum_{k=1}^{s} B_{k-1}(B_k - B_{k-1}) + \sum_{k=1}^{s} B_{k-1}(B_k - B_{k-1})$$
$$+ \sum_{k=1}^{s} (B_k - B_{k-1})(B_k - B_{k-1})$$

After some algebra we have

$$B^2(s) - B^2(0) = 2 \sum_{k=1}^{s} B_{k-1}B_k - 2 \sum_{k=1}^{s} B_{k-1}^2 + \sum_{k=1}^{s} (B_k - B_{k-1})^2$$
$$B^2(s) - B^2(0) = 2 \sum_{k=1}^{s} B_{k-1}(B_k - B_{k-1}) + \sum_{k=1}^{s} (B_k - B_{k-1})^2 \tag{3.18}$$

Set the last term of Equation (3.18) equal to $[B_k]$ and note that this is the quadratic variation of the Brownian motion process that, for fixed t, $[B]_t^s \to t$:

$$B^2(s) - B^2(0) = 2 \sum_{k=1}^{s} B_{k-1}(B_k - B_{k-1}) + [B_k] \tag{3.19}$$
$$I(s) = \lim_{s \to \infty} \sum_{k=1}^{s} 2B_{k-1}(B_k - B_{k-1}) = (B^2(s) - t) - B^2(0)$$

We obtain the usual result that the Ito integral is a martingale (this proof is left as an exercise):

$$I(s) = \int_0^t 2B(s)\mathrm{d}B(t)$$

Thus, once again the Ito integral can be interpreted as the limit of the partial sum in (3.19).

3.8.2 Ito lemma and Ito formula

The theory above shows that the Ito integral is well defined. If this is the case then we would also like to proceed to some operations on it. The Ito lemma accomplishes this task. The Ito lemma is a direct extension of the

Taylor expansion applied to stochastic processes. We start with an example of the Taylor rule to deterministic functions. Suppose the function $f(t)$ is twice differentiable and consider evaluating it over the interval $[t, t + dt]$. Using the Taylor rule, we have

$$f(t, t + dt) = f(t) + f'(t)dt + \frac{1}{2}f''(t)(dt)^2 + O(dt)^3 \qquad (3.20)$$

Obviously the last terms in Equation (3.20) will drop to zero very quickly by $dt \to 0$, so we can use a simple tangent approximation. Suppose now that we consider a function such as $f(B(t))$. Using the same approach as the one above, we have

$$f(B(t), B_{t+\Delta t}) = f(B(t)) + f'(B_t)dB(t) + \frac{1}{2}f''(B_t)(dB(t))^2 + \ldots \qquad (3.21)$$

Since $dB^2(t) = dt$, it follows that the quadratic term in (3.21) cannot be dropped. In fact, the contribution of this term to evaluate $f(B(t))$ is not negligible. We can now rewrite (3.21) in its integral form for $s < t$:

$$\int_0^t df(B(s)) = f(B(t)) - f(B(s)) = \int_0^t f'(B(s))dB(s) + \frac{1}{2}\int_0^t f''(B(s))ds$$

$$(3.22)$$

An interpretation of the integral in (3.22) is now necessary. We are already familiar with the integral on the left-hand side of (3.22). This is the Ito integral. We know that it is a suitable limit. The second integral is the so-called Riemann integral of $f''(B)$, which is also well defined. The formula described in (3.22) is the Ito formula, which we will use frequently in the next chapters. Now we will show a few applications of the Ito lemma.

Example 3.1

Consider the following stochastic process:

$$f(t, B(t)) = e^{(a-0.5\sigma^2)t+\sigma B(t)}$$

where $a, \sigma > 0$. Use the Ito lemma to find

$$f(t, B(t)) - f(0, B(0)) = \int_0^t f(s, B(s))ds$$

We first compute the first- and second-order derivatives:[9]

$$f'_t = f(t, B(t))(a - 0.5\sigma^2), \quad f'_B = f(t, B(t))\sigma, \quad f''_B = f(t, B(t))\sigma^2$$

Replacing these derivatives in the Ito formula above, we obtain

$$\int_0^t f(s, B(s))ds = (a - 0.5\sigma^2) \int_0^t f(s, B(s))ds + \sigma \int_0^t f(s, B(s))dB(s)$$

$$+ \frac{1}{2}\sigma^2 \int_0^t f(s, B(s))dB^2(s)$$

$$\int_0^t f(s, B(s))ds = (a - 0.5\sigma^2 + 0.5\sigma^2) \int_0^t f(s, B(s))ds + \sigma \int_0^t f(s, B(s))dB(s)$$

$$\int_0^t f(s, B(s))ds = a \int_0^t f(s, B(s))ds + \sigma \int_0^t f(s, B(s))dB(s)$$

If we set $f(s, B(s))a = A_1$ and $f(s, B(s))\sigma = A_2$, we have

$$\int_0^t f(s, B(s))ds = \int_0^t A_{1s}ds + \int_0^t A_{2s}dB(s) \tag{3.23}$$

Equation (3.23) describes an Ito process. In general, any stochastic process satisfying (3.23) is an Ito process.[10]

Example 3.2

Consider the stochastic process $f(t, X(t))$, where $X(t)$ satisfies

$$X(t) = X(0) + \int_0^t A_1(s)ds + \int_0^t A_2(s)dB(s)$$

Find

$$\int_0^t f(t, X(t))dX(t)$$

---

[9] Lower case indicates derivatives.

[10] Therefore the geometric Brownian motion considered at the beginning is an Ito process.

First let us work out the derivatives:

$$f_t'(t, X(t)) = \int_0^t f(s, X(s))ds$$

$$f_X' = \int_0^t A_1(s)f_y'ds + \int_0^t A_2(s)f_y'dB(s)$$

$$f_X'' = \int_0^t A_1^2(s)ds^2 + \int_0^t A_2^2(s)dB^2(s) = \int_0^t A_2^2(s)f_y''ds$$

Thus, it follows that

$$\int_0^t f(t, X(t))dX(t) = \int_0^t f(s, X(s))ds + \int_0^t A_1(s)f_y'ds + \int_0^t A_2(s)f_y'dB(s)$$

$$+ \frac{1}{2}\int_0^t (A_2(s))^2 f_y'ds$$

$$\int_0^t f(t, X(t))dX(t) = \int_0^t \left[f(s, X(s)) + A_1(s)f_y' + \frac{1}{2}(A_2(s))^2 f_y' \right] ds$$

$$+ \int_0^t A_2(s)f_y'dB(s)$$

APPENDIX A3.1   THE RIEMANN–STIELJES INTEGRAL

Define the following partition $0 = t_0 < t_1 < \ldots < t_n = T$ and consider the integral

$$\int_0^T f(t)dB(t) \tag{A3.1}$$

where $f(t)$ is a deterministic function, say, for example, $f(t) = \sigma$. As in Section 3.4, consider the mesh $\|H\|$ and write

$$\int_0^T f(t)dB(t) = \lim_{\|H\| \to 0} \sum_{k=0}^{k-1} f(t_k^*)[B(t_{k+1}) - B(t_k)] \tag{A3.2}$$

The mean value theorem justifies, in this case, the convergence of the partial sums above to the integral, regardless of the position of $f(t_k^*)$ within the interval $t_k \leq t_k^* \leq t_{k+1}$. The sum above is known as the Riemann–Stieljes sum and the integral as the Riemann–Stieljes integral. This result has noticeable implications. Suppose the stock price $S(t)$ follows the process

$$dS(t) = \mu dt + \sigma dB(t) \tag{A3.3}$$

By integrating we obtain

$$\int_0^T dS(t) = \mu \int_0^T dt + \sigma \int_0^T dB(t)$$

Its solution is given by

$$S(T) = S(0) + \mu T + \sigma B(T) \tag{A3.4}$$

What happens if $f(t) = S(t)\sigma$, as it is when stock prices are driven by geometric Brownian motion? As we shall see, the choice of the position of $f(t_k^*)$ is an important matter now. To see this, consider first the following integral:

$$\int_0^T B(t) dB(t), \quad \text{with } f(t) = B(t) \tag{A3.5}$$

Let us take partial sums at the edge of the interval $t_k \leq t_k^* \leq t_{k+1}$:

$$I_1 = \sum_{k=0}^{k-1} B(t_k)[B(t_{k+1}) - B(t_k)] \tag{A3.6}$$

$$I_2 = \sum_{k=0}^{k-1} B(t_{k+1})[B(t_{k+1}) - B(t_k)] \tag{A3.7}$$

Taking the expectations of their difference we have

$$E[I_2 - I_1] = T$$

with the variance given by

$$\text{Var}[I_2 - I_1] = T^2 - T^2 = 0$$

The expectation above depends on T. This result implies that the convergence of the partial sums to the integral crucially depends on the choice of $f(t_k^*)$ in $t_k \leq t_k^* \leq t_{k+1}$. We can construct a variety of possible integrals by choosing the position of $f(t_k^*)$.

The Ito integral discussed in this chapter chooses $t_k^* = t_k$, and therefore

$$I = \sum_{k=0}^{k-1} f(t_k)[B(t_{k+1}) - B(t_k)] = \int_0^T f(t)\mathrm{d}B(t)$$

The function $f(t_k)$ is said to be nonanticipating. This integral, as already discussed, can also have an intuitive meaning in finance as opposed to other integrals, since choosing $f(t_{k+1})$ might be more difficult to justify practically.

4

The Black and Scholes Economy

4.1 INTRODUCTION

In this chapter we shall introduce some key theorems such as the fundamental theorem of asset pricing, the Girsanov theorem and trading strategies.

4.2 TRADING STRATEGIES AND MARTINGALE PROCESSES

We start with the following assumptions.

Assumption 4.1

Suppose there are $d + 1$ assets in the market with prices given by the vector $(s_t^0, s_t^1, \ldots, s_t^d)'$, with $s_t^0 = 1$ (i.e. \$1 invested at the risk-free rate is what we call the numeraire). Trading dates are indexed by $t = 1, 2, \ldots, T$, with T finite but large.

Assumption 4.2

Suppose that the process $\{s_t\}_{t=1}^T$ is adapted to $\{F_t\}_{t=1}^T$.

We also need the following definitions.

Definition 4.1

A trading strategy $\phi_t = (\phi_1^0, \phi_2^1, \ldots, \phi_3^d)_{t=1}^T$ is a vector of predictable events (i.e. measurable under F_{t-1}).

Definition 4.2

The probability space (Ω, F, P), the filtration $\{F_t\}_{t=1}^T$ and $(s_t^0, s_t^1, \ldots, s_t^d)'$ form what we call the market model Π.

Definition 4.3

The portfolio value in t is defined by $\{s_t^i \phi_t^i\}_{i=1}^d$ or also $v_t(\phi) = \sum_{i=1}^d \phi_t^i s_t^i$.

Definition 4.4

We say that the market is viable (arbitrage-free) if, given $\phi_{1t} = (\phi_t^0, \phi_t^1, \ldots, \phi_t^d)$ and $\phi_{2t} = (\phi_t^0, \phi_t^1, \ldots, \phi_t^d)$, we have $v_{1t}(\phi) = v_{2t}(\phi)$ for all t.

Definition 4.5

We define a numeraire as an increasing stochastic process $s_t^0 = (s_t^0; t = 0, 1, \ldots, T)$, with $s^0 = \$1$. This is defined as the time t value of \$1 invested at a risk-free rate today.[1] One property of a numeraire is its invariance. Note that in the next sections we shall assume $s_t^* = s_t/s_0$.

Definition 4.6

A trading strategy is self-financing if $\phi_{t-1} s_{t-1} = \phi_t s_t$.

Definition 4.7

A portfolio is self-financing if $V_t(\phi) = V_0(\phi) + \sum_{j=1}^t \phi_j \Delta s_t$.

4.3   THE FUNDAMENTAL THEOREM OF ASSET PRICING

We are now ready to introduce the following important theorem.

Theorem 4.1   The fundamental theorem of asset pricing (FTAP)

The market model is viable if, and only if, there is a probability measure Q equivalent to the physical measure P such that the discounted asset price is a martingale under Q.

Remark 4.1

In a binomial model the equivalent martingale measure (EMM) is the consequence of the 'nonarbitrage argument'. Firstly, to what extent does this property apply to other market models? Secondly, if Q exists, is the market then 'viable'? The answers to these questions were only given in 1999 by Elliott and Kopp.

---

[1] We shall define this in the next section as B_t; therefore $s_t^* = (B_t^{-1} s_t^1, B_t^{-1} s_t^2, \ldots, B_t^{-1} s_t^d)$.

Remark 4.2

The existence of EMM Q ensures that the discounted asset price is a martingale process (and therefore the market is viable). We shall see the importance of this result when pricing derivatives.

Proof of Theorem 4.1

We proceed as follows. We assume that such a probability measure exists and that under Q the market is viable. In this case $s_t^{i*} = s_t^{1*}, s_t^{2*}, \ldots, s_t^{d*}$ is a martingale under Q. Therefore, by the martingale transform (see Lemma 4.1), the portfolio process should also be a martingale under Q.

We use an intuitive simple approach to prove this theorem. Assume that Q exists and the process s_t^{i*} is a martingale. As a consequence the market model is viable. First note that under a self-financing strategy the value of a portfolio is given by

$$v_t^*(\phi) = v_0^*(\phi) + \sum_{j=1}^{t} \phi_j \Delta s_j^*$$

Using Lemma 2.2 in Chapter 2, $v_t^*(\phi)$ is a martingale and $E^Q(v_T^*(\phi)) = E^Q(v_0^*(\phi))$ (this proof is left as an exercise).

Lemma 4.1

A probability measure Q on (Ω, F) is a martingale measure for the market model Π if it is also a martingale measure for the spot price process s_t^*.

To understand Lemma 4.1, define by $G_t^*(\phi)$ the cumulative discount gain under the self-financing trading strategy $\phi = (\phi_t^1, \phi_t^2, \ldots, \phi_t^d)$:

$$G_t^* = \sum_{j=1}^{t} \left(\phi_j^1 \Delta s_j^{*1} + \phi_j^2 \Delta s_j^{*2}, \ldots, \phi_j^d \Delta s_j^{*d} \right) \tag{4.1}$$

Suppose that $E^Q(G_t^*)$ exists; then it must be true that if $v_t^*(\phi)$, $\phi = (\phi_t^1, \phi_t^2, \ldots, \phi_t^d)$ is a martingale

$$E^Q(G_t^*) = E^Q \left(\sum_{j=1}^{t} (\phi_j \Delta s_j^*) \right) = 0 \tag{4.2}$$

Thus, for any trading strategy (ϕ), we have that $E^Q(G_t^*) = 0$ and the market is viable. Consequently, the existence of a martingale measure, Q, and of a viable market are the conditions for a market to be arbitrage free.

Note that, given the invariance of the numeraire, one could reach the same conclusion using a different numeraire. Therefore, changing the numeraire has no implications for the model.

Remark 4.3

The theorem above suggests that if there is a martingale, Q, the market model is viable and therefore it is arbitrage free. We should distinguish between building a mathematical model and using it for risk management purposes. It is clear that for a risk management purpose one should be projecting cash flows under P rather than Q.

4.4   MARTINGALE MEASURES

As we shall see, one important consequence of the FTAP is that if the market is arbitrage free (i.e. there is a martingale Q), the value of a contingent claim (for example an option) should be equal to the cost of the trading strategy used to replicate the claim itself. Contingent claims can therefore be priced by discounting their expected cash flows (under Q) at the risk-free rate of interest. Note that this implies that we can always find a portfolio $v_t(\phi)$ that can be used to replicate a contingent claim. Indeed, one can prove that if Q exists such a portfolio also exists and its cost is the price of the option.

Note that if Q is an equivalent martingale measure with respect to P, it is true that, for $\omega \in F$, $P(\omega) = Q(\omega) = 0$. In this case P and Q belong to the same null set and consequently $Q \sim P$. In short, this means that if an event happens under P, it will also happen under Q. We shall now consider the implications of this result. We first consider discrete time processes and then we extend the result to continuous time processes.

Consider the market model Π and the measure Q, and let X be an F_T cash flow paid by a contingent claim. Define by $\phi(t)$ a self-financing trading strategy such that[2] $V_T(\phi) = X$. Define a bank account numeraire[3] B_t. Furthermore, suppose that the value of a discounted contingent claim (say a call option) is $C_T(X)$.

We know that the discounted portfolio value is given by

$$V_t^*(\phi) = E^Q(V_T^*(\phi)|F_t), \quad t = 0, 1, \dots, T \tag{4.3}$$

---

[2] This means that given the self-financing trading strategy, we can find a portfolio that will replicate the contingent claim.

[3] Refer to Section 4.5 for details. To avoid confusion in notations, note that in the next sections B is the numeraire bond and not a Brownian motion process, which we will identify in this chapter by $W(t)$.

with V_T^* being a Q martingale, $V_0^*(\phi) = E^Q(V_T^*(\phi)) = E^Q(B_T^{-1}X)$. Thus, in general,

$$V_t^*(\phi) = E^Q(B_T^{-1}X|F_t)$$

Note that since $V_t^*(\phi) = V_t(\phi)B_t^{-1}$, it follows that

$$V_t(\phi)B_t^{-1} = E^Q(B_T^{-1}X|F_t)$$
$$V_t(\phi) = B_t E^Q(B_T^{-1}X|F_t)$$

Because the cost of the portfolio above must be exactly equal to the price of the contingent claim, it follows that under the self-financing trading strategy the value of the call option is

$$C_T(X) = B_t E^Q(B_T^{-1}X|F_t) \tag{4.4}$$

Thus, an investor selling this option at time t for $V_t(\phi)$ can follow the strategy ϕ_t to replicate the claim at time T.

Remark 4.4

The result above has been obtained on discrete time. However, we shall see in the next sections that such a result can also be extended to continuous time processes. The Girsanov theorem is the starting point.

4.5   GIRSANOV THEOREM

In this section we generalize the result obtained above to processes that are continuous. The Girsanov theorem is probably one of the most interesting theorems in mathematical finance in recent years.

Theorem 4.2

Let $W(t)$ be a standard Brownian motion on $0 \leq t \leq T$ and define the following probability space (Ω, F, P). Suppose that $\gamma(t)$ is a stochastic process and that the following condition holds, $\int_0^t \gamma^2(u)du < \infty$. Define the following processes:

$$W^Q(t) = \int_0^t \gamma(u)du + W^P(t)$$

$$\phi(t) = \exp - \left(\int_0^t \gamma(u)dW^P(u) - \frac{1}{2}\int_0^t \gamma^2(u)du \right) \tag{4.5}$$

The probability measure Q is defined as

$$Q = \int_F \phi(t)\mathrm{d}P$$

Under the new measure Q, the process W^Q is a martingale.

Remark 4.5

This result is remarkable. We start with an initial Brownian motion defined on the physical measure P and using 4.5 we construct another Brownian motion, which is now defined on a new measure Q. The latter is the measure that is equivalent to the original physical measure. Thus, the main results we obtained in the previous sections will also hold in this case (i.e. when dealing with continuous time processes).

Proof of Theorem 4.2

The proof of this theorem consists in showing that under the new measure Q, the process W^Q is a martingale. Consider the original Brownian motion W^P and note that it is normally distributed with mean equal to zero and variance equal to t.

Define the density of this process as

$$f(W^P(t)) = \frac{1}{\sqrt{2\pi t}}e^{-1/2(W^P(t)/t)^2}$$

The goal is to change this Brownian motion process into another one defined over the measure Q. Define the following stochastic process under the original measure:

$$\phi(t) = \exp\left[\int_0^t \gamma(u)\mathrm{d}W^P(u) - \frac{1}{2}\int_0^t \gamma^2(u)\mathrm{d}u\right] \qquad (4.6)$$

This process is a martingale. Specifically, it is an exponential martingale. However, let us prove it. Apply the Ito lemma to the process $\phi(t)$:

$$\mathrm{d}\phi(t) = \frac{\partial \phi(t)}{\partial W(t)}\mathrm{d}W^P(t) + \frac{1}{2}\frac{\partial^2 \phi(t)}{\partial W(t)^2}\mathrm{d}W(t)^{P^2} \qquad (4.7)$$

Let us start with the first-order derivative in (4.7):

$$
\frac{\partial \phi(t)}{\partial W(t)^p} = \left[\frac{\partial}{\partial W(t)^p} \int_0^t \gamma(u) dW(u)^p \right] \exp\left[\int_0^t \gamma(u) dW(u)^p - \frac{1}{2} \int_0^t \gamma(u)^2 du \right]
$$

$$
= \phi(t) \frac{\partial}{\partial W(u)} \int_0^t \gamma(u) dW(u)^p
$$

$$
= \phi(t)\gamma(t)
$$

Consequently, the second-order derivative in (4.7) is equal to zero.

Substituting this result into (4.6) and integrating gives

$$
\int_0^t d\phi(u) = \int_0^t \phi(u)\gamma(u) dW(u)^p \tag{4.8}
$$

Note that the right-hand side of (4.8) at t is $\phi(t)\gamma(t)W^P(t)$. It follows that if we consider the expectations on both sides we obtain the martingale process:

$$
E^P(d\phi(t)) = 0
$$

or, for $s < t$,

$$
E^P(\phi(t)) = \phi(s)
$$

After using the martingale process $\phi(t)$, we can define a new Brownian motion on the measure Q. The key to achieve this goal is $\phi(t)$. The lemma below completes the proof of Theorem 4.2.

Lemma 4.2

The process W^Q is a martingale under the new probability measure Q (this proof is left as an exercise).

Remark 4.6

Note that after the transformation above the density of the process W^Q is given by

$$
f(W^Q(t)) = \frac{1}{\sqrt{2\pi t}} e^{-1/2(W^Q - \phi/t)^2} \tag{4.9}
$$

This suggests that the difference between the two densities under the initial measure is given by the drift in (4.9). To be more precise, we can calculate this drift since it has an explicit solution:

$$\frac{dQ(W)}{dP(W)} = \phi(W) \tag{4.10}$$

The expression in (4.10) is known as the Radon–Nikodym derivative. We shall come back to it in the following sections.

4.6   RISK-NEUTRAL MEASURES

We define the usual probability space (Ω, F, P) and assume that the variable $B(t) = \exp[\int_0^t r(u)du]$ is adapted to this space. Here r is the risk-free rate of interest. Suppose that a zero coupon bond pays \$1 at maturity and that its value at t is written as $B^{-1}(t) = D(t) = -\exp[\int_0^t r(u)du].$[4]

Consider a geometric Brownian motion driving the stock price process $S(t)$:

$$dS(t) = u(t)S(t)dt + \sigma(t)S(t)dW(t) \tag{4.11}$$

where $u(t)$ is the rate of growth of the stock price, $\sigma(t)$ the stock price volatility and $dW(t)$ are increments of a Brownian motion process. Given the process in (4.11), the objective is to obtain an expression for the discounted stock price process, $Z(t) = Z(S(t)D(t))$. Let us apply the product rule for the Ito lemma to get

$$dZ(t) = D(t)dS(t) + dD(t)S(t) + dS(t)dD(t)$$

Thus, after some algebra manipulation we obtain

$$dZ(t) = \sigma(t)D(t)S(t)\left[\frac{u(t) - r(t)}{\sigma(t)}dt + dW(t)\right] \tag{4.12}$$

Define the following process:

$$\phi(t) = \frac{u(t) - r(t)}{\sigma(t)}$$

(this is called the market price of risk). It follows that

$$dZ(t) = \sigma(t)D(t)S(t)\left[\phi(t)dt + dW(t)\right] \tag{4.13}$$

Equations (4.12) and (4.13) show that the discounted stock price grows at a rate that is equal to the expected rate of growth of the stock and the risk-free rate of interest. Thus, investors investing in risky assets will seek compensation for risk.

If we were able to estimate the market price of risk, we could replace it in (4.12) and (4.13) and the final process will be a martingale. However, the

---

[4] Note that since the interest rate is assumed to be deterministic, the numeraire is the money market account; see also Chapter 5.

estimation of the market price of risk turns out to be very difficult in practice. The Girsanov change of measure helps us at this point. To understand how, define the following process:

$$W^Q(t) = \int_0^t \phi(u)du + W(t) \tag{4.14}$$

If we replace (4.14) into (4.13), we obtain (in a differential form)

$$dZ(t) = \sigma(t)D(t)S(t)dW^Q(t) \tag{4.15}$$

Clearly now $Z(t)$ is a martingale (under Q). Thus, a shift from the initial measure to the new measure Q induces a change of the drift in (4.13) and under this change of drift the new process is a martingale. This is the risk-neutral measure.[5] If we consider a contingent claim with the payoff given by X, written on $Z(t)$, the value of this claim can be written as the expected value of its payoff at expiry, namely $C(t, Z(t)) = E^Q[X(T)|F(t)]$.

To obtain the original process under the martingale Q, substitute (4.14) into (4.11), and after some algebraic manipulation we obtain

$$dS(t) = r(t)S(t)dt + S(t)dW^Q(t) \tag{4.16}$$

Remark 4.7

This process is not a martingale. However, note that, in this case, the rate of growth of the stock price is no longer u but the risk-free rate.[6] This is an important result since practically u is unknown and is to be estimated. This rather obvious result shows that the rate of growth of the stock price under the martingale Q is just the risk-free rate of interest. In this case, investors no longer require 'extra return' to hold the stock. Of course, this suggests that there are no market frictions; that is the market is arbitrage free.

These examples show an important point. We can start with an initial probability measure, work with the discounted stock price process and use the Girsanov theorem to obtain an equivalent measure. Under this new measure, the new process will be a martingale. If we do not work with the discounted process but only change the measure, the process we obtain is not a martingale. If you use the former approach to obtain a martingale process and you want to price an option, the value of the option is simply given by its expected value under the new measure. Thus, you do not need to discount in this case.

---

[5] In effect the Girsanov theorem proves the existence of this measure.

[6] Note that the drift process u is affected by the heterogeneous preferences of investors in the economy.

However, as discussed previously, we can get away with changing the measure without discounting, but in this case the process will not be a martingale. Thus, you do not need to discount the process, otherwise you can use the original process and discount it later.[7] Although this approach might be mathematically elegant it involves tedious calculations that can be demanding. On the other hand, the former approach is less mathematically elegant, but working with martingale processes can be simpler.

Exercise 4.1

Prove that under the process in (4.16), the discounted portfolio process (under a self-financing trading strategy) is a martingale.

APPENDIX A4.1   THE RANDON–NIKODYM CONDITION

We now discuss a more intuitive interpretation of the Randon–Nikodym condition described in this chapter.

For simplicity of exposition, we shall be less formal. Suppose the random variable $X(t) \sim N(\mu, \sigma^2)$ has the following density:

$$f(X) = \frac{1}{\sqrt{2\pi t}} e^{-1/2(X-\mu/\omega)^2} \qquad (A4.1)$$

Using the moment generating function for normal variables we get

$$E[\exp(X)] = \exp\left(\mu + 1/2\sigma^2\right) \qquad (A4.2)$$

Suppose now that we shift the mean process of the variable $X(t)$ so that its new density becomes

$$f(X) = \frac{1}{\sqrt{2\pi t}} e^{-1/2(X-\mu-a/\omega)^2} \qquad (A4.3)$$

Apply again the moment generating function to obtain

$$E[\exp(Xa)] = \exp\left(\mu - a + 1/2\sigma^2\right) \qquad (A4.4)$$

Note that the shift has produced a new drift (i.e. $\mu - a$) but no change in the variance process. Also, note that

$$\frac{E[\exp(X)]}{E[\exp(Xa)]} = \exp(a)$$

---

[7] Note that this definition is more in line with the economic interpretation of the price of an asset as its discounted future price.

As well as

$$\exp(-a)E^P[\exp(X)] = \exp\left(\mu - a + 1/2\sigma^2\right)$$

The result above suggests that the two densities are the same if scaled by a factor. How do we determine the factor? Note that if you consider the exponent part of the two densities, you should notice that, after some calculations, the difference is equal to

$$\exp\left[\frac{1}{\sigma^2}(2aX - 2a\mu - a^2)\right] = \phi(aX)$$

The result suggests that you can recover the density under Q from the initial density if you multiply the latter by the factor $\phi(X)$. This is the same as saying that[8]

$$\frac{dQ}{dP} = \phi(aX) \tag{A4.5}$$

The factor in (A4.5) is the Randon–Nikodym derivative. This can be viewed as an adjustment factor that converts one probability measure into an equivalent one.[9]

APPENDIX A4.2   GEOMETRIC BROWNIAN MOTION

This appendix shows an application of geometric Brownian motion (see Equation (4.11)) using MATLAB. This process is widely used in financial derivatives to model asset prices. It is also widely used in computational finance to price a variety of derivatives.

The first line of this code specifies the function with the output (stock paths) and the inputs (the initial stock price, so; the risk-free rate of interest, r; volatility, sigma; the time to maturity, T; the number of steps, NSteps; and the number of replications, Rep):

```
function SPaths=GenPaths0(so,r,sigma,T,NSteps,Rep)
dt=T/NSteps;
nudt=(r-0.5*sigma^2)*dt;
%drift component
sidt=sigma*sqrt(dt);
%diffusion component.
RandMat=randn(Rep,NSteps);
Increments=[nudt+sidt*RandMat];
% The first part of the code is a Brownian
motion process.
```

---

[8] Note that if the probability distribution function of $f(X) = P(X)$ and if $f(Xa) = Q(X)$, we can write $dP/dX = f(X)$ and $dQ/dX = f(Xa)$.

[9] Obviously you need the two measures to be the same.

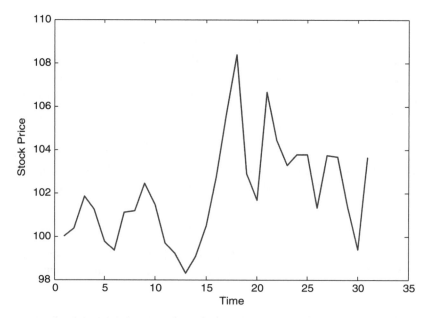

Figure A4.1   Geometric Brownian motion stock price path

```
LogPaths=cumsum([log(so)*ones(Rep,1), Increments],2);
% Prices are reverted into generate lognormals processes
SPaths=exp(LogPaths);
```

We now show an application of the code. We assume that the stock price today is $100, the risk-free rate of interest 5% and the stock price volatility 10% per annum. In order to use Equation (4.11) to simulate stock prices over the next year, we need to divide the time period (i.e. T = 1 year) into small intervals (NSteps). In this simulation, we have considered 30 time steps. The output (SPaths) for a single path is shown in the graph in Figure A4.1.

5

The Black and Scholes Model

5.1 INTRODUCTION

In this chapter we introduce the Black and Scholes model and discuss its practical use. The main assumptions underlying the model are:

(a) it is possible to short-sell the underlying stock;
(b) trading stocks is continuous;
(c) there are no arbitrage opportunities;
(d) there are no transaction costs or taxes;
(e) all securities are perfectly divisible (i.e. you can buy or sell a fraction);
(f) it is possible to borrow or lend cash at a constant risk-free rate;
(g) the stock does not pay a dividend.

5.2 THE BLACK AND SCHOLES MODEL

Define a standard Brownian motion $W(t)$, on $0 \le t \le T$, and a probability space (Ω, F, P). The process driving the stock price is a geometric Brownian motion:

$$dS(t) = \mu S(t)dt + \sigma S(t)dW(t) \qquad (5.1)$$

Suppose that $C(t) = C(S(t), t)$ is the value at t of an option on the stock $S(t)$. Changes in the value of the option on small intervals, $dC(t)$, are[1]

$$dC(.) = \frac{\partial C}{\partial t}dt + \frac{\partial C}{\partial S}dS + \frac{1}{2}\sigma^2 S^2 \frac{\partial^2 C}{\partial S^2}dt \qquad (5.2)$$

The term $(\partial C/\partial S)dS$ is stochastic. However, we can eliminate it from (5.2). Suppose we can construct the following portfolio P consisting of a long-position on the call option and a short-position on n units of stock:

$$P(t) = C(S(t), t) - n(t)S(t)$$

We can differentiate P to obtain

$$dP = dC - ndS(t) \qquad (5.3)$$

---

[1] For simplicity we drop the argument in the bracket and use (.).

Using (5.2) in combination with (5.3) we obtain

$$dP(.) = \left(\frac{\partial C}{\partial t} + \frac{1}{2}\sigma^2 S^2 \frac{\partial^2 C}{\partial S^2}\right) dt + \left(\frac{\partial C}{\partial S} - n\right) dS \tag{5.4}$$

Thus, setting n in (5.4) equal to $\partial C/\partial S$, we have

$$dP(.) = \left(\frac{\partial C}{\partial t} + \frac{1}{2}\sigma^2 S^2 \frac{\partial^2 C}{\partial S^2}\right) dt \tag{5.5}$$

The portfolio in (5.5) is risk free. Thus, it should earn the risk-free rate of return.[2] Since $dP = rP dt = r[C(S, t) - (\partial C/\partial S)S(t)]dt$, it follows that[3]

$$\frac{\partial C}{\partial t} + \frac{1}{2}\sigma^2 S^2 \frac{\partial^2 C}{\partial S^2} + rS\frac{\partial C}{\partial S} - rC = 0 \tag{5.6}$$

This result is known as the Black and Scholes partial differential equation. In the absence of arbitrage any derivative security having as an underlying stock S should satisfy (5.6).

5.3   THE BLACK AND SCHOLES FORMULA

For simplicity, we now set $T = 1$. We already know that if the market is arbitrage free, the value of an option can be written as the expected value of its cash flows (see Sections 4.3 and 4.5):

$$C(T) = E^Q[S(T) - K]^+ \tag{5.7}$$

where $S(T)$ is the stock price at T, K is the strike of the option and the expectation is taken under the measure Q. The idea is to evaluate the expectations in (5.7) for values of the stock price for which the option is in the money:

$$E^Q(C(T)) = E[S(T)|S(T) > K]$$

$$S(0)E\left[\frac{S(T)}{S(0)} > \frac{K}{S(0)}\right] \tag{5.8}$$

where $S(0)$ is the initial stock price.

First note that $S(T)/S(0) = e^{\log(S(T)/S(0))}$ and also that $\log(S(T)/S(0)) \sim N(\mu, \sigma^2)$. Define the following random variable:

$$q = \frac{\log(S(T)/S(0)) - \mu}{\sigma} \sim N(0, 1) \tag{5.9}$$

---

[2] This is the so-called nonarbitrage portfolio.

[3] Equation (5.6) follows from setting (5.5) equal to the portfolio process and simplifying.

Define by $N(q)$ the cumulative normal distribution

$$N(q) = \frac{1}{\sqrt{2\pi}} e^{-q^2/2}$$

Suppose that $f(q)$ is its density. We can rewrite (5.8) as

$$E^Q(C(T)) = \int \frac{S(T)}{S(0)} f(q)dq - \frac{K}{S_0} \int f(q)dq$$

Note that, from (5.8) and (5.9), we have

$$\frac{S(T)}{S(0)} = e^{q\sigma + \mu} = S_0 e^{q\sigma + \mu} > K$$

$$q > -\frac{\log(S_0/K) + \mu}{\sigma} \Rightarrow q > -d_2$$

Thus, the integral above is bounded as

$$E^Q(C(T)) = \int\limits_{-d_2}^{\infty} S_0 e^{q\sigma + \mu} f(q)dq - \frac{K}{S_0} \int\limits_{-d_2}^{\infty} f(q)dq \qquad (5.10)$$

Let us focus first on the first integral in (5.10) and write it as

$$S_0 \int\limits_{-d_2}^{\infty} e^{q\sigma + \varpi} f(q)dq = \frac{1}{\sqrt{2\pi}} S_0 \int\limits_{-d_2}^{\infty} e^{q\sigma + \mu} e^{-\frac{q^2}{2}} dq$$

$$= \frac{1}{\sqrt{2\pi}} S_0 \int\limits_{-d_2}^{\infty} e^{-1/2(q-\sigma)^2 + 1/2\sigma^2 + \mu} dq$$

Define a new variable $\gamma = q - \sigma$. After the change of variable the integral above can be written as

$$\frac{1}{\sqrt{2\pi}} e^{1/2\sigma^2 + \mu} S_0 \int\limits_{-d_2}^{\infty} e^{-1/2(q-\sigma)^2} dq = \frac{1}{\sqrt{2\pi}} e^{1/2\sigma^2 + \mu} S_0 \int\limits_{-d_2}^{\infty} e^{-1/2\gamma^2} d\gamma$$

However, following the change of variable we also have to change the bounds of the integral. Suppose that $q = \gamma + \sigma$ and note that so far we have been focusing on values of $q > -d_2$. Since $d_2 = d_1 - \sigma$, it follows that $q > -(d_1 - \sigma) \Rightarrow q > \sigma - d_1$, or $\gamma < d_1$. We can now rewrite the integral as

$$\frac{1}{\sqrt{2\pi}} e^{1/2\sigma^2 + \mu} S_0 \int\limits_{d_1}^{\infty} e^{-1/2\gamma^2} d\gamma$$

Since $1/2\sigma^2 + \mu = r$, under the arbitrage-free condition, it follows that

$$\frac{1}{\sqrt{2\pi}}e^r S_0 \int_{d_1}^{\infty} e^{-1/2\gamma^2} d\gamma = e^r S_0 N(d_1)$$

We are now left with handling the second integral in (5.10). Note that $q > -d_2 \Rightarrow q < d_2$. It follows that

$$K \int_{d_2}^{\infty} f(q)dq = KN\left[\frac{\log(S/K) + (r + \sigma^2/2)}{\sigma}\right] = KN(d_2)$$

This is the probability that the call option is in the money at expiry. Assuming that the option expires at T, we have

$$C(T) = e^{rT} S_0 N(d_1) - KN(d_2)$$

Discounting back to $T = T_0$:

$$C(T_0) = S_0 N(d_1) - e^{-rT} KN(d_2) \qquad (5.11)$$

where we have defined

$$d_1 = \frac{\log(S/K) + (r + \sigma^2)T}{\sigma\sqrt{T}} \quad \text{and} \quad d_2 = d_1 - \sigma\sqrt{T}$$

Remark 5.1

Note that $\partial C/\partial S_0 = N(d_1)$ is the so-called delta of the option.

5.4   BLACK AND SCHOLES IN PRACTICE

The Black and Scholes model is based on a set of assumptions that might be too restrictive in practice. Nevertheless, it is by far the most widely used model to price options. In this section we shall try to shed some light on the reasons for its popularity. Obviously options within the Black and Scholes model can be priced in closed form. There is no need for simulations. This has noticeable implications in terms of efficiency. This reason alone may be sufficient to justify its large use in practical applications.

Let us now consider what happens to a trader if he or she uses the Black and Scholes formula and the model happens to be mis-specified. We shall be using an example from Davis (2007).

The option value is given by $C(t, S_0, \sigma)$. Consider a trader who sells the option at implied volatility σ^* and suppose that this is higher than the implied volatility that satisfies the price function above. Also suppose that the trader uses the Black and Scholes model to hedge the option. If the model is not mis-specified then he or she will make a profit with probability one. The question is what happens if instead the model used is mis-specified? To answer this question we shall calculate the difference in the value of the hedging portfolio in the case where the model is correct and the hedging portfolio using the implied volatility at which the option has been sold. The difference in the value of the hedging portfolio $\Phi(T)$ is

$$\Phi(T) = \int_0^T e^{rT} \frac{1}{2} S^2(t) \Gamma(\sigma^{*2} - \sigma^2) dt \qquad (5.12)$$

where $\Phi(t)$ is the difference between the two portfolios and $\partial^2 C/\partial S^2 = \Gamma$ is the gamma of the option.

Equation (5.12) shows an interesting result. The hedging mis-specification highly depends on the gamma of the portfolio. For small gamma, the hedging error may not be crucial. For large gamma the impact will be more significant.

5.5   THE FEYNMAN–KAC FORMULA

An alternative way of obtaining the Black and Scholes formula uses the solution of the partial differential equation (PDE) (5.6) under the boundary condition $C(T) = [S(T) - K]^+$. Therefore, one can prove that the Black and Scholes solution (5.11) satisfies the PDE (5.6)[4] and that it is also a relationship between PDEs and conditional expectations. The Feynman–Kac formula generalizes the Kolmogorov equations to processes that are generally used in finance. We provide here an introduction to the study of stochastic differential equations.[5]

We know that the price of a contingent claim $C(t)$ can be written as

$$C(t) = E_t^Q \left[e^{-r(T-t)} (S(T) - K)^+ \right] \qquad (5.13)$$

Consider a constant interest rate r. Given (5.13) and an Ito diffusion process for the stock price $S(t)$, we are interested in the PDE that corresponds to (5.13). Appendix A5.1 shows that the solution takes the following form:

$$\frac{\partial g}{\partial t} = \mu(t) \frac{\partial g}{\partial S} + \frac{1}{2} \sigma^2(t) \frac{\partial^2 g}{\partial S^2} \qquad (5.14)$$

Theorem 5.1 below clarifies this result.

---

[4] After a change of the original probability measure in the geometric Brownian motion process for the stock price.

[5] See Appendix A5.1 for details.

Theorem 5.1

Consider the following conditional expectation, $C(t) = E[g(S(T))|S(t) = s]$, with $S(t)$ satisfying $dS(t) = \mu(t)(S(t))dt + \sigma(t)(S(t))dW(t)$ and the initial condition $S(t) = s$. The solution $C(.) = g(t, s)$ is given by the following PDE:

$$C_t + \mu C_s + 1/2\sigma^2 C_{ss} = 0 \tag{5.15}$$

where we have used lower case to indicate derivatives with respect to the argument and $g(.) = [S(t) - K]^+$.

Remark 5.2

Note that Theorem 5.1 holds for general cases. However, one may also restrict the investigation to the space spanned by the measure Q by using a change of variable.

Example 5.1

Let us use (5.15) to find the PDE satisfied by the conditional expectation in (5.13) when the stock price follows a geometric Brownian motion process with drift equal to the risk-free rate of interest. Apply the Ito lemma to the process $e^{-rt}C(t)$ and using (5.14) we obtain

$$d(e^{-rt}C(t)) = e^{-rt}\frac{\partial C}{\partial t} + e^{-rt}\frac{\partial C}{\partial S}dS + e^{-rt}\sigma^2\frac{1}{2}\frac{\partial^2 C}{\partial S^2}dS^2 - re^{-rt}C(t)$$

After some algebra and considering Equation (A5.1) in the appendix we obtain

$$d(e^{-rt}C(t)) = e^{-rt}AC(t)dt + e^{-rt}\frac{\partial C}{\partial t}dt + e^{-rt}\frac{\partial C}{\partial S}\sigma dW(t) - re^{-rt}C(t)dt \tag{5.16}$$

The process in (5.16) simplifies to

$$d(e^{-rt}C(t)) = e^{-rt}\frac{\partial C}{\partial S}\sigma dW(t) \tag{5.17}$$

This process is a martingale and therefore satisfies the PDE in (5.13). The same result can be obtained if stochastic interest rates[6] were considered. If the process is a martingale at t and considering the interval $T - t$, taking the conditional expectation,[7] we have

$$C(t) = E_t^Q \left[e^{-r(T-t)}C(T, S(T)) \right] \tag{5.18}$$

---

[6] A similar result was reached in the previous section when we considered discounted stock price processes.

[7] Note that the integrability condition is met for this integral. Therefore the expectation exists.

This result proves that there is a relationship between the initial conditional expectation and the PDE. We know that the solution to (5.18) gives the Black and Scholes formula. An important conclusion follows. The Black and Scholes formula is the solution of the Feynman–Kac PDE.

APPENDIX A5.1   THE KOLMOGOROV BACKWARD EQUATION

Consider the following diffusion process:

$$dS(t) = \mu(t)dt + \sigma(t)dW(t)$$

and the expectation:

$$g(t, S(t)) = E[g(S(t))|S(t-1)]$$

Define the generator of the Ito diffusion as A, such that

$$A = \mu(t)\frac{\partial g}{\partial S} + \frac{1}{2}\sigma^2(t)\frac{\partial g^2}{\partial S^2} \tag{A5.1}$$

Equation (A5.1) shows the expected (not actual) evolution over time of the Ito diffusion. Suppose that $g(.)$ is the solution of the boundary problem[8]

$$\frac{\partial g}{\partial t} + Ag(.) = 0 \tag{A5.2}$$

with the boundary condition given by

$$g(T, s) = h(s)$$

This shows that there is a link between expectations and PDEs. We discuss this further in the following example.

Example A5.1

Suppose that the stochastic process is a geometric Brownian motion:

$$dS(t) = \mu S(t)dt + \sigma S(t)dW(t)$$

Find the Kolmogorov PDE for this specific case. From (A5.1) we have

$$\frac{\partial g}{\partial t} = \mu(t)\frac{\partial g}{\partial S} + \frac{1}{2}\sigma^2(t)\frac{\partial^2 g}{\partial S^2}$$

---

[8] Note that the process in (A5.1) is a consequence of applying the Ito lemma to $g(.)$ when S_t satisfies the Ito process under consideration.

Using the Ito lemma and some algebra we obtain the Kolmogorov backward equation:[9]

$$\frac{\partial g}{\partial t} = S(t)\mu(t)\frac{\partial g}{\partial S} + \frac{1}{2}S^2(t)\sigma^2(t)\frac{\partial^2 g}{\partial S^2} \tag{A5.3}$$

Using Equation (A5.2) and the boundary condition we finally obtain

$$g(.) = E[g(T, S(T))] = h(S(T))$$

APPENDIX A5.2   CHANGE OF NUMERAIRE

This appendix shows an application of the Girsanov theorem, which is useful when pricing derivatives using computational methods.

To see why this technique is important in finance, consider a d-dimensional vector of stock prices. We assume that it is defined on the probability space (Ω, F, P) and the dynamics are specified by a d-dimensional process equivalent to Equation (5.1).

Consider the numeraire $s_t^0 = B(t)$ with $dB(t) = rB(t)dt$ or $B(t) = B_0 e^{rt}$ and $B_0 = 1$. This is \$1 invested at the risk-free rate r until time t in a money market account. Define now by $\beta(t)$ a stochastic interest rate, and write $B(t)/\beta(t)$; clearly this process is a martingale. Impose the following normalization: $\beta_0 = B_0 = 1$. Clearly the process above is a positive martingale and it defines a measure. Define this new measure by $dP^B/dP = B(t)/\beta(t)$. Under this new measure the price at time t of a contingent claim can be written as

$$E^B(V(t)) = E^p\left[\frac{V}{\beta(t)}B(t)\right] \tag{A5.4}$$

This process is also a martingale and the measure p^B is called a risk-neutral measure and is equivalent to the physical measure P. However, a closer inspection of Equation (A5.4) shows that to evaluate the expectation we have to compute a stochastic discount factor. This involves a considerable amount of difficulty since it involves solving a sequence of integrals. However, since we know that the two measures above are equivalent, we can write the price today of a contingent claim under the risk-neutral measure as

$$V_0 = e^{-rT}E^B[V(T)]$$

---

[9] Note that the result in (A5.3) is evident if we use an integral form. In fact, in this case, after using the Ito lemma, the last term in the equation is the Ito integral. Therefore, its expected value is zero. Using this result, Equation (A5.2) and the boundary condition, the final result is obtained.

Theorem A5.1

Let B be a numeraire. Then it follows that

$$P^B = \frac{1}{B(0)} \int_F \frac{B(T)}{\beta(T)} dP$$

is a risk neutral measure for B and that

$$E^B(S(t)/B(t)|F(t)) = \frac{S(t)}{B(t)}$$

Remark A5.1

Note that the original measure P and the new measure P^B are equivalent; therefore

$$P = B(0) \int_F \frac{\beta(T)}{B(T)} dP^B$$

Proof of Theorem A5.1

We divide the proof into two parts. In the first part we prove that P^B is a measure. In the second part we prove Theorem A5.1. Define the discounted price process for an asset by $B(t)/\beta(t)$. This process is a martingale under P^B. Then it follows that

$$\begin{aligned}
P^B(F) &= \frac{1}{B(0)} \int_F \frac{B(T)}{\beta(T)} dP \\
&= \frac{1}{B(0)} E^B \left[\frac{B(T)}{\beta(T)} | F(t) \right] \\
&= \frac{1}{B(0)} \frac{B(0)}{\beta(0)} = 1
\end{aligned}$$

This completes the first part of the proof. Now we have to prove that the discounted price of an asset under this new measure (i.e. P^B) is a martingale. Let us now consider an asset $S(t)$ and write the expectations in t under the measure P^B as

$$E^B(S(t)/B(t)) = B(t) \int \frac{\beta(T)}{B(T)} dP$$

An application of Baye's rule gives

$$E^B(S(t)/B(t)|F(t)) = \frac{\beta(t)}{B(t)}E\left[\frac{B(T)}{\beta(T)}\frac{S(T)}{B(T)}|F(t)\right]$$

$$= \frac{\beta(t)}{B(t)}E\left[\frac{S(T)}{\beta(T)}|F(t)\right]$$

$$= \frac{\beta(t)}{B(t)}\frac{S(t)}{\beta(t)} = \frac{S(t)}{B(t)}$$

APPENDIX A5.3   BLACK AND SCHOLES AND THE GREEKS

This appendix shows an application of the Black and Scholes formula (see Equation (5.11)) to price a call and put option written on a stock. The code also shows the computation of the call/put option deltas (cd/pd) and the gamma (gamma).

This function uses inputs such as the initial stock price (so), interest rate (r), stock price volatility (sigma), time (T) expressed in days, dividend and strike price (X), to calculate the call/put option price, deltas (cd/pd) and gamma.

```
function [call,put,cd,pd,gamma]=bs(so,r,sigma,T,
dividend,X)
% this function computes the Black and Scholes
price for call/put (European) equity
% option. It also computes the delta and the gamma.
Note that T should be
% expressed in days (i.e. T=30, 60, 365...
d1=(log(so/X)+(r-dividend+0.5*(sigma.^2))*(T/365))/
(sigma*(T/365).^0.5);
d2=d1-sigma*(T/365).^0.5;
Nd1=normcdf(d1); Nd2=normcdf(d2);
% call option price.
call=so*exp(-dividend*(T/365))*Nd1-exp(-r*(T/365))*X*Nd2;
%put option price using the put/call parity condition.
put=call-exp(-dividend*(T/365))*so+X*exp(-r*(T/365));
% call delta.
cd = exp(-dividend.*T).*normcdf(d1);
% put delta.
pd = cd - exp(-dividend.*T);
gamma = (normpdf(d1).*exp(-dividend.*T/365))./
(so.*sigma.*sqrt(T/365));
```

We assume that the initial stock price so = \$100, the risk-free rate of interest r = 5%, the stock price volatility sigma = 10% per annum, time to expiry of the option T = 365 (one year) and the strike price is X = 100. We assume that the stock does not pay a dividend (dividend = 0). Using the function 'bs' we obtain: call = 6.80, put = 1.93, call delta (cd) = 0.71, put delta (pd) = −0.29 and gamma = 0.03.

6

Monte Carlo Methods

6.1 INTRODUCTION

Monte Carlo methods are generally used in mathematics to solve complex problems where analytical solutions are difficult to obtain. In these cases we can obtain approximate solutions. This methodology has become very common in many areas of social science and in finance. In this chapter, we introduce Monte Carlo methods and review the main applications of this methodology to price derivatives.

Consider a function $g(x)$ that is not tractable analytically and suppose that we want to solve the integral in the following equation:

$$\int_a^b g(x)\mathrm{d}x = c \qquad (6.1)$$

where c is a constant. Consider the following random variable $y \in [a, b]$ with known density $f(.)$ and the following estimator $\psi = g(y)/f(y)$; then

$$E(\psi) = \int_a^b \left[\frac{g(x)}{f(x)}\right] f(x)\mathrm{d}x = c \qquad (6.2)$$

In general, to solve Equation (6.1), we replace it by (6.2) and sample from a known distribution. Thus, the deterministic problem in (6.1) is transformed into a stochastic one (6.2). The estimator preserves the sampling distribution and therefore it is inexact. This may lead to further estimation errors. Furthermore, in many practical applications the underlying process is continuous. In this case the sampling approach may also lead to estimation errors.

In this chapter we try to shed some light on some of these issues and suggest practical alternatives to implement this methodology.

6.2 THE DATA GENERATING PROCESS (DGP) AND THE MODEL

When designing an experiment, we specify the so-called data generating process (DGP) for the model under investigation.

A DGP may consist in a single equation as well as a set of equations. The DGP is generally known to the designer of an experiment.[1] Denote the parameters of a DGP by (λ, T) and denote the parameter space by $\Theta \times \mathfrak{I}$. A set of DGPs form what we call a 'model M'. Denote by μ a generic element, or DGP, of a model M. Now suppose that using Monte Carlo and the DGP you generate random samples from a known distribution. Also suppose that the object of your experiment is to estimate the sample average λ. The average λ. is said to be *pivotal* if its distribution is the same for each DGP $\mu \in M$. We denote by λ^* the realization of λ calculated from the data generated by some known DGP μ_0. Thus, using the realization λ^*, the sample average can be easily estimated.

Note that there is a unique correspondence between a DGP and λ. In this case we say that λ is *pivotal*. In general, most of the estimators in statistics or finance are pivotal and therefore we can use Monte Carlo to obtain estimates. However, there might be cases when this assumption fails to hold and Monte Carlo, if used, may provide very poor results – even worse than asymptotic theory. In these cases bootstrap can be used.[2] In fact bootstrap requires a much weaker assumption of 'asymptotically pivotal' (see Davidson and McKinnon, 2001).

6.3   PRICING EUROPEAN OPTIONS

The Monte Carlo method in finance was first introduced by Boyle (1997). Suppose that the paths generating the asset prices $S(t)$ follow a geometric Brownian motion process:

$$dS(t) = \mu S(t)dt + \sigma S(t)dW(t) \tag{6.3}$$

where μ is the drift process, σ the stock price volatility and $W(t)$ a standard Brownian motion on the usual probability space. Suppose also that the process $S(t)$ takes the following form:

$$F(S(t)) = \ln S(t) \tag{6.4}$$

An application of the Ito lemma to (6.4) leads to

$$dF = \left(\mu - \frac{1}{2}\sigma^2 dt\right) + \sigma\sqrt{dt}dz \tag{6.5}$$

After some algebra, the process in (6.5) can be written as

$$S(t + dt) = S_0 \left(\exp \mu - 0.5\sigma^2\right) dt + \sigma\sqrt{dt}dz \tag{6.6}$$

---

[1] It will be unknown if we were to use nonparametric methods.

[2] We do not discuss bootstrap methods in this chapter.

The process in (6.6) can be used as a DGP to generate M random paths for $S_j(t + dt)$, $j = 1, 2, \ldots, M$ and $t = 0, 1, 2, \ldots, T$. For each j, we calculate the option payoff, $\max(0, S_j - K) = V_j$. Discounting the payoff back to today gives V_{j0}^*.

Averaging the discounted payoff gives the estimated option price

$$\hat{V}_0 = \frac{1}{M} \sum_{j=1}^{M} V_j^*$$

with its variance given by

$$\hat{s}^2 = \frac{1}{M-1} \sum_{j=1}^{\hat{M}} (V_j - \hat{V}_0)^2$$

An application of the central limit theorem shows that for a large number of replications (i.e. $M \rightarrow \infty$)

$$\frac{\hat{V}_0 - V}{\sqrt{\hat{s}^2/M}} \rightarrow N(0, 1)$$

where V is the observed option price.

The simplicity and flexibility of this methodology makes it a reasonable choice when pricing various complex derivative instruments. Additionally, it also has the advantage that we can easily compute standard errors that can be used to evaluate point estimates. Indeed, the standard error is given by $\hat{s}/\sqrt{M}$ and it can be used to compute confidence intervals. A closer look at the standard error above shows that one can reduce the confidence interval by increasing the number of replications (i.e. M). Therefore, to reduce the confidence interval by a factor of 10, for example, we should increase the number of replications by 100.

6.4 VARIANCE REDUCTION TECHNIQUES

6.4.1 Antithetic variate methods

Rewrite equation (6.5) using its discrete version:

$$S(t + \Delta t) = S(t) \left(\exp v \Delta t + \sigma \sqrt{\Delta t} \varepsilon \right)$$

where $v = 1/2\mu - \sigma^2$, Δt is a small time interval and $\varepsilon \sim N(0, 1)$.

Suppose we use the above DGP to generate ε_T paths for stock prices, but we split these paths into two sequences, for example ε_1 and $-(\varepsilon_2)$, such that $\varepsilon_1 + \varepsilon_2 = \varepsilon$. Note that ε_1 and ε_2 are from the same path ε but with opposite sign. Assume also that, by using these two paths, we get two estimators for the option price, say $\hat{V}_{01}$ and $\hat{V}_{02}$.

An application of the law of large numbers shows, as $M \to \infty$, that the two estimators are normally distributed with mean, say V,[3] and standard deviations σ_1 and σ_2, respectively. Thus, in the limit, as $M \to \infty$, $\hat{V}_{01}$ and $\hat{V}_{02}$ will be unbiased estimators for V, and they are also negatively correlated. The negative correlation between the two paths plays a fundamental role in *antithetic variate techniques*. In fact, it implies that if one estimator overestimates V, the other is likely to underestimate V, thus we can adjust our estimator for the bias by using the following estimator of V:

$$C^* = \frac{\hat{V}_{01} + \hat{V}_{02}}{2}$$

where C^* is the sample estimator using antithetic techniques. The variance of the estimator is given by

$$\mathrm{Var}(C) = \frac{1}{4}\mathrm{Var}(\hat{V}_{01}) + \frac{1}{4}\mathrm{Var}(\hat{V}_{02}) + \frac{1}{2}\mathrm{Cov}(\hat{V}_{01}\hat{V}_{02})$$

Hence, it follows that in the case when the two estimators are negatively correlated, the variance will be lower than the case when the two estimators are independent.

6.4.2 Control variate methods

This methodology is particularly suitable when the objective is to price an option for which there is no analytical formula but its price is strongly correlated to that of a similar option for which an analytical formula is obtainable.

Suppose we want to estimate the price of an option, for which there is no analytical formula, using the control variate estimator, say V_{1CV}^*. Furthermore, suppose that there is a similar option traded in the market for which an analytical formula exists. Assume that the analytical and Monte Carlo prices of this option are V_2 and V_2^* respectively. We can obtain an estimate of V_{1CV}^* as

$$V_{1CV}^* = V_1^* + (V_2 - V_2^*) \tag{6.7}$$

where V_1^* is the simulated option price.

This quantity is obtained using the same simulated path as for V_2^*. The difference $(V_2 - V_2^*)$ can be viewed as a control for the error made in the estimation process when using the Monte Carlo method. The variance of V_{1CV}^* is

$$\mathrm{var}(V_{1CV}^*) = \mathrm{var}(V_1^*) + \mathrm{var}(V_2^*) - 2\mathrm{cov}(V_1^*V_2^*)$$

---

[3] Suppose this is the true option price we are trying to estimate.

Thus, the control variate estimator will reduce the variance of the option price estimate if $\text{var}(V_2^*) < 2\text{cov}(V_1^* V_2^*)$. This means that the stronger the correlation between the two options the lower the variance of the estimator V_{1CV}^*.

Example 6.1

Asian options[4] display a very high degree of path dependency since their payoffs generally depend on the average price of the underlying over part of the life of the option. Furthermore, arithmetic average options have no analytical solutions for the price, even within a Black and Scholes framework.

Suppose that A_a is the arithmetic average (stock) price at T:

$$A_a = \frac{1}{T} \int_0^T S(t)\mathrm{d}t$$

and A_g is the geometric price at T given by

$$A_g = \exp\left[\frac{1}{T} \int_0^T \ln S(t)\mathrm{d}t\right]$$

Suppose that V_a is the value of an arithmetic option and V_g the value of a geometric option. We can obtain V_g using analytical formulae.[5] In fact under the assumption that $S(t)$ is lognormal, it can be shown that V_g is lognormal.[6] The same is not true for V_a. However, although the distribution of V_a is not lognormal, it looks very similar to a lognormal distribution. This means that even if closed-form solutions for arithmetic average options are not obtainable, we can still approximate the distribution of V_a using Monte Carlo simulation.

Consider only one simulated path and an estimate of the discounted option payoff $\Phi(V_a^*)$ and $\Phi(V_g^*)$. The option value using control variates V_{CV_a} is

$$V_{CVa} = \Phi_a + (V_g - \Phi_g) \tag{6.8}$$

where V_g is the value of the equivalent geometric average option obtained by an analytical formula and Φ_a and Φ_g are the simulated option prices for arithmetic and geometric options respectively.

This result exploits the analytical solution for geometric average options. Note that this approach is not computationally intensive.

---

[4] We shall discuss Asian options in the following chapters.

[5] This holds provided that it is a European option. For American options, computational solutions are rather expensive in terms of time. However, in the next sections we shall look at methods available to accelerate the process.

[6] The distribution of the geometric price for a set of lognormally distributed variables is still lognormal.

6.4.3 Common random numbers

This method is similar to the antithetic variate method introduced above. It is generally used when the objective is to compare two different methods or also, for example, in mechanical engineering – two different systems. The idea is to compare two systems using the same random numbers. Suppose that X and Y are two random variables, and suppose that the goal is to evaluate $X - Y$. First note that if the DGP for X and Y is conditioned on the same set of random numbers, we should have that $\text{Cov}(X, Y) > 0$.

The variance of the process is

$$\text{Var}(X - Y) = \text{Var}(X) + \text{Var}(Y) - 2^*\text{Cov}(X, Y)$$

Thus, it follows that

$$\text{Var}(X - Y) < [\text{Var}(X) + \text{Var}(Y)]$$

6.4.4 Importance sampling

This method is particularly useful when the objective is to approximate densities of random variables whose outcome is rare. Suppose we want to estimate $E[h(X)]$, where X is a random variable, and $E[h(X)] = \int h(X)f(X)\mathrm{d}X$, where $f(X)$ is the joint density. Suppose we know the density $g(X)$ and also that $g(X) > 0$ each time $f(X) > 0$. Then we can use this information to write $E[f(X)]$ as

$$\begin{aligned} E[f(X)] &= \int \frac{h(X)f(X)}{g(X)} g(X)\mathrm{d}X \\ &= E_g\left[\frac{h(X)f(X)}{g(X)}\right] \end{aligned} \tag{6.9}$$

where we use the notation g as a reminder that the expectation is taken over $g(X)$. Thus, there is a change in the underlying measure.

The choice of $g(X)$ plays an important role in order to obtain $E[f(X)]$. To understand (6.9) consider the following example. Suppose we want to calculate the probability that a certain event occurs. We can summarize such an event, depending on a set of variables $[\alpha_1, \alpha_2, \dots, a_N]'$ defined on the measure P. We can represent it using an indicator function $I(\alpha)$, with $I = 1$ if the event occurs, $I = 0$ otherwise. P is then given by the following N-dimensional integral:

$$P = \int I(\alpha)P(\alpha)\mathrm{d}\alpha \tag{6.10}$$

where $P(\alpha)$ is an unbiased joint probability.

With importance sampling we replace $P(\alpha)$, with the biased joint probability $P^*(\alpha)$ and replace the integrand in (6.10) with $I(\alpha)\pi(\alpha)P^*(\alpha)$, where $\pi(\alpha) = P(\alpha)/P^*(\alpha)$.

Finally, Monte Carlo methods can be used to estimate

$$P^* = \frac{1}{M} \sum_{m=1}^{M} I(\alpha_m)\pi(\alpha_m) \qquad (6.11)$$

Note that if $P^*(\alpha) = P(\alpha)$, it follows that $\pi(\alpha) = 1$. Thus Equation (6.11) is just the relative frequency of the M experiments. This is what one would expect when using a crude Monte Carlo method.[7]

However, if, as assumed at the beginning, the probability of occurrence of an event is very rare, using the crude Monte Carlo method we would need a very large number of trials to be certain that the event we are interested in occurs. On the other hand, using a biased probability as in (6.11), we avoid this problem. In fact, the region of interest is now more likely to be visited by the event. Thus, using a *distorted distribution* it is more likely that the event will be captured more often.

Note that the use of a distorted distribution does not pose any problems. In fact, each time the event occurs and is recorded by the indicator function the likelihood function $\pi(\alpha)$ automatically adjusts the result such that the realizations receive a correct weight.

Applications of this method are rather useful when dealing with risk management of rare event phenomena such as earthquakes.

APPENDIX A6.1   MONTE CARLO EUROPEAN OPTIONS

This code uses the following inputs, such as initial stock price (so), strike (X), interest rate (r), volatility (sigma), time to maturity (T), number of replications (Rep), to calculate the call/put European option value. The second part uses some strikes (x) to calculate options call prices. The model used to generate stock prices is a geometric Brownian motion process (see Equation (6.6)). In this example, stock prices are only simulated at time T. Using the simulated path, the code computes the price of a call and put option (first part). The second part of the code simulates the (call) option payoff for different levels of strike prices.

```
function [call,put,P]=optionp(so,X,r,sigma,T,Rep);
T=T/365;
z=randn(Rep,1);
St=so.*exp((r-sigma.^2/2)*T+sigma.*sqrt(T).*z);
Payoff1=max(St-X,0);Payoff2=max(X-St,0);
optionprice1=exp(-r*T).*Payoff1;optionprice2=exp
```

---

[7] That is, each randomly generated number is weighted using the relative frequency of trials.

```
(-r*T).*Payoff2;
% call option value (strike X)
call=mean(optionprice1);
% put1 option value (strike X)
put=mean(optionprice2);
% calculate option values for different strikes x
x=[47 48 49 50 51 52 53];
St=so.*exp((r-sigma.^2/2)*T+sigma.*sqrt(T).*z);
for i=1:length(St)
    for j=1:length(x)
payoff(i,j)=max(St(i)-x(j),0);
        end
    i=i+1;
optionprice=exp(-r*T).*payoff;
P=mean(optionprice);
end
% one can use the command plot(x,P) to plot the
option payoff given the strike x.
```

As an example we use the code above to price a call and put option written on a stock that does not pay a dividend. The initial stock price is assumed to be so = \$48, the risk-free rate of interest r = 5%, the stock price volatility sigma = 10% per annum, the time to expiry of the European option is assumed to be T = 1 year and the strike price is \$50. The call option is out of the money and its price is therefore equal to zero. The put option is in the money and its value is \$1.99. Figure A6.1 shows the (call) option payoff for different levels of strike price.

APPENDIX A6.2   VARIANCE REDUCTION TECHNIQUES – FIRST PART

This appendix provides a code for the application of some of the variance reduction techniques discussed in Section 6.4. It uses the code listed in Appendix A6.3 and the code 'GenPaths0' in Appendix A4.1 in Chapter 4.

```
function SPaths=GeneratePaths(so,r,sigma,T,NSteps,Rep,
PType)
%generates different paths for Monte Carlo simulations.
switch PType
    case 1
        SPaths=GenPathsA(so,r,sigma,T,NSteps,Rep);
% Antithetic technique
    case 2
```

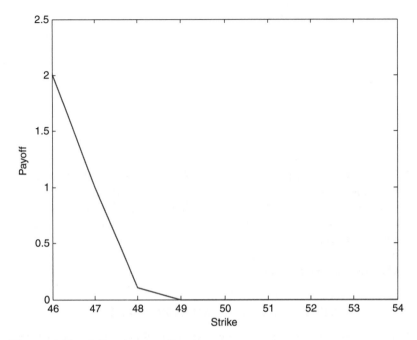

Figure A6.1   Call option payoff

```
[price]=LongstaffschwartzE3CV(so,X,r,T,sigma,NSteps,Rep)
% control variate
    SPaths=GenPathsA(so,r,sigma,T,NSteps,Rep);
  otherwise
    SPaths=GenPaths0(so,r,sigma,T,NSteps,Rep);
% No Variance reduction
end
```

APPENDIX A6.3   MONTE CARLO 1

This function is an extension of Brandimarte's (2006) antithetic variate
(case 1). We use it as a general device in combination with the code in
Appendix A6.2. We provide an example of how to use it in the case of an
anthitetic variate (case 1 in GenPaths). The code generates stock prices paths
using Monte Carlo simulation (with an antithetic variate) and assuming that
stock prices are driven by a geometric Brownian motion.

```
function SPaths=GenPathsA(so,r,sigma,T,NSteps,Rep)
dt=T/NSteps;
```

```
nudt=(r-0.5*sigma^2)*dt;
sidt=sigma*sqrt(dt);
RandMat=randn(round(Rep/2),NSteps);
Increments=[nudt+sidt*RandMat ; nudt-sidt*RandMat];
%generate lognormals stock prices
LogPaths=cumsum([log(so)*ones(Rep,1), Increments],2);
% revert back the log-prices
SPaths=exp(LogPaths);
```

To run the code(s) above set the inputs: so = \$48, r = 5%, sigma = 10% and T = 1 year. We consider 20 time steps (i.e. NSteps = 20) and set the number of replications to 100 000 (i.e. rep = 100 000). If one specifies type = 0 (i.e. no variance reduction), the code will call the function 'GenPaths0' in Appendix A4.1 in Chapter 4. If the user specifies type 1, the code will call the function GenPathsA above.

In the following chapters we shall see how the output of these simulations can be used for option pricing.

APPENDIX A6.4   MONTE CARLO 2

This function uses the control variate estimator discussed in Section 6.4 to compute the price of a (European) arithmetic average option. The code uses the function 'GeneratePaths' in Appendix A6.2 with PType = 0.[8]

```
%Asian option using control variates.
function price=LongstaffschwartzE3CV(so,X,r,T,sigma,
NSteps,Rep,dividend,PType)
dt=T/NSteps; % number of time steps
discount=exp(-r*dt);
SPaths=GeneratePaths(so,r,sigma,T,NSteps,Rep,PType);
%generate stock prices paths
SPaths(:,1)=[];
ar_average=mean(SPaths,2); %arithmetic average
Asian_Mont=max(X-ar_average,0);% option cash flow
Asian_Mont1=mean(Asian_Mont*discount); % simulated
arithmetic option price
ge_average=geomean(SPaths,2); %geometric average
Asian_Geome=max(X-ge_average,0); % cash flow
Asian_Geome1=mean(Asian_Geome*discount); %simulated
geometric option price
```

---

[8] Thus, we generate stock prices paths using a *crude* Monte Carlo approach. However, one can also combine two different variance reduction techniques by specifying PType = 1.

```
% geometric option price using closed form as in Kemna
and Vorst (1990)
sigma_bar=sigma/sqrt(3); b_bar=0.5*(r-dividend-
0.16666*sigma^2);
d1=(log(so/X)+(b_bar+0.5*sigma_bar^2)*T)/sigma_bar*sqrt
(T); d2=d1-sigma_bar*sqrt(T);
p_closedform=X*exp(-r*T)*normcdf(-d2)-so*exp(b_bar-r)
*T*normcdf(-d1);
%Apply Control Variate
price = Asian_Mont1 +p_closedform-Asian_Geome1;
```

As an example, suppose we want to price an arithmetic average option and the stock price is \$100, strike price \$100, the risk-free rate of interest 5%, stock price volatility 10% per annum and the stock does not pay any dividend. Using 200 time steps and 100 000 replications we obtain

so = 100; X = 100; r = 0.05; T = 1; sigma = 0.1; Nsteps = 200; Rep = 100 000;

Ptype = 0; dividend = 0;

Price = LongstaffschwartzE3CV(so,X,r,T,sigma,NSteps,Rep,dividend, PType);

price = 1.222

7

Monte Carlo Methods and American Options

7.1 INTRODUCTION

The Monte Carlo method for pricing American options is a relatively new topic. In fact, this methodology was considered unsuitable for pricing American options. Fundamentally, pricing American options is equivalent to solving an optimal stopping problem and, as always occurs in these cases, the optimal policy should be determined recursively. However, computational methods using Monte Carlo rest on generating forward paths for stock prices. Thus, it was unclear until a few years ago how these two different features could be reconciled. Recently a number of researchers (see Longstaff and Schwartz, 2001; Glasserman and Broadie, 2003, 2004; Cerrato, 2009) have proposed different solutions to this problem.

7.2 PRICING AMERICAN OPTIONS

Pricing American options is one of the oldest problems in financial mathematics. An American option grants the holder the right but not the obligation to exercise it at *any time* during the option's life. Fundamentally, pricing American options is equivalent to solving an optimal stopping problem. The option holder, at any time during the option's life, has to decide whether it is appropriate to exercise the option or continue to hold it until the next period. Thus, a decision is taken after comparing the payoff of the option if immediately exercised and the expected payoff of the option. The optimal policy is to exercise the option if its payoff (at the present time) is larger than the expected payoff.

This problem can be formalized in a simple framework. Suppose that C^p is the price of an American put option and $S(t)$ the stock price at time t. Also suppose that the option can be exercised at any time during the option life $0 \leq t \leq T$. Assume that the strike price is K. The put option price payoff is given by

$$C^p = \sup E(e^{-rt}(K - S_t)) \qquad (7.1)$$

where r is the risk-free rate of interest that we assume to be constant over the period under consideration.

Pricing an American put option fundamentally consists in solving (7.1) at each possible stopping time in $0 \leq t \leq T$. One possible way to approach the problem is the following. Suppose that S^* is the critical stock price for the early exercise, that is $C^P(S_t^*, t) = K - S^*$. If no arbitrage is assumed and the stock follows a geometric Brownian motion, one can show that the put option of the partial differential equations is given by

$$\frac{1}{2}\sigma^2 S^2 C_{ss}^P + r S C_s^P + C_t^P - rC^P \quad \text{for } S_t \geq S_t^* \text{ continuation region}$$

(7.2)

$$\frac{1}{2}\sigma^2 S^2 C_{ss}^P + r S C_s^P + C_t^P - rC^P = -rK \quad \text{for } S_t \leq S_t^* \text{ stopping region}$$

(7.3)

In the continuation region, the option can be easily priced using the Black and Scholes formula. The main problem is determining its value at each possible stopping time and therefore in the stopping region. This problem could be solved using finite difference methods, for example. Finite difference methods use (7.2) and (7.3) and the values of $S^*(t)$ are chosen using a grid search.

Otherwise, we can formulate the option pricing problem using the so-called *integral representation* of the option price:

$$C^P = C^{Ep} + \int_0^T e^{-rt} K \Pr(S \leq S^*) \mathrm{d}s$$

(7.4)

where C^{Ep} is the price of an equivalent European put option, K is the strike price of the options and $\Pr(S \leq S^*)$ indicates the probability that the stock price S is below its critical exercise value S^*.

With this formulation one can now use Monte Carlo to solve the integral, while C^{Ep} can be obtained in closed form.

7.3 DYNAMIC PROGRAMMING APPROACH AND AMERICAN OPTION PRICING

Consider a probability space (Ω, F, P) with a filtration $(F(t_k))_{k=0}^K$. The model we consider is a Markovian model with state variables $(S(t_k))_{k=0}^K$ adapted to $(F(t_k))_{k=0}^K$ and recording all the relevant information about the stock price. We assume that g_k is the payoff function of the option at t_k and with $V_k(x)$ the option value when the stock price $S = x$. The state vector $(S(t_k))_{k=0}^K$ can be augmented to increase its dimensionality and include additional state variables.[1] We also define a vector of possible stopping times over $0 \leq t \leq T$, that is $\tau \in T$. The

---

[1] Stochastic volatility processes or stochastic interest rates can be included in the model.

optimal stopping time is defined as $\tau^* = \inf(t \geq 0 : S(t) \leq S^*(t))$ for some optimal exercise boundary $S^*(t)$. Thus, the optimal stopping time is a function of the current state variable (x). Finally, the option we consider is a Bermudan option. Thus we restrict the exercise times to be discrete.

As generally happens with dynamic programming problems, the option value $V_0(x)$ is determined recursively using

$$V_K(x) = g_K(x) \tag{7.5}$$

$$V_k(x) = \text{Max}(g_k(x), E(V_{k+1}(S_{k+1})|S_k = x) \tag{7.6}$$

Equation (7.5) states that the option value at the time the option expires is given by the payoff function g_K. At any exercise time k the option holder has to decide between the immediate exercise or continuing to hold the option alive until the next period (i.e. Equation (7.6)). The second element on the right-hand side of (7.6) is the so-called continuation value:

$$C_k(x) = E(V_{k+1}(S_{k+1})|S_k = x) \tag{7.7}$$

with $C_K = 0$ at $t_k = t_K$. Equation (7.7) defines the option continuation value. The continuation value is the value to continue to hold the option alive until the next period. To determine the optimal policy, the option holder has to compare the continuation value $C_k(x)$ and the payoff $g_k(x)$ at each t_k and exercise the option if $C_k(x) \leq g_k(x)$. In general, we can write the solution to this problem as

$$V_k(x) = \max(g_k(x), C_k(x)) \tag{7.8}$$

7.4   THE LONGSTAFF AND SCHWARTZ LEAST SQUARES METHOD

A direct application of the dynamic programming scheme above is rather difficult. Indeed, the estimation of the continuation value of the option is not obvious. Longstaff and Schwartz (LS) (2001) suggest a simple way to estimate the continuation value. They suggest combining Monte Carlo with a technique known in statistics as the projection method.

In what follows we assume that the payoff function $(g_k(x))_{k=0}^{k=K}$ is a square integrable function adapted to F. LS consider (7.8) and suggest an approximation for the conditional expectation in Equation (7.6) (i.e. V_{k+1}) using orthogonal projection on the space generated by a finite number of basis functions $\psi_{ik}(x)$, $k = 0, 1, \ldots, K$ and $i = 1, \ldots, n$, such that

$$V_{k+1}(S_{k+1}) = \sum_{i=0}^{n} c_{k,i} \psi_{k,i}(S_k) \tag{7.9}$$

where c_k are the coefficients to be estimated.

Replacing Equation (7.7) by Equation (7.9) simplifies the problem. In fact, coefficients in (7.9) can be estimated using a simple cross-sectional regression and ordinary least squares (OLS):

$$(c_{k,0}^*, c_{k,1}^*, .., c_{k,n}^*) = E[V_{k+1}^*(S_{k+1})\psi_k(S_k)'][\psi_k(S_k)\psi_k(S)']^{-1}$$

where c_k^* are the estimated coefficients.

LS (2001) show that under certain assumptions[2] and by choosing a sufficiently large number of basis functions, as $M \rightarrow \infty$:

$$\lim_{M \rightarrow \infty} \Pr[|V_k(S) - \frac{1}{M} \sum_{j=1}^{M} \psi_{k,i}(S)| > \varsigma] = 0 \qquad (7.10)$$

for any $\varsigma > 0$ and where pr stands for probability, while M denotes the number of replications. Thus, the conditional expectation can be approximated by choosing a large enough M and the value of the American option can be obtained within ς of the true price. LS (2001) provide a simple proof of convergence of the proposed estimator of the option to its true price. Indeed, the proof only holds within a single period context.

Recently Clement et al. (2002) prove convergence within a multiperiod framework. The main limitation of this analytical proof is that it uses a sequential limit approach (i.e. letting the number of simulated paths increase while holding the number of basis functions). This approach is rather odd on practical grounds. Indeed, it does not show joint convergence but rather sequential convergence of the estimator. This would, for example, imply that (7.9) holds exactly at each k without considering sampling error.[3]

Glasserman and Yu (2004) prove convergence of the LS estimator by letting both the number of basis functions and the number of paths increase. They consider cases where the basis functions are polynomials and the underlying process is a Brownian motion or geometric Brownian motion. They show that in the geometric Brownian motion setting the number of simulated paths, that is M, must increase much faster than the number of basis functions k, of the order $\sqrt{\log M}$ (or $\exp(k^2)$ the number of paths).[4]

A closer inspection of Equation (7.10) shows that the option price using the LS method converges to the true option price if the estimated conditional expectation $V_k^*(S)$ converges (in probability) to the true expectation $V_k(S)$ at

---

[2] Refer to Longstaff and Schwartz (2001) for an analysis of the underlying assumptions of the model.

[3] By letting the number of basis functions increase we approximate the conditional expectation. However, the evaluation of the approximation is carried out using Monte Carlo and sample paths. Therefore, one should really look at the convergence of this algorithm by allowing both the number of sample paths and the number of basis functions to increase jointly.

[4] Note that Glasserman and Yu (2004) consider martingales basis functions as well as Hermite polynomials and multiples of powers.

each k. Stentoft (2004) noted that since the value of the American option is based on choosing a stopping rule that maximizes the value of the option, any other rules (including the one used by the LS method) will produce biased prices since in finite samples it is not an optimal rule:

$$V(S) \geq \lim_{m \to \infty} \frac{1}{m} \sum_{i=1}^{m} LS(k, \tau) \qquad (7.11)$$

7.5   THE GLASSERMAN AND YU REGRESSION LATER METHOD

In Equation (7.9) the conditional expectation is approximated using current basis functions, that is $\psi_k(S_k)$. However, one would expect option prices at t_{k+1} to be more correlated with the basis functions $\psi_{k+1}(S_{k+1})$ than $\psi_k(S_k)$. We can exploit the information contained in the correlation structure by regressing discounted option values at t, on the basis function at $t + 1$ (i.e. $\psi_{k+1}(S_{k+1})$). Glasserman and Yu (2004) call this method 'regression later' to distinguish it from the LS method, which they call 'regression now'.

They show that the weighted Monte Carlo method proposed in Brodie *et al.* (2000), under certain assumptions, has a 'regression later' representation and therefore it is equivalent to their regression later approach. Note that Equation (7.9) does not consider sampling error. Suppose that we want to consider it and rewrite Equation (7.9) as

$$V_{k+1}(S_{k+1}) = \sum_{i=0}^{n} c_{k,i} \psi_{k+1,i}(S_{k+1}) + \varepsilon_{k+1} \qquad (7.12)$$

The least square estimator is then given by

$$(c_{k,0}^*, c_{k,1}^*, \ldots, c_{k,n}^*) = E[(V_{k+1}^*(S_{k+1})\psi_{k+1}(S_{k+1})'][\psi_{k+1}(S_{k+1})\psi_{+1k}(S_{k+1})']^{-1}$$

Glasserman and Yu (2004) introduce martingales representations of the basis functions, that is $E(\psi_{k+1}(S_{k+1})|S_k) = \psi_k(S_k)$, for all k, in Equation (7.12). Under a martingale assumption for the basis functions they were able to prove analytically (in a single period framework) that their method produces less dispersed estimates of the option than the 'regression now' method. However, note that no small sample analysis of their estimator is provided.

Cerrato (2009) compares the 'regression now' (i.e. LS estimator) and the 'regression later' estimator to conclude that they both perform remarkably well. However, the LS estimator appears to perform best. Convergence of the estimated option price to the true price was found to be of a nonuniform type. Finally, he extends the two estimators above using different variance reduction techniques to show that when the LS (2001) method is implemented using control variates, it produces very accurate option prices.

7.6   UPPER AND LOWER BOUNDS AND AMERICAN OPTIONS

The main estimators discussed in the previous sections produce an estimate of the option price that is downwards biased, as evident from Equation (7.11). This result implies that one can use these estimators to compute a lower bound for the true price of the American option. Consider the stopping rule $\tau^* = \min(t_k \geq 0 : g_k(x) \geq C_k^*(x))$; i.e. this is the first time the process $g_k(x) \geq C_k^*(x)$, where C_k^* is the estimated continuation value at time t_k. The stopping rule does not only depend on the history of $S_k = x$ but also on the estimated coefficients c_k^* (note that these are estimated using sample paths). It turns out that this rule is not an optimal rule and in general $E[g_{\tau^*}(S_{\tau^*})|c^*] \leq V_0$, where V_0 is the true option price at t_0.

Rogers (2002) uses a similar model to the one described in Equations (7.5) and (7.6). Consider the following approximation for the conditional expectation in (7.6) at t_k:

$$C_k^*(.) = \sum_{i=0}^{n} c_{k,i}^* \psi_{k,i}(.) \quad \text{for all } k = 1, 2, \ldots \tag{7.13}$$

where ψ_k are basis functions. The expected value of the option at time $t_k + 1$ is

$$V_{k+1}^*(.) = \sum_{i=0}^{n} c_{k,i}^* \psi_{k+1,i}(.) \quad \text{for all } k = 1, 2, \ldots \tag{7.14}$$

Define the following difference M :

$$M_n = \sum_{k=0}^{n-1} [V_{k+1}^*(.) - C_k^{+*}(.)] \quad \text{for all } n = 1, 2, \ldots \tag{7.15}$$

Since (7.15) is a martingale difference, it follows that if $M_0 = 0$, $M_0, M_1, M_2, \ldots$ is a martingale.[5] We also assume that basis functions in (7.13) and (7.14) are martingales. In particular, since $[E(M_n)|M_{n-1}] \leq M_{n-1}$, the optional stopping theorem for martingales tells us that it is a sequence of supermartingales. Thus, for any stopping time τ^*,[6]

$$E[g_{\tau^*}(S_{\tau^*})] \leq \inf E[\max_{n=0,1,2\ldots}(g_n(S_n) - M_n)] \tag{7.16}$$

The right-hand side of Equation (7.16) defines an upper bound for the true option price. A confidence interval for the option price can therefore be

---

[5] For example, $E(M_0) = E(M_1) = \ldots$. However, Glasserman (2004) shows that, in order for M to be a valid martingale, we should use regression later and not regression now.

[6] Note that the term on the right-hand side is taken over the supremum, $\text{Sup}_{\tau^* \in k}(g_{\tau^*}(S))$, while the second term is taken on the maximum. The two definitions coincide if the supremum belongs to the set we consider; otherwise the supremum and the maximum do not coincide.

determined if we use option price estimates from Equation (7.16) and estimates using the methodologies described in the previous sections. Rogers (2002) shows that if the martingale we consider is an optimal martingale, that is $M_n = M_n^*$, where M_n^* is an optimal martingale, it follows that

$$V_0(S) = \inf E[\max_{n=0,1,2..}(g_n(S_n) - M_n)] \qquad (7.17)$$

In theory, an optimal martingale will allow one to estimate the option price exactly. Although this is an important result, it rests completely upon the choice of an optimal martingale, but it is still unclear how to obtain it.

Cerrato and Abbasyan (2009) suggest that optimal martingales are the ones spanning the Hilbert space.[7] They suggest a simple way of obtaining martingales using the residuals from Equation (7.12) and the same approach as in (7.14) to (7.16). They also show that their methodology produces very fast and accurate option prices.

APPENDIX A7.1   MULTIASSETS SIMULATION

This code is an extension of the one in Chapter 4, Appendix A4.1 and allows one to simulate stock price paths (under geometric Brownian motion) for a basket of five stocks. It can be used jointly with the code in Appendix A7.2 to price American basket options using the LS regression approach presented in Section 7.4.

```
function [SPaths]=GPaths(so,r,sigma,T,NSteps,Rep,q)
%part1 MonteCarlo analysis American basket Options.
%Generate Rep random paths based on Brownian Motion
%Generally used for a call on 5 stocks, see LS (2001).
noofassets=size(so);
dt=T/NSteps;
nudt=(r-q-0.5*sigma.^2)*dt;
sidt=sigma.*sqrt(dt);
Increments=[];
%run for each asset one by one
for i=1:1:noofassets(2)
   randn('state',sum(100*clock));
   RandMat=randn(round(Rep/2),NSteps);
   iIncrements=[nudt(i)+sidt(i)*RandMat ;
nudt(i)-sidt(i)*RandMat];
%generate lognormals stock prices
   LogPaths=cumsum([log(so(i))*ones(Rep,1),
```

---

[7] In fact, these martingales retain some nice properties that are very important when pricing options. See the discussion in Cerrato and Abbasyan (2009).

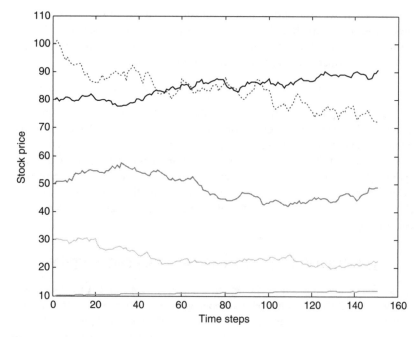

Figure A7.1 Simulated stock prices

```
iIncrements],2);
% revert back the log-prices
  SPaths(:,:,i)=exp(LogPaths);
end
```

We show an application of the code to simulate geometric Brownian motion paths for five stock prices. To run the code first specify a vector of (initial) stock prices so = [100, 80, 50, 30, 10] and volatilities sigma = [0.2, 0.1, 0.15, 0.25, 0.05]. We have set the time to expiry T = 1 year, the risk free equal to 10% and the dividend yield equal to zero. Figure A7.1 shows the simulated stock prices.

APPENDIX A7.2   PRICING A BASKET OPTION USING THE REGRESSION METHODS

This code can be used jointly with the code in Appendix A7.1 to price American basket options and using the LS regression approach presented in Section 7.4.

```
%Basket options using exponential polynomial
```

```
function price=LSmb2(so,X,r,T,sigma,NSteps,Rep,q)
% LSmb2 pricing an American option on the maximum of a
collection of assets using the Least Square methodology
dt=T/NSteps;lenso=length(so);
discount=exp(-r*dt);
discountVet=exp(-r*dt*(1:NSteps)');
SPaths=GPaths(so,r,sigma,T,NSteps,Rep,q);
%eliminate the first column
SPaths(:,1,:)=[];
%order prices for each set of prices at each time point
SPaths=sort(SPaths,3);
CashFlows=SPaths(:,NSteps,lenso);
CashFlows=max(0,CashFlows-X);
ExerciseTime=NSteps*ones(Rep,1);
for step=NSteps-1:-1:1
  InMoney=find(SPaths(:,step,lenso)>X);
  if ~isempty(InMoney)

Xd5=SPaths(InMoney,step,5);Xd4=SPaths(InMoney,step,4);
Xd3=SPaths(InMoney,step,3);Xd2=SPaths(InMoney,step,2);
Xd1=SPaths(InMoney,step,1);
  dimXd=size(Xd5);
  % Xd5 is the highest stock price, Xd4 the 2nd
  highest, etc...
  RegrMat=[ones(dimXd(1),1), Xd5,Xd5.^2, Xd5.^3, Xd5.^4,
 Xd5.^5, Xd4,Xd3,Xd2,Xd1,Xd4.^2,Xd3.^2,Xd2.^2,Xd1.
^2,Xd5.*Xd4,Xd4.*Xd3,Xd3.*Xd2,Xd2.*Xd1,Xd5.
*Xd4.*Xd3.*Xd2.*Xd1];
  YData=CashFlows(InMoney).*discountVet(ExerciseTime
  (InMoney)-step);
  a=RegrMat\YData;
  IntrinsicValue=Xd5-X;
  ContinuationValue=RegrMat*a;
  Exercise=find(IntrinsicValue>ContinuationValue);
  k=InMoney(Exercise);
  CashFlows(k)=IntrinsicValue(Exercise);
  ExerciseTime(k)=step;
 end
end
price=mean(CashFlows.*discountVet(ExerciseTime));
```

We present an application of the LS methodology to price a basket option. We consider three different options with initial stock prices of 90, 100 and 110

Table A7.1   American basket option LS (2001)

S	Exponential	Hermite	Exponential	Hermite	Exponential	Hermite
Simulations	30 000		50 000		75 000	
90	16.70	16.70	16.66	16.62	16.66	16.64
100	26.18	26.17	26.17	26.10	26.08	26.12
110	36.77	26.77	36.78	36.75	36.82	36.75

respectively (see Table A7.1). The assets pay a 10% proportional dividend, the strike price of the option is 100, the risk free rate of interest is 10% per annum and volatility is 20%. Confidence intervals in Broadie and Glasserman (1997) are [16.602, 16.710] when the initial asset value is 90, [26.101, 26.211] with an initial asset value of 100 and finally [36.719, 36.842] when the initial value is 110.

In order to implement the LS (2001) methodology, we have used two different basis functions, exponential and Hermite. All the estimated option prices fall within the Broadie and Glasserman (1997) confidence intervals.

American Option Pricing: The Dual Approach

8.1 INTRODUCTION

This chapter builds on Chapter 7 and proposes a methodology to price American options that is an extension of the recent methodology showed in Rogers (2002). We shall first introduce a general theoretical framework and thereafter describe the methodology and present some empirical results.

8.2 A GENERAL FRAMEWORK FOR AMERICAN OPTION PRICING

Consider the following probability space (Ω, F, P) and the filtration $(F_i)_{i=0,...,n}$, with n being an integer. Define by $X_0, X_1, \ldots, X_n$ an R^d valued Markov chain representing the state variable recording all the relevant information on the price of an asset. Assume that $V_i(x)$, $x \in R^d$, is the value of an American option exercised at time i under the state x and $\Theta(X)$ is its payoff. Write the value of the option as[1]

$$V_i(x) = \sup_{\tau \in \Gamma} E\left[\Theta_\tau(X_\tau)|X_i = x\right] \qquad (8.1)$$

$$V_n(x) = \Theta(x) \qquad (8.2)$$

Thus, the value of an American option at time t_i under the state $X_i = x$ is given by maximizing its expected payoff over all possible stopping times $\tau \in \Gamma$. After combining Equations (8.1) and (8.2), the value of an American option at time t_i is given by the maximum between its value if immediately exercised and its expected value (i.e. the continuation value)

$$V_i(x) = \max\{\Theta_i(x), E[V_{i+1}(X_{i+1})|X_i = x]\} \qquad (8.3)$$

As pointed out in Chapter 7, we can replace the above equation by the simple regression:

$$E\left[V_{i+1}(X_{i+1})|X_i = x\right] = \sum_{K=0}^{k} \beta_{ik}\psi(x) \qquad (8.4)$$

---

[1] For simplicity we do not consider discounted payoffs.

Otherwise, we can use the option's continuation value C_i:

$$C_i(x) = E\left[V_{i+1}(X_{i+1})|X_i = x\right] \tag{8.5}$$

where C_i is a linear combination of the coefficients in (8.4)

$$C_i(X_i) = \beta_i'\psi_i(X_i)$$

with $\beta_i' = (\beta_{i1}, \beta_{i2}, \dots \beta_{iK})'$, $\psi_i(X_i) = [\psi_1(X_1), \psi_2(X_2), \dots, \psi_K(X_K)]$.

Computing the option price from (8.2) and (8.3) or (8.4) and (8.5) is difficult and in general one has to rely on approximations. The typical assumption made is that $V_i(.)$ is a function spanning the Hilbert space; therefore the conditional expectation above can be approximated by the orthogonal projection on the space generated by a finite number of basis functions ϕ_{ik}, $i = 1, 2, .., n$ and $k = 0, 1, \dots, K$. If we replace (8.1) to (8.3) above with their sample quantities, we obtain

$$V_n^*(x) = \phi_n(x) \tag{8.6}$$
$$V_i^*(x) = \max\{\phi_i(x), E[V_{i+1}(X_{i+1})|X_i = x]\} \tag{8.7}$$

The expectation in (8.7) can be estimated using a simple regression:

$$E[(V_{i+1}(X_{i+1})|X_i)] = \sum_{k=0}^{K} \beta_{ik}\phi_{ik}(X) + \varepsilon_{i+1} \tag{8.8}$$

Equation (8.8) will hold exactly if we consider the error term ε_{i+1}. The advantage of working with Equation (8.8) rather than (8.2) and (8.3) is that, in this way, we transform a complex problem into a simpler one consisting of estimating the $K + 1$ coefficients of (8.8). Lemma 8.1 defines the asymptotic convergence of the least squares estimator.

Lemma 8.1

If $E(\varepsilon_{i+1}|X_i) = 0$ and $E[\phi_i(X_i)\phi_i(X_i)']$ is finite and nonsingular then $V_i^* \to V_i$ for all i. See Glasserman and Yu (2004b) for a proof.

As discussed in Chapter 7, proofs of convergence of the option price estimator have been discussed in Longstaff and Schwartz (2001), Clement et al. (2002a), and Glasserman and Yu (2004a). Furthermore, we also saw that Glasserman and Yu (2004b) developed a method based on Monte Carlo simulations where the conditional expectation is approximated by $\phi_{i+1}(X_{i+1})$ and where the regression representation is given by

$$\hat{V}_{i+1}(X_{i+1}) = \sum_{k=0}^{K} \varpi_{ik}\phi_{i+1,k}(X_{i+1}) + \widehat{\varepsilon_{i+1}} \tag{8.9}$$

Definition 8.1   *Martingale property of basis functions*

$$E(\phi_{i+1}(X_{i+1}) \,|\, (X_i) = \phi_i(X_i) \text{ for all } i$$

Under Definition 8.1, Glasserman and Yu show that regressions (8.8) and (8.9) are equivalent but the standard errors from regression later are smaller. The option prices obtained from regression (8.8) or (8.9) are linear combinations of the same basis functions. They only differ in the way coefficients are estimated. Glasserman and Yu (2004a) call this method regression later, since it involves using $\phi_{i+1}(X_{i+1})$; on the other hand, they call the Longstaff and Schwartz (LS) (2001) method regression now since it uses the functions $\phi_i(X_i)$. Note that as a consequence of Assumption 1 in Glasserman and Yu (2004b) it is now true that $E(\hat{\varepsilon}|X_i) = 0$ and therefore the conditional expectation is approximated exactly. However, the finite variance assumption imposed on the basis functions may now become rather restrictive. We believe our martingale approach should make Assumption 2 in Glasserman and Yu (2004b) more likely to hold.

Rogers (2002) shows that the option pricing problem can be formulated in terms of minimizing a penalty function, given by a class of martingales over the lifetime of the option. Any martingales would generate an upper bound for the true option price, while an optimal martingale would permit its exact estimation.

To see this, note that a consequence of the dynamic programming framework in (8.1) to (8.3) is that the option price is a supermartingale Therefore one can use the Doob–Meyer decomposition for martingales and write

$$V_i = V_0 + M_i - A_i \tag{8.10}$$

where M_i is a martingale with $M_0 = 0$ and A_i a pre-visible process with $A_0 = 0$. Rogers (2002) shows that under the dual the value of the option at t_0 is given by

$$V_0 = \inf_{M \in H_0} E[\sup(V_i - M_i)] \tag{8.11}$$

where H_0 is the space of all martingales and the infinitum is obtained when an optimal martingale $M = M^*$ is chosen.

Therefore under this martingale measure one can price the option exactly. However, this result holds if the martingale chosen is an optimal martingale. As noted in Rogers (2002), determining an optimal martingale turns out to be at least as difficult as solving the original option pricing problem! In this chapter we build on Glasserman and Yu (2004b) and Rogers (2002) and propose a simple way to design optimal martingales.

8.3   A SIMPLE APPROACH TO DESIGNING OPTIMAL MARTINGALES

Let us first clarify what we mean by an 'optimal martingale'. Following Glasserman and Yu (2004b), define the following random variable M^*:

$$M_i^* = V_i(X_i) - E[V_i(X_i)|X_{i-1}] \tag{8.12}$$

with $M_0 = 0$.

Lemma 8.2

Let μ^2 be the space of martingales M^* bounded in L^2 such that any M_i^* in μ^2 is an R martingale and therefore $\sup E(M_i^{*2}) < \infty$. The space μ^2 inherits the Hilbert structure from $L^2(\infty)$.

See Appendix A8.1 for a proof.

Note that the process M_i^* in (8.12) is a martingale. In fact, if we rewrite (8.12) as

$$M_i^* = C_i(X_i) - E[V_i(X_i)|X_{i-1}] \tag{8.13}$$

$$= C_i(X_i) - \sum_{k=0}^{K} \beta_{ik}[\psi_{i+1,k}(X_{i+1})] \tag{8.14}$$

under Definition 8.1, we have

$$M_i^* = C_i(X_i) - \beta_i' \psi_i(X_i) \tag{8.15}$$

and therefore it follows that

$$E[(M_{i+1}^*)|X_1, X_2, \ldots X_i, \ldots, \beta] = M^* \tag{8.16}$$

An immediate consequence of Lemma 8.2 is that the martingale M^* belongs to a specific class of martingales. This is a completely different, and well-defined, martingale than others suggested in the literature (see, for example, Rogers, 2002).

8.4   OPTIMAL MARTINGALES AND AMERICAN OPTION PRICING

Using M_i^* one can design basis functions $M_{ik}^*(X_i)$ and re-write the regression in Section 8.3 as

$$C_i(X_i) = \sum_{k=0}^{K} a_{i,k} M_{ik}^*(X_i)$$

Consider now the sample version of

$$C_i^*(X_i) = \sum_{k=0}^{K} a_{ik}^* M_{ik}^*(X_i) \qquad (8.17)$$

where $a_i^* = (a_{i0}^*, a_{i1}^*, \ldots, a_{iK}^*)'$ are least squares coefficients.

Theorem 8.1

If M_i^* is a martingale process and Lemma 8.2 holds then $C_i^* \to C_i$ and $V_i^* \to V_i$ for all i.

See Appendix A8.1 for the proof.

Remark 8.1

The proposed approach is similar in spirit to Glasserman and Yu (2004b) but the important difference is that we are able to obtain martingales that are bounded in L^2 and also suggest a novel algorithm based on this martingale to compute the dual.

8.5   A SIMPLE ALGORITHM FOR AMERICAN OPTION PRICING

Before describing our dual approach, let us first start by implementing the Longstaff and Schwartz (2001) or Glasserman and Yu (2004b) methodologies. The proposed algorithm uses multiple regressions. We describe it below:

(1) At each time t_i, in a recursive fashion, use a regression approach with M_i^* as a martingale. Start, for example, with two basis functions and obtain residuals.
(2) Repeat the regression in (8.1) and increase the number of basis from two to three. Save the residuals.
(3) Use the residuals in (8.1) and (8.2) to obtain two L^2 martingales. Run a new regression using the two martingales basis and estimate the conditional expectation.
(4) Use (8.1) to (8.3) in a recursive fashion.

Remark 8.2

The proposed approach seems to be computationally more intensive than Rogers (2002), for example. However, note that this multiple regression approach does not impact massively on the computational speed. The approach in Rogers (2002) is more computationally intensive than ours. Intuitively, using

Table 8.1 Black and Scholes basis

	Order	3	4	Bin	LS price
$S = 36$	Value	4.469	4.479	4.4867	4.472
$K = 40$	SE	*[10.009]*	*[10.0065]*		
$V = 0.02$	RMSE	*[0.0198]*	*[10.0101]*		
$T = 1$					
$S = 36$	Value	4.827	4.832	4.8483	4.821
$K = 40$	SE	*[0.006]*	*[0.011]*		
$V = 0.02$	RMSE	*[0.0226]*	*[0.0195]*		
$T = 2$					
$S = 36$	Value	7.098	7.116	7.1092	7.091
$K = 40$	SE	*[0.0093]*	*[0.0077]*		
$V = 0.04$	RMSE	*[0.0143]*	*[0.0100]*		
$T = 1$					
$S = 36$	Value	8.495	8.501	8.5142	8.488
$K = 40$	SE	*[0.0123]*	*[0.0121]*		
$V = 0.04$	RMSE	*[0.0229]*	*[0.0180]*		
$T = 2$					

our approach we expect that each basis obtained by iterative least squares regressions will have a smaller and smaller variance in each subsequent regression.

Table 8.1 shows the empirical results. We have used five and six basis functions in the first regression and three and four in the second.[2]

8.6 EMPIRICAL RESULTS

We price an American put option written on a stock. The empirical example follows very closely that of Longstaff and Schwartz (2001) and therefore assumes the same parameters as in that study. Some of the parameters such as stock price, strike, volatility and time to maturity are reported in the tables. S is the initial stock price, K is the strike, v the stock price volatility and finally T is the time to expiry of the option.[3]

The short-term interest rate is assumed to be 6% per annum and we use a fixed number of replications that is equal to 100 000 with antithetic variates. Standard errors and root mean squares errors were calculated as in Cerrato (2008) and obtained from 50 trials.

---

[2] Note that numbers appearing at the top of the tables are the number of basis functions we have used in the two regressions.

[3] We have also calculated standard errors (SE) and root mean squares errors (RMSE). These are reported in brackets.

We first start with a simple martingale. We use the discounted Black and Scholes price as a martingale basis. In fact, this is the first martingale basis that one should consider. Estimated options prices are reported in Table 8.1

We price long-dated options since it is well known that standard methodologies, such as the one proposed in Barone-Adesi and Whaley (1987), do not perform well in this case. On the other hand, binomial or finite difference methods are rather inefficient and not applicable to multidimensional problems. We compare two regression methods. The first uses Black and Scholes prices as martingales and the second uses simple exponential basis functions. We consider three and four basis functions. We also report prices obtained by binomial methods with 10 000 time steps, which we assume to be our true price. First we note that the estimated prices using the Black and Scholes basis are in general higher than the ones obtained by the LS method. Root mean squares errors (RMSE) are very small when four basis functions are considered.

We now consider the basis functions proposed in this chapter. Table 8.2 shows the empirical results. We use up to five basis functions in the first regression and three and four martingales basis functions in the second and, finally, up to six basis functions in the first regression and three martingales basis functions. Three basis seem to be sufficient to obtain a good fit. Standard errors are very small and overall of the same order of magnitude as the RMSE. This could indicate that none of the errors (i.e. the sample error and the error for the estimation of the conditional expectation) overcomes the other. These results may indicate that our simple martingale approach can reduce the probability of choosing a suboptimal strategy when determining the stopping times. To implement our method one has to apply a double regression. Furthermore, basis functions in the first regression must be martingales. Following Cerrato (2008) we use martingales obtained from exponential functions under geometric Brownian motion:

$$\phi_{ik}(X_i) = (X_i)^k \exp{-(kr + k(k-1)\sigma^{2/2})(t_i - t_0)}$$

8.7 COMPUTING UPPER BOUNDS

Following Rogers (2002), researchers have proposed different methodologies to compute the option price dual. Glasserman and Yu (2004b), for example, show that, if Assumption 1 in Glasserman and Yu (2004b) holds, we can use simulation methods to obtain upper and lower bounds with a minimal effort. The proposed martingale approach in this chapter can also be extended to this case in a very simple fashion. We first describe our algorithm; subsequently we discuss the main differences with the existing methods. Our approach follows Rogers (2002) and is based on an additive dual as opposed to the multiplicative dual suggested in Jamshidian (2003). We use this approach since, as discussed

Table 8.2 Martingales basis functions

	Order	5 and 3	5 and 4	6 and 3	Bin	LS price
$S = 36$	Value	4.473	4.482	4.4809	4.4867	4.472
$K = 40$	SE	[0.007]	[0.006]	[0.005]		
$V = 0.02$	RMSE	[0.0153]	[0.0076]	[0.0077]		
$T = 1$						
$S = 36$	Value	4.832	4.838	4.832	4.8483	4.821
$K = 40$	SE	[0.003]	[0.004]	[0.006]		
$V = 0.02$	RMSE	[0.0166]	[0.0110]	[0.0200]		
$T = 2$						
$S = 36$	Value	7.103	7.117	7.101	7.1092	7.091
$K = 40$	SE	[0.012]	[0.009]	[0.009]		
$V = 0.04$	RMSE	[0.0138]	[0.0117]	[0.0121]		
$T = 1$						
$S = 36$	Value	8.501	8.518	8.491	8.5142	8.488
$K = 40$	SE	[0.01]	[0.01]	[0.009]		
$V = 0.04$	RMSE	[0.0166]	[0.0117]	[0.0257]		
$T = 2$						
$S = 38$	Value	3.252	3.253	3.247	3.2572	3.244
$K = 40$	SE	[0.008]	[0.008]	[0.009]		
$V = 0.02$	RMSE	[0.0098]	[0.0089]	[0.0136]		
$T = 1$						
$S = 38$	Value	3.735	3.754	3.748	3.7514	3.3735
$K = 40$	SE	[0.006]	[0.009]	[0.009]		
$V = 0.02$	RMSE	[0.0174]	[0.0094]	[0.0097]		
$T = 2$						
$S = 38$	Value	6.147	6.156	6.148	6.1545	6.139
$K = 40$	SE	[0.007]	[0.001]	[0.009]		
$V = 0.04$	RMSE	[0.0105]	[0.0102]	[0.0112]		
$T = 1$						
$S = 38$	Value	7.666	7.68	7.66	7.6749	7.669
$K = 40$	SE	[0.01]	[0.008]	[0.009]		
$V = 0.04$	RMSE	[0.0134]	[0.0095]	[0.0174]		
$T = 2$						

Order refers to the polynomial order. S is the stock price, K the option strike, V the stock price volatility and T the time to maturity. SE and RMSE are standard errors and root mean squares errors.

in Chen and Glasserman (2006), it produces estimators of the upper bound with the lowest variance. Our goal is to obtain a fast algorithm to compute upper bounds and an estimator with the lowest possible variance. Following Rogers (2002) the dual is given by the right-hand side below:

$$E[\Theta_\tau(X_\tau) \leq V_0(X_0)] \leq E[\max_{i=0,1\ldots}(\Theta_n(X_n) - M_n)] \qquad (8.18)$$

As discussed in Rogers (2002), any martingales will generate an upper bound in (8.18). However, Equation (8.18) will hold with equality only if the martingale used is an optimal martingale. Our approach is rather simple and can be summarized as follows:

(1) Use the algorithm described in the previous section to compute at each t_i estimates of the conditional expectation and martingales basis.
(2) Use the output from step 1 above to obtain an estimate of Equation (8.5).
(3) Along each path, compute the summation $M_n^* = \sum_{i=0}^{n-1} [C_i(X_i) - V^*(X_i)]$
(4) Along each path, compute $\Theta_n^* = \max(\Theta n, V_n(X_n))$.
(5) Estimate the right-hand side of Equation (8.18) along each path.
(6) Repeat steps 1 to 5 and iterate across each simulated path to compute the option price.

Remark 8.3

The dual estimator proposed in this study is similar in spirit to the one suggested in Glasserman and Yu (2004b) but the martingale M_n^* is designed in a different way. Furthermore, it is also similar to the one proposed in Chen and Glasserman (2006).[4] The rationale for choosing this iterative regression scheme is that by designing martingales from ordinary least squares residuals one would expect to obtain martingales with smaller and smaller variance as the number of basis functions increases. Thus, the iterative scheme is similar in spirit to the one proposed in Chen and Glasserman (2006). Proposition 6.6 in Chen and Glasserman (2006) could also hold in this context. If the martingale used is an optimal martingale, we expect the difference between the upper (Table 8.3) and lower (Table 8.2) bounds to be very small.

Proof of convergence of this estimator can be obtained using Theorem 8.1 above along the lines used by Rogers (2002).

8.8 EMPIRICAL RESULTS

Table 8.3 shows the empirical results for the upper bounds using the dual algorithm described in this chapter.

Table 8.3 shows the results with five martingales basis functions in the first regression and three in the second regression. We use 100 000 replications and prices in Table 8.3 are averages of 50 trials. The upper bounds are very close to the true price. Indeed, the absolute error is small for all the combinations of parameters. The standard errors show that the sample uncertainty is relatively modest. The computation of the upper bound takes about 4 seconds on a standard Intel Core 2 processor.

---

[4] They both rely on iterations.

Table 8.3 Dual method and upper bounds

	Order	5 and 3	Bin	LS price
$S = 36$	Value	4.488	4.4867	4.472
$K = 40$	SE	[0.006]		
$V = 0.02$	RMSE	[0.0013]		
$T = 1$				
$S = 36$	Value	4.849	4.8483	4.821
$K = 40$	SE	[0.007]		
$V = 0.02$	RMSE	[0.0004]		
$T = 2$				
$S = 36$	Value	7.11	7.1092	7.091
$K = 40$	SE	[0.011]		
$V = 0.04$	RMSE	[0.0001]		
$T = 1$				
$S = 36$	Value	8.519	8.5142	8.488
$K = 40$	SE	[0.008]		
$V = 0.04$	RMSE	[0.0057]		
$T = 2$				
$S = 38$	Value	3.258	3.2572	3.244
$K = 40$	SE	[0.009]		
$V = 0.02$	RMSE	[0.0001]		
$T = 1$				
$S = 38$	Value	3.752	3.7514	3.3735
$K = 40$	SE	[0.009]		
$V = 0.02$	RMSE	[0.0001]		
$T = 2$				
$S = 38$	Value	6.158	6.1545	6.139
$K = 40$	SE	[0.011]		
$V = 0.04$	RMSE	[0.0035]		
$T = 1$				
$S = 38$	Value	7.681	7.6749	7.669
$K = 40$	SE	[0.013]		
$V = 0.04$	RMSE	[0.0057]		
$T = 2$				

Order refers to the polynomial order. S is the stock price, K the option strike, V the stock price volatility and T the time to maturity. SE and RMSE are standard errors and root mean squares errors.

APPENDIX A8.1

Proof of Lemma 8.2

Lemma 8.1 is an intuitively simple result and we report it for completeness.

First note that if M^* is in L^2 then $\sup_{i>0} EM^{*2} < \infty$. Define with $\|M^*\|^2 = E(M_\infty^{*2})$ the norm for the μ^2 martingales M^*. Jensen inequality implies

$$E(M_\infty^{*2} | F_i) \geq E(M_\infty^* | F_i)^2 \tag{8.19}$$

$$E(M_i^*)^2 \leq E(M_\infty^{*2} | F_i) \tag{8.20}$$

Then it follows that

$$M_i^* : \mu^2 \to L^2(F_\infty) \tag{8.21}$$

Proof of Theorem 8.1

First note that if the process $M_1, M_2, \ldots$ is a martingale then it follows that C_i^* is a martingale and therefore $\sup EC_i^{*2} = \|C_\infty^{*2}\|_2^2 = E[C_\infty^{*2}] < \infty$.

Definition A8.1

Let $C^*(C_i^*)$ be a martingale such that $E[C_I^{*2}] < \infty$. It follows, using Lemma 8.1, that $C^* \in \mu^2 \to L^2(\infty)$. Also, let $C_i := E(C_\infty | F_i)$, where we have defined with C_∞ the limit of the sequence C_i^*.

Doob's L^2 inequality implies

$$\sup_{i>0} |C_i^* - C_i| \to 0 \tag{8.22}$$

is in L^2. Define the value function as

$$V_i^*(X_i) = \max(\Theta_i, C_i^*(X_i)) \tag{8.23}$$

with X_0 fixed. We have

$$C_0^*(X_0) = \frac{1}{R} \sum_{j=1}^{R} V_1^*(X_{ij}) \tag{8.24}$$

$$V_0^*(X_0) = \max(\Theta_0(X_0), C_0^*(X_0)) \tag{8.25}$$

Since $C_0^* \to C_0$, it follows that $V_0^* \to V_0$.

9

Estimation of Greeks using Monte Carlo Methods

9.1 FINITE DIFFERENCE APPROXIMATIONS

In this chapter we follow Glasserman (2003). One of the simplest and direct ways of estimating Greeks by simulation is using the so-called finite difference approximation method. Consider a simple European call option and its delta $\Delta = \frac{dC}{dS_0}$. The delta measures the sensitivity of the option to small changes of the underlying stock price. To obtain an estimate of the delta we simulate two independent paths for the stock price S_T. If we consider a lognormal process[1] for S_T, we can simulate stock paths as

$$S(T) = S_0 \exp^{\left(r-(1/2)\sigma^2\right)T + \sigma\sqrt{T}\varepsilon} \qquad (9.1)$$

where ε are standard normal numbers. After using small perturbation (ψ), we obtain

$$S(T) = (S_0 + \psi) \exp^{\left(r-(1/2)\sigma^2\right)T + \sigma\sqrt{T}\varepsilon'} \qquad (9.1)'$$

The simulated payoffs from (9.1) and (9.1)' are

$$g(S(T)) = \max(S(T) - K, 0)$$
$$g(S(T) + \psi) = \max(S(T)(\psi) - K, 0)$$

Thus a forward estimator of the delta can be obtained as

$$\Delta^* = \psi^{-1}[C^*(S(T)(\psi)) - C^*(S(T))] \qquad (9.2)$$

The forward estimator in (9.2) is biased in that

$$E[\Delta^* - \Delta] = \frac{1}{2}\frac{\partial^2 C}{\partial S^2(0)}\psi + O(\psi^2)$$

The convergence rate can be improved by considering a central difference estimator with simulations at $S(0) + \psi$ and $S(0) - \psi$:

$$E[\Delta^* - \Delta] = O(\psi^2)$$

---

[1] This assumption could be relaxed and the same approach as the ones described in the following sections adopted.

Since paths are uncorrelated, the variance of the estimator is given by the sum of the variances of the individual estimators. Thus, choosing a smaller ψ may help reducing the bias, but will increase the variance of the estimator. In fact, consider the function $n^*(\Delta)$, as $\psi \to 0$:

$$\text{Var}[n^*(\Delta + \psi) - n^*(\Delta - \psi)]/2\psi$$
$$= \frac{1}{4\psi^2}[\text{Var}(n^*(\Delta + \psi)) + \text{Var}(\Delta - \psi)] \to \infty$$

Common random numbers can be used in practical applications to reduce the variance.

The finite approximation method can be used to estimate various Greeks for European options and it is rather simple to implement. The main drawback with this methodology is that we need to carry out, in general, $1 + s$ simulations for each parameter s we consider. The first simulation is necessary to compute an estimate of the parameter of interest, furthermore, s additional simulations are necessary to compute estimates of the perturbed parameters.[2] Note, however, that this methodology uses an approximation of Δ rather than computing the appropriate derivative.

9.2   PATHWISE DERIVATIVES ESTIMATION

The methodologies presented in this and the next section offer the advantage that a simulation at a single point allows us to estimate both the price of the security and the respective Greek of interest. Glasserman (2003) and Broadie and Glasserman (1996) show how these methodologies can be used to compute Greeks for a variety of options. The first method we discuss is based on the direct estimation of the Greeks, the pathwise method.

Let us consider Equation (9.2) and take its limit as

$$\frac{dC^*}{dS_0} = \lim_{\psi \to 0} \psi^{-1}[C^*(S(T) + \psi) - C^*(S(T))] = \frac{dC}{dS_0} \qquad (9.3)$$

Equation (9.3) suggests that we can consider the discounted payoff function $C(S_T) = e^{-rT} E[\max(S(T) - K)^+]$ and apply the chain rule to obtain

$$\frac{dC}{dS(0)} = \frac{dC}{dS(T)} \frac{dS(T)}{dS(0)} \qquad (9.4)$$

The derivative above vanishes if $S(T) = K$; however, since this event occurs with probability zero, we are certain that the derivative in (9.4) exists. Let us work out each of the components in Equation (9.4). We start with $dC/dS(T)$. Suppose that I is an indicator function taking on the value $I = 1$ if $S(T) > K$.

---

[2] In effect, we need to simulate at ψ and then at $-\psi$. Furthermore, if we are also interested in the estimate of the option price, we will also need an additional simulation.

It follows that

$$\frac{dC}{dS(T)} = e^{-rT} I(S(T) > K) \tag{9.5}$$

The second term in Equation (9.4) can be easily computed from (9.1):

$$\frac{dS(T)}{dS(0)} = e^{(r-(1/2)\sigma^2)T + \sigma\sqrt{T}\varepsilon} \tag{9.6}$$

Since $e^{(r-(1/2)\sigma^2)T + \sigma\sqrt{T}\varepsilon} = S_T/S_0$, it follows that

$$\frac{dS(T)}{dS(0)} = \frac{S(T)}{S(0)}$$

Finally, an estimator of the delta can now be defined:

$$\frac{dC}{dS_0} = e^{-rT} \frac{S(T)}{S(0)} I(S(T) > K) \tag{9.7}$$

The estimator in (9.7) is an unbiased estimator and its expected value is therefore the Black and Scholes delta:

$$E\left(\frac{dC}{dS_0}\right) = \frac{d}{dS_0} E(C) \tag{9.8}$$

Other Greeks can be computed using the same approach.[3]

Remark 9.1

Note that this methodology uses the simulated values

$$\frac{1}{M} \sum_{i=1}^{M} e^{-rT} \left[\frac{S(T_i)}{S(0)} I(S(T_i) > K)\right]$$

Taking the expectations and using Equation (9.6) to eliminate ε yields the Black and Scholes delta (this proof is left as an exercise). This implies that the pathwise estimator does have the correct limit.

We provide a further example where we consider a floating strike lookback[4] put option. This has a discounted payoff given by

$$C^p = e^{-rT}(S_{\max} - S(T)) \tag{9.9}$$

with

$$S_{\max} = \max_{1 < i < T} S(t_i) \tag{9.10}$$

---

[3] Note that we cannot use this approach to compute gammas or Greeks for options whose payoff is discontinuous (i.e. digital, barriers, etc.). In fact, the gamma of a plain vanilla option is equivalent to the delta of a digital option.

[4] We shall introduce exotic options in the following chapters.

An application of the chain rule gives

$$\frac{dC^P}{dS(0)} = \frac{dC^P}{dS_{max}}\frac{dS_{max}}{dS(0)} \tag{9.11}$$

It follows from (9.9) that

$$\frac{dC^P}{dS_{max}} = e^{-rT} \tag{9.12}$$

and also that

$$\frac{dS_{max}}{dS(0)} = \frac{\max dS(t_i)}{dS(0)} = \frac{\max S(t_i)}{S(0)} = \frac{S\,max}{S(0)} \tag{9.13}$$

Combining (9.12) and (9.13), we obtain

$$\frac{dC^P}{dS(0)} = e^{-rT}\frac{S\,max}{S(0)} \tag{9.14}$$

Equation (9.14) has the following interpretation. Suppose you buy plain vanilla put options with strike equal to the maximum price reached by the underlying stock and the same maturity as an equivalent lookback option. Also, suppose that, at discrete intervals, you sell the option and use the money to buy a new one with strike equal to the maximum price reached by the stock over that interval. Using this rolling-down strategy you can replicate (9.14) which can now be rewritten as

$$\frac{dC^P}{dS(0)} = \frac{e^{-rT(S\,max - S(T))}}{S(0)} = \frac{P}{S(0)} \tag{9.15}$$

The pathwise delta estimator above is an unbiased estimator. One can use a similar approach to find delta estimators for Asian options and barrier options, for example, as well as other Greeks.

9.3   LIKELIHOOD RATIO METHOD

The likelihood ratio method (LR) is an alternative method to estimate Greeks. To introduce the method, consider the following European call option:

$$C = e^{-rT}\max(S(T) - K, 0) \tag{9.16}$$

Assume a Black and Scholes economy and thus a lognormal process for the stock price. Under the risk-neutral measure, the density for the stock price, $S(T)$, is

$$g(x) = \frac{1}{x\sigma\sqrt{T}}n(d(x))$$

where $n(.)$ is the standard normal density:

$$d(x) = \frac{\ln(x/S(0)) - (r - \frac{1}{2}\sigma^2)T}{\sigma\sqrt{T}}$$

Once the density is known, the Greeks can be easily computed. In fact, consider the payoff in Equation (9.16). Given the density, the value of a call option C can be written as

$$C = \int_0^\infty e^{-rT} \text{Max}(x - K, 0) \frac{\partial g(x)}{\partial S(0)} dx$$

Multiply and divide the integrand by $g(x)$ (note that $(\partial g/\partial S(0))/g = \partial \ln g/\partial S(0)$):

$$C = E\left[e^{-rT}\text{Max}(S(T) - K, 0)\frac{\partial \ln(g(S(T)))}{\partial S(0)}\right] \tag{9.17}$$

where in (9.17) we have replaced the integral with the expectation. Equation (9.17) is the likelihood estimator of the delta and it is an unbiased estimator:

$$\frac{\partial}{\partial S(0)} E(.) = E\left[(.)\frac{\partial \ln(g(S(T)))}{\partial S(0)}\right] \tag{9.18}$$

where $E(.) = e^{-rT}\text{Max}(S(T) - K, 0)$.

One can use the same approach to obtain estimators for a variety of Greeks. In the case of the delta

$$\frac{\partial \ln(g(x))}{\partial S(0)} = -d\left(\frac{\partial d}{\partial S(0)}\right)$$

with

$$\frac{\partial d}{\partial S(0)} = -\frac{\sigma\sqrt{T}}{S(0)\sigma^2 T}$$

Thus, the score function in Equation (9.17) is

$$\frac{\partial \ln(g(x))}{\partial S(0)} = \frac{\ln(S(T))/S(0) - (r - 0.5\sigma^2)T}{S(0)\sigma^2 T} \tag{9.19}$$

An estimator for the delta can now be easily computed using (9.17).

Remark 9.2

Note that, unlike the pathwise method, the likelihood method does not consider an explicit dependence between the parameter of interest and the underlying asset price. This means that we can use Equation (9.19) to compute delta estimators for a variety of options other than plain vanilla options. We shall see this in the next chapters.

9.4   DISCUSSION

The two methodologies presented in this chapter suggest two easy ways of computing Greeks by simulation. The main difference between the two is that pathwise methods rely on differentiating the payoff function with respect to the parameter of interest, while the likelihood ratio method relies on differentiating the density with respect to the parameter of interest. Thus, the former assumes that the parameter of interest belongs to the payoff function, while the latter assumes it is part of the density. The interchange of the derivative with the expectation, as in (9.8) and (9.18), requires that the smoothness condition for the payoff function and/or the density is satisfied. One can show that in general cases of interest in finance, these conditions are rarely a problem for the density.[5] The likelihood method can be used in applications in which the option payoff does not easily satisfy the smoothness condition.

Broadie and Glasserman (1996) compare Greeks for a European call option obtained using the methodologies introduced above with the respective analytical Black and Scholes values. They note that the estimated Greeks are accurate but the standard errors from the likelihood ratio method are generally greater than the standard errors from the other methodologies.[6] Also, they note that the use of variance reduction techniques seems to be sensitive to the methodology used.[7]

APPENDIX A9.1   PATHWISE GREEKS USING MONTE CARLO

This function computes the delta/vega estimator for call/put (European) options using the pathwise and the likelihood ratio methods discussed in Sections 9.2 and 9.3.

```
function [deltaC,deltaP, deltaLC, deltaLP, vega_C,
vega_P, VegaLC, VegaLP]=path(so,X,r,sigma,T,Rep);
%out put: deltaC/deltaP call/put delta using pathwise
methods.
%deltaLC/deltaLP call/put delta using Likelihood ratio
methods.
```

---

[5] See Broadie and Glasserman (1996) for a discussion of these conditions.

[6] This may be due to the likelihood ratio method not depending on the form of the option payoff.

[7] Particularly where the impact on the likelihood ratio method seems to be somewhat less.

```
%vega_C/vega_P vega using pathwise. VegaLC/VegaLP
vega using Likelihood
%ratio methods.
epsi=randn(Rep,1);% generate normal random numbers
St=so.*exp((r-0.5*sigma.^2)*T+sigma.*sqrt(T).*epsi);
% log normal stock price paths
Payoff1=max(St-X,0);payoff2=max(X-St,0);
I=St>X; I1=St<X;
ratio=St/so;
% call/put deltas pathwise method
delC=I.*ratio; delP=I1.*ratio;
dellC=delC*exp(-r*T);dellP=delP*exp(-r*T);
deltaC=mean(dellC);deltaP=-mean(dellP);
%call/put vegas pathwise method
vega=(St/sigma).*(log(ratio)-(r+0.5*sigma.^2).*T);
vegaC=vega.*I; vegaP=vega.*I1;
vegaCC=vegaC*exp(-r*T); vegaPP=vegaP*exp(-r*T);
%note the difference between the two vegas as Rep-?inf.
vega_C=mean(vegaCC); vega_P=abs(mean(vegaPP));
% Likelihood ratio method to compute deltas/vegas.
% we start computing the score function.
SF=(log(St/so)-(r-0.5*sigma.^2)*T)/(so*sigma.^2*T);
% multiply it by the payoffs.
dp1=Payoff1*exp(-r*T); dp2=payoff2*exp(-r*T);
dp11=dp1.*SF;
dp22=dp2.*SF;
% Average the paths to estimate the price
deltaLC=mean(dp11);
deltaLP=mean(dp22);
% Call/Put vegas using Likelihood ratio methods
d1=(log(St/so)-(r-0.5*sigma.^2)*T)/(sigma*sqrt(T));
d2=(log(so./St)+(r+0.5*sigma.^2)*T)/(sigma.^2*sqrt(T));
d3=(-d1.*d2-1/sigma).*Payoff1; d33=(-d1.*d2-1/sigma).
*payoff2;
discounted_VC=d3.*exp(-r*T); discounted_VP=d33.
*exp(-r*T);
VegaLC=mean(discounted_VC); VegaLP=mean(discounted_VP);
```

We show an application of the function 'path' presented above in Figure A9.1.

We have computed pathwise and likelihood ratio estimates of the delta for a call option with an initial stock price $100, strike price $100, risk-free rate of interest 5%, stock price volatility 10% and time to expiry 1 year. The stock does

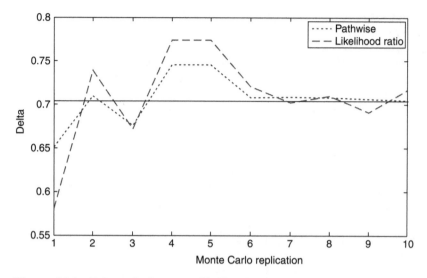

Figure A9.1   Delta pathwise versus likelihood ratio method

not pay a dividend and the number of Monte Carlo simulations ranges from 100 up to 1 000 000. The Black and Scholes delta is 0.7088 and is shown by the solid line. The pathwise estimator of the delta, after the initial 100 replications, shows a uniform type of convergence.

10

Exotic Options

10.1 INTRODUCTION

The market for exotic options is in continuous expansion. These options are used for hedging or speculation also embedded in a variety of structured products. It is essential to price and hedge these options properly. The list of exotic options is so extensive that it would be impossible to cover all of them in this chapter. We shall only look at the most common ones, namely digital, average, forward starting and barrier options, and we shall only focus on European style options.

10.2 DIGITAL OPTIONS

These are options whose payoff is discontinuous. As we shall see, this has implications for pricing and hedging. Suppose that $S(t)$ is the stock price at time t and that it follows the process in Equation (4.11). Suppose you buy a call option with strike K and that the option gives you the right to receive \$1 at the expiry date T if $S(T) \geq K$ or zero if $S(T) < K$. The option value at expiry is

$$C(T) = E^Q[f(S(T) \geq K)] \tag{10.1}$$

Consequently, the value of the option at expiry is given by $P_r(S(T) \geq K))$. Note that this corresponds to $N(d_2)$ in Equation (5.11). It follows that we can rewrite Equation (10.1) as

$$C(T) = N(d_2)$$
$$C(t) = e^{-r(T-t)} N(d_2)$$

The Greeks can be derived by differentiating the price with respect to the parameter of interest of the cumulative normal distribution. In the same way we can also obtain the value of a put option:

$$P(t) = e^{-r(T-t)} N(-d_2)$$

Binary options offer the buyer the possibility to know in advance the amount of money that will be received at expiry (if the option is in the money). However, hedging these options is rather challenging since the delta and gamma are not bounded.[1] While the delta and the gamma of an out-of-the-money digital are

---

[1] As an exercise, derive and discuss the limit of the delta and gamma functions as $T \to 0$.

very small as we approach maturity, the delta and gamma of an in-the-money digital are very large. Furthermore, if the stock price, close to maturity, oscillates around the strike, the large value of the delta and the gamma will force a trader to trade stocks excessively in order to hedge his or her option position.[2]

Digital options are the building blocks of many structured products and synthetic exotic options.

10.3   ASIAN OPTIONS

In the case of Asian options, the underlying is not the stock price but the average of the stock price calculated over an agreed period (generally over the lifetime of the option). The average price can be calculated using geometric or arithmetic averages, and it can be continuous or discrete. Practically, the continuous average is replaced by the discrete average.[3] Define by $G(t, T)$ the geometric average price over the interval $(T - t)$, and assume it is given by

$$G(.) = \prod_{i=0}^{n-1} S(t_t)^{1/n} \quad \text{with } t_i = t_1, t_2, \ldots, t_n = T \tag{10.2}$$

where we assume that the stock price is generated by a geometric Brownian motion process.

The payoff of a geometric average call option at maturity T is given by

$$C(T) = E^Q(G(.) - K)^+ \tag{10.3}$$

Equation (10.2) can be written as

$$G(.) = aS_0 \exp\left(\frac{1}{n}\sigma \sum_{i=0}^{n-1} (n - i - 1)\left(W_{t_{i+1}}^Q - W_{t_i}^Q\right)\right) \tag{10.4}$$

For any constant a the distribution of the average in (10.2) remains lognormal. If the average follows a lognormal process, using the same argument as discussed in Chapter 5, we can evaluate the expectation in (10.3) in closed form.

In the same way, the payoff of the geometric average put option is

$$P(T) = E^Q(K - G(.))^+$$

---

[2] Obviously this is one of the assumptions underlying the Black and Scholes world. However, practically this has huge implications. Hedging digitals is one of the examples where the limitation of the assumptions underlying the Black and Scholes model is more evident.

[3] This is particularly convenient when simulation methods are used since computing the continuous average implies solving a computationally intensive integral.

which can also be priced in closed form. Arithmetic average options, on the other hand, are more challenging to price. In fact, if we define the arithmetic average on the same interval as above, then

$$A(.) = \frac{1}{n} \sum_{i=0}^{n-1} S(t_i)$$

The value of a call option at expiry is given by the following expectation:

$$C(T) = E^Q (A(.) - K)^+ \tag{10.5}$$

However, now the distribution of $A(.)$ is not lognormal. In fact, the product of lognormal variables is not itself lognormal. Therefore, a closed-form evaluation of (10.5) is possible.[4] Different approaches have been suggested in this case, including Fourier transform and Monte Carlo, among others.

10.4   FORWARD START OPTIONS

Suppose you buy at time t a call option with expiry at T. Also, suppose that the strike of the option is only set at T_0, with $t \leq T_0 \leq T$. The value of the option at expiry is given by

$$C(T) = E^Q (S(T) - S(T_0))^+ \tag{10.6}$$

Thus, the value of the option at time t is

$$C(t) = E^Q [e^{-r(T-t)}(S(T) - S(T_0))] \tag{10.7}$$

Note that (10.6) can be evaluated in closed form (as shown in Chapter 5). Therefore, the price of the call option in (10.7) can be obtained easily. Thus, adjusting the Black and Scholes formula we obtain

$$C(.) = KN(d_1) + K e^{-r(T-T_0)} N(d_2)$$

The value of a put can be obtained in the same way.[5]

10.5   BARRIER OPTIONS

Barrier options are among the most widely used exotic options. There are different types of barrier options and they are very common both as hedging instruments and investment instruments embedded in structured products. A typical up-and-out barrier call option, for example, is an option that pays the

---

[4] Note, however, that all moments of $A(.)$ have been computed in closed form by Geman and Yor (1992, 1993).

[5] Note that this corresponds to an at-the-money call option issued at time T_0. We shall discuss forward start options in the following chapters.

difference $(S(T) - K)^+$ if a fixed barrier H is never reached over the lifetime of the option. Otherwise, the reward payoff will be zero:

$$C_{UO} = (S(T) - K)^*_{I_{S_{\max} \leq H}} \tag{10.8}$$

where $S_{\max} = \max_{0 \leq u \leq t} S(t)$ and I is an indicator function taking the value zero if the option reaches the barrier. The payoff of an equivalent up-and-in barrier call option is

$$C_{UI} = (S(T) - K)^*_{I_{S_{\max} > H}} \tag{10.9}$$

Thus, the value of a plain vanilla European option C_E is given by

$$C_E = C_{UO} + C_{UI}$$

(this proof is left as an exercise).

Generally, these options can be priced in closed form within a Black and Scholes framework.[6] Recall the reflection principle for Brownian motions and the joint density of a Brownian motion with its maximum/minimum value. We know that the transition density of a Brownian motion and its maximum are given by

$$F(W) = P(W_{\max} > H, W(t) < W)$$
$$= 1 - N\left(\frac{2H - W}{\sqrt{t}}\right) = N\left(\frac{W - 2H}{\sqrt{t}}\right) \tag{10.10}$$

where $W_{\max} = \max_{0 \leq s \leq t} W(s)$ and H is the barrier value.

The symmetry argument of Brownian motion only applies if the process does not contain a drift. In the absence of a drift we can use the result in (10.10) and the same argument as in Chapter 5 with the Black and Scholes formula to work out a formula to price the option. This is not possible for processes containing a drift term. However, an application of the Girsanov theorem simplifies all the calculations. Define the original Brownian motion process as

$$W(t) = ut + W^Q(t)$$

where u is the drift.

Now, write it as $f(W(t))$ and define the following random variable:

$$\frac{dP}{dQ} = \exp\left(uW^Q(T) - \frac{1}{2}u^2T\right)$$

The Girsanov theorem then implies the following:

$$E^P[f(W(T)_{I_{W_{\max} \leq H}})] = E^Q\left[f(W(T))\frac{dP}{dQ}_{I_{W_{\max} \leq H}}\right] \tag{10.11}$$

---

[6] Note that in the case of an up-and-out barrier option we require that $S_0 < H$ and also that $K < H$.

which integrated gives

$$= \int_{-\infty}^{H} f(W)e^{(uW-\frac{1}{2}u^2T)}N\left(\frac{W-2H}{\sqrt{T}}\right)dW \tag{10.12}$$

As $N(W) = e^{-\frac{1}{2}W^2}/\sqrt{2\pi}$ a few calculations lead to the following:

$$F^u(.) = \frac{1}{\sqrt{2\pi T}}\exp\left(-\frac{1}{2T}(W-2H)^2 + uW - \frac{1}{2}u^2T\right)$$

$$= \frac{e^{2Hu}}{\sqrt{T}}N\left(\frac{W-2H-uT}{\sqrt{T}}\right) = P^u(.) \tag{10.13}$$

We now have an explicit result, showing the joint distribution function of a Brownian motion with drift and its maximum, which can be used to price a barrier option. Note that the stock price process can be written as follows:

$$S(T) = S_0e^{\sigma[uT+W^Q(T)]}$$

$$S(T) = S_0e^{\sigma W(T)}$$

It follows that the call option payoff is given by

$$C_{UO} = (S(T) - K)^+_{I_{S_{max} \leq H}}$$

$$C_{UO} = (S_0e^{\sigma W^Q(T)} - K)^+_{I_{max} \leq H}$$

The value today of the call is given by the following:

$$V_{UO}(0) = e^{-rT}\int_{x_0}^{x_1}(S_0e^{\sigma W^Q(T)} - K)^+_{I_{S_{max} \leq H}}g(W) \tag{10.14}$$

where $g(W) = \frac{d}{dW}F^u(W)$ and we have used the bounds (x_0, x_1) to define an in-the-money call, i.e.

$$\frac{1}{\sigma}\log\left(\frac{K}{S_0}\right) = x_0 \leq W(T) \leq \frac{1}{\sigma}\log\left(\frac{H}{S_o}\right) = x_1$$

Solving the integral in (10.14) (as we did in Chapter 5) gives a formula to price barrier options.

10.5.1 Hedging barrier options

Hedging barrier options is a challenging task. Indeed, because of the unique structure of these options, a standard hedging approach does not always work. The main difficulty is the discontinuous payoff which generates big spikes in the delta function when the price of the underlying is close to the barrier threshold. A dynamic hedging scheme, in this case, consists of selling/buying a continuously increasing amount of the underlying asset. Clearly this is not practically feasible.[7]

A different part of the literature has focused on implementing static hedging strategies for barrier options. For example, one could implement a calendar spread strategy using plain vanilla options with strikes equal to the barrier but with different expiry times. However, the main (practical) problem with this strategy is that, since we do not know when or if the barrier will be hit, it is difficult to design a portfolio with options having the same expiry as the time when the asset crosses the barrier. In theory this would only be possible if the portfolio contains an infinite number of plain vanilla options with different maturities.

Carr and Chou (1997) take a different approach and suggest designing a portfolio of different plain vanilla options with different strikes. The adjusted payoff of this portfolio will replicate the barrier option position. However, practically, this strategy can result in a high hedging error. Hedging barrier options continues to attract a significant amount of research effort.

APPENDIX A10.1   DIGITAL OPTIONS

This code shows an application of Monte Carlo methods to price the digital option introduced in Section 9.2. The function 'digital' uses the function 'GeneratePaths' introduced in Chapter 6, Appendix A6.2. Note that, in this case, you do not need to simulate stock prices at each time step; therefore you can set NSteps $= 1$.

```
function CD=digital(so, X, r, sigma, T,NSteps,Rep,PType)
%so initial stock price, X the strike, r the risk free
rate of interest,
%sigma is the stock price volatility, NSteps is the
number of time steps,
%Rep the number of replications.
discount=exp(-r*T);
SPaths=GeneratePaths(so,r,sigma,T,NSteps,Rep,PType);
%generate stock prices paths
SPaths(:,1)=[];
I=(SPaths>X); %this is an indicator function
optionprice=discount*I;
% the option price using antithetic is the average of
the two prices.
CD=mean(optionprice); %option price
```

---

[7] Obviously, this would involve continuous trading, which is impossible in practice. Furthermore, it will also involve high transaction costs. For prices of the underlying asset close to the barrier, the trader will trade the underlying far too often and in increased amounts of the underlying asset.

We show an application of the code above to price a digital call option with an initial stock price equal to $100, strike price equal to $100, a risk-free rate of interest equal to 5% and stock price volatility equal to 30%; the stock does not pay a dividend and the expiry date of the option is 1 year. After running 100 000 replications we obtain CD = 0.4819.

11

Pricing and Hedging Exotic
Options

11.1 INTRODUCTION

This chapter discusses various applications of Monte Carlo simulation to price exotic options. We know that, for most of these options, one can obtain an analytical price (within a Black and Scholes economy). However, Monte Carlo can be extended to more general cases where closed-form solutions are difficult to obtain or are obtained at the cost of imposing restrictions on the model. Although the chapter only focuses on some of the most common exotic options, such as Asian, barrier and forward start options, the same methodologies can also be extended to price a broader variety of exotics. The final sections describe ways of computing Greeks for exotic options using pathwise and likelihood ratio methods.

11.2 MONTE CARLO SIMULATIONS AND ASIAN OPTIONS

There is no analytical formula to price arithmetic Asian options. Thus, Monte Carlo simulation can be an attractive method in this case.

An application of Monte Carlo simulation to price Asian options proceeds in the following way. We assume that the stock price follows a geometric Brownian motion process given by

$$dS(t) = rS(t)dt + \sigma S(t)dW(t)$$

Thus, its solution is given by

$$S(t + dt) = S_0 \left(\exp r - 0.5\sigma^2 \right) dt + \sigma \sqrt{dt} z \qquad (11.1)$$

We can use (11.1) as a DGP to compute $S_j(t + dt)$, $j = 1, 2, \ldots, M$ and $t = 0, 1, 2, \ldots, T$. $A(.) = 1/n \sum_{i=0}^{n-1} S(t_i)$ can then be computed using the simulated stock paths. For each j, we calculate the option payoff, max$(0, A(.) - K) = V_j$. Discounting the payoff using the risk-free rate gives the price of the option.

Remark 11.1

This example assumes discrete monitoring of the average as opposed to the continuous case. Although the latter case is far more demanding to deal with, it is also less common in practice.

The simulation scheme above can be improved using one of the variance techniques discussed in Chapter 8. We now show an application of control variates. The appendix shows a MATLAB code that implements this approach.

Kenna and Vorst (1990) suggest a simple method to price geometric Asian options within the Black and Scholes framework. We use this formula to compute its analytical price as a control in our simulation. A Monte Carlo application to price Asian options using a control variate is presented in Chapter 6, Appendix A6.2.

11.3 SIMULATION OF GREEKS FOR EXOTIC OPTIONS

The pathwise and likelihood ratio methods discussed in the previous chapters can be easily extended to compute Greeks in this case. The computation of the option delta follows along this line. With a little extra effort, the approach can also be extended to compute the gamma and the vega of the option. Consider the discounted payoff of an Asian call option:

$$C(.) = E[e^{-rT} \max(0, A(.) - K)]$$

As we did in Chapter 8, and using the chain rule, the delta is computed as

$$\frac{\partial C}{\partial S(0)} = \frac{\partial C}{\partial A(.)} \frac{\partial A(.)}{\partial S(0)}$$

It follows that

$$\frac{\partial}{\partial A(.)} \max(0, A(.) - K) = 0 \qquad \text{if} \quad A(.) < K$$

$$\frac{\partial}{\partial A(.)} \max(0, A(.) - K) = 1 \qquad \text{if} \quad A(.) > K$$

If we define the indicator function I, we have

$$I = 0 \quad \text{if} \quad A(.) < K$$
$$I = 1 \quad \text{if} \quad A(.) > K$$

and it follows that

$$\frac{\partial}{\partial A(.)} = e^{-rT} I(A(.) > K)$$

To implement this delta estimator we also need

$$\frac{\partial A(.)}{\partial S(0)} = \frac{\partial}{\partial S(0)} \frac{1}{n} \sum_{i=1}^{n} S(t_i) = \frac{1}{n} \frac{\partial}{\partial S(0)} \sum_{i=1}^{n} S(t_i) \qquad (11.2)$$

From (11.2), it follows that

$$\frac{\partial A(.)}{\partial S(0)} = \frac{A(.)}{S(0)}$$

Hence, the delta is given by

$$\frac{\partial C}{\partial S(0)} = e^{-rT} \frac{A(.)}{S(0)} I(A(.) > K) \qquad (11.3)$$

Equation (11.3) can be applied to the simulated stock price paths in order to compute the option delta.

Likelihood ratio methods can also be used in this case. Remember that this estimator does not depend on the specific payoff function since it focuses on the density. Thus, within a Black and Scholes economy, the score function obtained in Chapter 9, Equation (9.18), can still be used here. Thus, combining the payoff function above and Equation (9.18), we obtain

$$\Delta = e^{-rT} \left[\text{Max}(A(.) - K, 0) \frac{\partial \ln(g(S(T)))}{\partial S(0)} \right] \qquad (11.4)$$

Equation (11.4) is the likelihood ratio estimator of the Asian delta.

11.4   MONTE CARLO SIMULATIONS AND FORWARD START OPTIONS

With a forward start option we can use the same approach as the one in Section 11.2. However, we simplify it by following Broadie and Kaya (2004). Recall the option payoff under the measure Q:

$$C(T) = E^Q (S(T) - kS(T_0))^+$$

where k is a constant that determines the strike.[1]

At time T_0 the strike price, the stock price and the expiry date are known. Thus, one can use the Black and Scholes formula to find the price of the option. Call this price $C_{BS}(S(0), K, T)$. The option price is linearly homogeneous with respect to the strike and the initial price (i.e. $C_{BS}(S(0), kS(0), T) = S(0)C_{BS}(1, k, T)$), so the forward option price formula can be written as

$$C(T) = E^Q[S(0)C_{BS}(1, k, T - T_0)]^+ \qquad (11.5)$$

Equation (10.4) can be used to compute a Monte Carlo price of the option.

---

[1] Note that, if $k = 1$, the option is in-the-money option at time T_0.

11.5 SIMULATION OF THE GREEKS FOR EXOTIC OPTIONS

Pathwise and likelihood ratio methods can also be used to compute Greeks for forward start options. For example, the delta is given by

$$\Delta = e^{-rT_0} C_{BS}(1, k, T - T_0 - 1) \frac{S_0}{s} \tag{11.6}$$

where s is the stock price at time t_0. On the other hand, the gamma of a forward start option is equal to zero (this proof is left as an exercise).

The likelihood ratio estimators of the delta and the gamma follow the same approach as described above. Since there is no dependence of these estimators on the payoff function, the likelihood ratio for the delta is given by the following:

$$\Delta = \left[e^{-rT} (S(T) - kS(T_0))^+ \frac{\partial \ln(g(S(T)))}{\partial S(0)} \right] \tag{11.7}$$

Gamma can be obtained in a similar fashion (this proof is left as an exercise).

11.6 MONTE CARLO SIMULATIONS AND BARRIER OPTIONS

Discrete barrier options can also be priced using Monte Carlo simulation. Assuming a Black and Scholes world and a simple plain vanilla Monte Carlo approach, the simulation starts by using Equation (6.5) to generate stock paths over the discrete interval $t_0, t_1, \ldots, t_T = T$. Given the option under consideration (i.e. up and out, down and in, etc.), one can monitor the stock price crossing a pre-defined barrier. For example, for a knockout barrier option with strike K, expiry time T and barrier $H > S(0)$, we monitor at each time step the barrier for the condition $I[\max_{t_1 \le i \le t_T} S(t_i) < H]$. Thus, the discounted final payoff is given by $C(S(t_m)) = e^{-rT} (S(T) - K)^+ I[\max_{t_1 \le i \le t_T} S(t_i) < H]$, and it is calculated using the paths that have survived the stated condition.

When dealing with barrier options, the main problem with this approach is that in the case of many paths not surviving, the payoff is calculated using very few paths. Hence, this will increase the variance of the Monte Carlo estimator. Glasserman and Staum (2001) suggest implementing Monte Carlo methods using importance sampling. This methodology is illustrated below. In addition, a MATLAB code demonstrating this approach is reported in Appendix A11.2.

Consider again the barrier option introduced above and assume a Black and Scholes economy. Also, assume equal spaced intervals denoted by Δ. The importance sampling estimator proposed in Glasserman and Staum (2001) relies on simulating stock paths conditional on $I_{t+1} = 1$ (assuming that the conditional distribution is known).[2] Thus, it follows that for stock prices at maturity the condition $I_T = 1$ is preserved. However, as this distribution is biased the option price computed using this distribution is also biased. For this reason an adjustment is necessary. Define the likelihood ratio function $L_i = \prod_{j=0}^{i-1} p_r(S_j)$, where $p_r(s) = P_r[S_{j+1} \neq \Delta | S_j = s]$. The likelihood ratio shows the probability for a given stock path to survive the next period.

We shall see that within the Black and Scholes world such a probability can be easily computed. For example, the adjusted payoff $L_T C(S(T))$ can be computed and the option priced. Consider the simulation of forward stock prices under a lognormal process using

$$S(t_{i+1}) = S(t_i) \exp \left((r - 0.5\sigma^2)\Delta t + \sigma\sqrt{\Delta t}\Phi^{-1}(U) \right) \tag{11.8}$$

where U is a uniformly distributed random term and Φ is the standard cdf. Different algorithms are available to deal with the inverse transform problem in (11.8).

Suppose that $U = (1 - p_r(S(t_i))) + V p_r(S(t_i))$, where V is uniformly distributed and

$$p_r(S(t_i)) = P_r(S(t_{i+1}) \geq H | S(t_i))$$
$$= \Phi \left((\ln \frac{S(t_i)}{H}) + (r - 0.5\sigma^2)\Delta t / (\sigma\sqrt{\Delta t}) \right)$$

This transformation guarantees that stock prices (in the next period) are at least as large as necessary to prevent a knockout. The methodology can also be extended, with very little effort, to the case of continuous monitoring (see Glasserman and Staum, 2001, for details).

Remark 11.2

Glasserman and Staum (2001) show that the estimator is unbiased and efficient (compared with the simple Monte Carlo estimator). They also present an empirical example where they show that the methodology works well (in reducing the variance of the estimator) when the variance reduction is associated with the knockout. However, when the variance of the payoff is much higher and also dominant, the methodology becomes less effective. They also point out that the probability of knockout is dominant when the underlying asset is close to the barrier relative to its volatility and maturity. In this situation the payoff variance can be higher and dominant. Therefore, in these cases, they suggest combining importance sampling with other variance reduction techniques.

---

[2] See Glasserman and Staum (2001) for an example when the conditional distribution is unknown.

APPENDIX A11.1   THE PRICE AND THE DELTA
OF FORWARD START OPTIONS

In the following code we show an application of the methodology presented in Chapter 10, Section 10.4 to compute the delta of a forward start option. The function 'forward' uses the initial stock price (so), the interest rate (r), volatility (sigma), the time to maturity (T) and the dividend yield (dividend).

```
function [price, delta]=forward(so,r,sigma,T,dividend,
NSteps,Rep,To)
% this simply uses the GenPathsA function to
generate stock prices.
SPaths=GenPathsA(so,r,sigma,T,NSteps,Rep);
SPaths(:,1)=[];
% compute the Black and Scholes price.
d1=(log(1/1)+(r-dividend+0.5*(sigma.^2))*
(T-To))/(sigma*(T-To).^0.5);
d2=d1-sigma*(T-To).^0.5;
Nd1=normcdf(d1); Nd2=normcdf(d2);
% call option price.
call=exp(-dividend*(T-To))*Nd1-exp(-r*(T-To))*Nd2;
Strike=SPaths(:,round(To*NSteps));
price1=call.*Strike.*exp(-r*To);
% call price
price=mean(price1);
% call delta
delta1=exp(-r*To)*call*Strike/so;
delta=mean(delta1);
```

As an example, consider an initial stock price so $= 60$; $r = 0.08$; sigma $= 0.3$; $T = 1$; NSteps $= 100$; Rep $= 100000$; To $= 0.25$; and dividend $= 0$. The price and the delta of the option are: price $= 7.93$ and delta $= 0.13$.

APPENDIX A11.2   THE PRICE OF BARRIER OPTIONS
USING IMPORTANCE SAMPLING

As a second example, we show an application of the methodology presented in Chapter 10, Section 10.6 to compute the price of a down-and-out call option.

```
function barrierC=barrier1(so,K,r,sigma,T,NSteps,Rep, bar)
% This code computes the price-barrierC-of a barrier
option (down-and-out call)using
%control variate (importance sampling). so is the
initial stock price, K the option strike, r the risk free
```

rate of interest,
%sigma the stock price volatility, NSteps the number of
steps in the
%simulation, Rep the number of simulations and bar the
barrier.

```
dt=T/NSteps;
SPaths=zeros(Rep,NSteps);
SPaths(:,1)=so;
psii=zeros(Rep,NSteps); U1=zeros(Rep,NSteps);
for step=1:Rep
    st=so;  %initialize the simulation
    curtime=0;
    for step1=1:NSteps
    curtime=curtime+dt;
psi=normcdf((log(st/bar)+(r-0.5*sigma.^2)*dt)/
(sigma*sqrt(dt)));
psii(step,step1)=psi;
U=(1-psi)+rand.*psi; %generate uniform random numbers
U1(step,step1)=U;
st=st*exp((r-0.5*sigma.^2).*dt+sigma*sqrt(dt)*norminv(U));
% use inverse transform to compute stock prices
SPaths(step,step1)=st;
minn(step)=min(SPaths(step,:)); % define the barrier
minn1=minn';
    end
end
Li=prod(psii(:,1:NSteps-1),2); % define the likelihood
ratio
I=(minn1>bar); % indicator function-one can also not
consider it in this case
payoff=max(SPaths(:,NSteps)-K,0);
payoff1=payoff.*I; payoff2=payoff.*Li;
barrierC=mean(payoff2.*exp(-r*T));
```

As an example we price a down-and-out call option when the initial stock price is $100, the strike price is $100, the barrier is set at 80, the time to expiry is 1 year, the risk-free rate of interest is 5% per annum and stock price volatility 30%. Using crude Monte Carlo 100 time steps and 100 000 replications, the price (standard error in parentheses) of the option is 13.79 (0.0103). We now use the function 'barrier1' to price the same option but we set the number of replications equal to 10 000. The option price (standard error in parentheses) is: price $= 13.60$ (0.0022).

Note that if the number of replications in the crude Monte Carlo is set at 10 000, the option price is (standard error in parentheses) 13.34 (0.0788). The importance sample can help to reduce the sample error of the option price estimator.

12

Stochastic Volatility Models

12.1 INTRODUCTION

The Black and Scholes formula is widely used to price European style options. Recently some empirical studies have shown that stock returns show a higher degree of kurtosis than is assumed in the normal distribution. This has led to a search for different models that can explain the excess kurtosis.

Different approaches have been suggested in the literature. One approach which has been widely used makes the volatility stochastic. Stochastic volatility models have been found to fit the implied skew in the market better. However, although in very general cases, as discussed in this chapter, closed-form solutions have been proposed to price derivatives, in many other cases computational methods are still required.

The aim of this, and the following chapter, is to introduce some relevant issues in the computational analysis of stochastic volatility models.

12.2 THE MODEL

In general, stochastic volatility models (SVM) can be analysed within the following framework:

$$dS(t) = \mu S(t)dt + \sigma(t)S(t)dW_1(t) \tag{12.1}$$

$$\sigma(t) = f(V(t)) \tag{12.2}$$

$$dV(t) = a(t, V(t))dt + b(t, V(t))dW_2(t) \tag{12.3}$$

$$dW_1(t)dW_2(t) = \rho dt \tag{12.4}$$

where $W_1(t)$ and $W_2(t)$ are two correlated Brownian motions (satisfying Equation (12.4)) with correlation coefficient ρ, the variance process V and time varying parameters a, b. Using a Cholesky decomposition, Equation (12.4) can be rewritten as

$$W_1(t) = \rho W_2(t) + \sqrt{1 - \rho^2}Z(t) \tag{12.5}$$

where $Z(t)$ is a standard normal variable.

Hull and White (1987) (HW) consider the following stochastic process driving the variance in Equation (12.3):

$$dV(t) = aV(t)dt + bV(t)dW(t) \tag{12.6}$$

where a and b are constants. Assuming no correlation (i.e. $\rho = 0$), HW derive an analytical formula for pricing options. However, this is rather restrictive. Some empirical studies show evidence that the correlation is not equal to zero and, generally, in the equity case, the correlation is negative.[1] In theory, the model can be extended to the case where $\rho \neq 0$, but then closed-form solutions can no longer be obtained (i.e. numerical methods would then be required). Note that the HW model does not consider the possibility that volatility is mean-reverting (some empirical studies have shown that, generally, that is indeed the case).

Heston (1993) proposes a square root diffusion process with some convenient characteristics that better address the criticisms mentioned above. However, before introducing the model, it is convenient to discuss some of the main features of a square root diffusion process.

12.3   SQUARE ROOT DIFFUSION PROCESS

Feller (1951) analysed the following class of models for the variance process:

$$dV(t) = k(\theta - V(t))dt + \xi \sqrt{V(t)}dW(t) \tag{12.7}$$

where θ is the long-run variance, k is the rate of mean reversion and ξ is the volatility of the volatility or even the volatility of variance. With this model, if $V_0 > 0$, then $V(t)$ will never be negative and if $2k\theta \geq \sigma^2$, $V(t)$ will almost surely be positive. The drift in Equation (12.7) suggests that the variance process $V(t)$ is pulled back towards the long-run equilibrium θ at a rate controlled by the parameter k.

The stochastic differential equation (SDE) in (12.7) has no explicit solution but its transition density is known. In fact, Cox et al. (1985) show that, conditional on V_s, V_t with $s < t$ has a noncentral chi-square distribution. We shall see that this property can be exploited to compute prices and Greeks for options under stochastic volatility.

When Monte Carlo simulation is used to solve Equation (12.7), one generally relies on the so-called Euler discretization processes (or similar schemes). Define n time steps as $t_0 < t_1 < \ldots < t_n$. Equation (12.7) can be solved numerically at each time t_i using

$$V(t_{i+1}) = V(t_i) + k(\theta - V(t_i))[t_{i+1} - t_i] + \xi\sqrt{V(t_i)} + \sqrt{t_{i+1} - t_i}Z(t+1) \tag{12.8}$$

---

[1] Note that we do not introduce all the stochastic volatility models, but rather focus on the two main ones described in this and the following section.

where $Z_1, Z_2, \ldots, Z_n$ are independent standard normal variables. Note that when using (12.8) for simulations, $V(t)$(inside the square root) can be negative. In fact, if $V(t) > 0$:

$$P_r(V(t + \Delta t) < 0) = N\left(\frac{-k(\theta - V(t))\Delta t - k\theta}{\xi\sqrt{V(t)}\Delta t}\right)$$

where N is the standard normal cumulative distribution function.

The probability that the variance will turn into negative territory decreases as we increase the number of steps (i.e. as Δt becomes smaller). When we calibrate stochastic volatility models and ξ is set quite high, the problem that the process may switch into negative territory is real.

Generally one relies on the *absorption* (which involves setting the variance process equal to zero whenever a path takes on a negative value (i.e. $v^+ = \max(v, 0)$) or *reflection* (i.e. reflecting it in the origin and continuing from there, $|v|$) to fix the problem. Lord *et al.* (2008) suggest an alternative method called the *full truncation* scheme. The full truncation scheme relies on truncating the drift in the variance process such that the drift becomes $-k(v_i^+ - \theta)\Delta t_i$.

Cerrato (2009) extends the Longstaff and Schwartz (2001) approach to price American options under stochastic volatility. The framework used is the Heston model with the variance process given by Equation (12.8). To reduce the implicit error within the Euler equation (12.8), and at the same time to keep the empirical model consistent with the theoretical model, Cerrato (2009) suggests a drift transformation in Equation (12.8) above as follows:

$$V(t_{i+1}) = V(t_i) + k^*(\theta^* - V(t_i))[t_{i+1} - t_i] + \xi\sqrt{V(t_i)} + \sqrt{t_{i+1} - t_i}Z(t + 1)$$

where the market price of risk is $\Lambda(S, V, t) = \lambda V, \lambda = k\xi, k^* = k(1 + \xi)$ and $\theta^* = \theta/k^*$. Cerrato (2009) suggests applying the Ito lemma to the log stock price to avoid stock prices becoming negative martingales:

$$Ln(S(t_{i+1})) = Ln(S(t_i)) + (r - 0.5V(t_i))[t_{i+1} - t_i]$$
$$+\sqrt{V(t_i)} + \sqrt{t_{i+1} - t_i}Z(t_{i+1})$$

Lastly, a reflection rule can be used to deal with negative variance processes and the scheme can be implemented using control variates. This final Euler scheme proves to be very effective and efficient when pricing European and American style options.

12.4   THE HESTON STOCHASTIC VOLATILITY MODEL (HSVM)

This is probably the most widely known stochastic volatility model. The model is very popular among practitioners because of its simplicity when extended to include jumps for example. The variance process follows a square root diffusion process, given by

$$dS(t) = \mu S(t)dt + \sqrt{V(t)}S_t dW_1(t) \tag{12.9}$$

$$dV(t) = k(\theta - V(t))dt + \xi\sqrt{V(t)}dW_2(t) \tag{12.10}$$

$$dW_1(t)dW_2(t) = \rho dt \tag{12.11}$$

Within this framework, Heston shows that one can obtain a closed-form solution for pricing options under stochastic volatility. Note that, in the Black and Scholes economy, we only have one source of uncertainty (the standard Brownian motion $W_1(t)$), driving the state variable process $S(t)$. Also, as stocks are traded assets, the market in this case is complete. However, the Heston market is different. Here, there are two sources of uncertainty ($W_1(t)$ and $W_2(t)$) driving variables such as stock price and volatility, of which only the former is a traded asset. The market is incomplete and, hence, we are short of one traded asset.

Consider a market for options on volatility and call this option VO. As with the Black and Scholes case, we can design a portfolio Π consisting, say, of a long position on a given option O (this is the option we want to price) and a short position on Δ_1 units of stocks and Δ_2 units of option VO:

$$\Pi(t) = O(t) - \Delta_1 S(t) - \Delta_2 VO(t) \tag{12.12}$$

In differential form:

$$d\Pi(t) = dO(t) - \Delta_1 dS(t) - \Delta_2 dVO(t) \tag{12.13}$$

with $O(t) = f(t, S(t)V(t))$ and $VO(t) = f(t, S(t), V(t))$. An application of the multidimensional Ito lemma to (12.13) gives[2]

$$
\begin{aligned}
d\Pi = {} & \frac{\partial O}{\partial t}dt + \frac{\partial O}{\partial S}dS + \frac{\partial O}{\partial V}dV \\
& + \frac{1}{2}\left[\frac{\partial^2 O}{\partial t^2}dt^2 + \frac{\partial^2 O}{\partial S^2}dS^2 + \frac{\partial^2 O}{\partial V^2}dV^2 + 2\frac{\partial^2 O}{\partial S\partial V}dSdV\right]\ldots \\
& -\Delta_1 dS - \Delta_2\left[\frac{\partial VO}{\partial t}dt + \frac{\partial VO}{\partial S}dS + \frac{\partial VO}{\partial V}dV\right. \\
& \left. + \frac{1}{2}\left(\frac{\partial^2 VO}{\partial t^2}dt^2 + \frac{\partial VO}{\partial S^2}dS^2\frac{\partial^2 VO}{\partial V^2}dV^2 + 2\frac{\partial^2 VO}{\partial S\partial V}dSdV\right)\right]
\end{aligned}
$$

---

[2] For simplicity, in what follows we drop the time component t from the equations describing the portfolio process.

Using the processes in (12.9) and (12.10):

$$d\Pi = \left[\frac{\partial O}{\partial t} + \frac{1}{2}V^2S^2\frac{\partial^2 O}{\partial S^2} + \frac{1}{2}\xi^2\frac{\partial^2 VO}{\partial V^2} + \rho VS\xi\frac{\partial V^2 O}{\partial S\partial V}\right]dt + \frac{\partial O}{\partial S}dS$$

$$+\frac{\partial O}{\partial V}dV - \Delta_1 dS - \Delta_2\left[\left(\frac{\partial VO}{\partial t} + \frac{1}{2}V^2S^2\frac{\partial^2 VO}{\partial S^2} + \frac{1}{2}\xi^2\frac{\partial^2 VO}{\partial V^2}\right.\right.$$

$$\left.\left. + \rho VS\xi\frac{\partial^2 VO}{\partial S\partial V}dt\right) + \frac{\partial VO}{\partial S}dS + \frac{\partial VO}{\partial V}dV\right]$$

Finally, after collecting the terms together we obtain

$$d\Pi = \left[\frac{\partial O}{\partial t} + \frac{1}{2}V^2S^2\frac{\partial^2 O}{\partial S^2} + \frac{1}{2}\xi^2\frac{\partial^2 VO}{\partial V^2} + \rho VS\xi\frac{\partial V^2 O}{\partial S\partial V}\right]dt$$

$$-\Delta_2\left[\frac{\partial VO}{\partial t} + \frac{1}{2}V^2S^2\frac{\partial VO}{\partial S^2} + \frac{1}{2}\xi^2\frac{\partial^2 VO}{\partial V^2} + \rho VS\xi\frac{\partial^2 VO}{\partial S\partial V}dt\right]$$

$$+\left[\frac{\partial O}{\partial S} - \Delta_2\frac{\partial VO}{\partial S} - \Delta_1\right]dS + \left[\frac{\partial O}{\partial V} - \Delta_2\frac{\partial VO}{\partial V}\right]dV \quad (12.14)$$

Equation (12.14) shows the evolution of $\Pi(t)$ over time. The sources of uncertainty in (12.14) are linked to changes in the stock price and variance process (i.e. dS and dV). If we can find a way to eliminate them, the equation will be deterministic. To achieve this we need

$$\frac{\partial O}{\partial S} - \Delta_2\frac{\partial VO}{\partial S} - \Delta_1 = 0 \quad (12.15)$$

$$\frac{\partial O}{\partial V} - \Delta_2\frac{\partial VO}{\partial V} = 0 \quad (12.16)$$

and

$$d\Pi = \left[\frac{\partial O}{\partial t} + \frac{1}{2}V^2S^2\frac{\partial^2 O}{\partial S^2} + \frac{1}{2}\xi^2\frac{\partial^2 O}{\partial V^2} + \rho VS\xi\frac{\partial^2 O}{\partial S\partial V}\right]dt$$

$$-\Delta_2\left[\frac{\partial VO}{\partial t} + \frac{1}{2}V^2S^2\frac{\partial^2 VO}{\partial S^2} + \rho VS\xi\frac{\partial^2 VO}{\partial S\partial V}\right]dt \quad (12.17)$$

Solving (12.15) and (12.16) for Δ_1 and Δ_2 gives

$$\Delta_2 = \frac{\delta O/\delta V}{\delta VO/\delta V} \quad (12.18)$$

$$\Delta_1 = \frac{\partial O}{\partial S} - \frac{\partial VO}{\partial S}\frac{\delta O/\delta V}{\delta VO/\delta V} \quad (12.19)$$

The portfolio can be rebalanced using the results in (12.18) and (12.19) to set up a risk-free portfolio. It follows that the rate of return of this portfolio should be equal to the risk-free rate. We can now rewrite equation (12.17) as

$$d\Pi = r d\Pi \tag{12.20}$$

and after substituting (12.18) and (12.19) into (12.20), we obtain

$$\left[\frac{\partial O}{\partial t} + \frac{1}{2} V^2 S^2 \frac{\partial^2 O}{\partial S^2} + \frac{1}{2} \xi^2 \frac{\partial O}{\partial V^2} + \rho V S \xi \frac{\partial^2 O}{\partial S \partial V} - r O + r S \frac{\partial O}{\partial S} \right] \Big/ \frac{\partial O}{\partial V}$$

$$= \left[\frac{\partial VO}{\partial t} + \frac{1}{2} V^2 S^2 \frac{\partial^2 VO}{\partial S^2} + \frac{1}{2} \xi^2 \frac{\partial O}{\partial V^2} \right.$$

$$\left. + \rho V S \xi \frac{\partial^2 VO}{\partial S \partial V} - r VO + r S \frac{\partial VO}{\partial S} \right] \Big/ \frac{\partial VO}{\partial V} \tag{12.21}$$

The identity in (12.20) is justified if we consider the function, say, $k(t, S, V)$ such that

$$\frac{\partial O}{\partial t} + \frac{1}{2} V^2 S^2 \frac{\partial^2 O}{\partial S^2} + \frac{1}{2} \xi^2 \frac{\partial O}{\partial V^2} + \rho V S \xi \frac{\partial^2 O}{\partial S \partial V} - r O$$

$$+ r S \frac{\partial O}{\partial S} = -k(t, S, V) \frac{\partial O}{\partial V} \tag{12.22}$$

It follows that in a risk-neutral world the value of any options must satisfy equation (12.22). If we now conjecture a functional form for $k(t, S, V)$, for example

$$k(t, S, V) = k(\theta - V(t)) - \Lambda(S(t), V(t), t) \xi(t) \sqrt{V(t)}$$

Equation (12.22) can be rewritten as

$$\frac{\partial O}{\partial t} + \frac{1}{2} V^2 S^2 \frac{\partial^2 O}{\partial S^2} + \frac{1}{2} \xi^2 \frac{\partial O}{\partial V^2} + \rho V S \xi \frac{\partial^2 O}{\partial S \partial V}$$

$$- r O + r S \frac{\partial O}{\partial S} + (k[\theta - V]) - \Lambda(S, V, t) \xi \sqrt{V} \frac{\partial O}{\partial V} = 0 \tag{12.23}$$

$\Lambda(S, V, t)$ is the market price of volatility risk. If we set $\Lambda(S, V, t) = k \sqrt{V}$ or $\Lambda(S, V, t) \xi \sqrt{V} = k \xi V$, Equation (12.23) can be rewritten as

$$\frac{\partial O}{\partial t} + \frac{1}{2} V^2 S^2 \frac{\partial^2 O}{\partial S^2} + \frac{1}{2} \xi^2 \frac{\partial O}{\partial V^2} + \rho V S \xi \frac{\partial^2 O}{\partial S \partial V}$$

$$- r O + r S \frac{\partial O}{\partial S} + (k[\theta - V]) - k \xi V \frac{\partial O}{\partial V} = 0 \tag{12.24}$$

Equation (12.24) can now be solved using the method of characteristic functions. The solution of the characteristic function involves solving a tricky integral; generally numerical methods are used.

12.5 PROCESSES WITH JUMPS

Although SV models perform well in matching the sample paths, nevertheless empirical evidence shows that asset prices are discontinuous and therefore subject to jumps. Merton (1976) considers jumps as idiosyncratic shocks. Consider the model below:

$$dS(t) = \mu S(t)dt + S(t)dW(t) + dJ(t) \qquad (12.25)$$

$$J(t) = \sum_{j=1}^{N(t)} (Y_j - 1)$$

where $Y_1, Y_2 \ldots$ are random variables and $N(t)$ is a counting process. This process allows for random arrival times $0 < \tau_1 < \tau_2 \ldots$ and $N(t) = \sup\{n : \tau_n \leq t\}$ counts the number of arrivals in the interval [0,t].

Simulation of the jump model in (12.25) at fixed dates $0 = t_0 < t_1 < \ldots$ uses the following equation:

$$s(t_{i+1}) = s(t_i) + \left(\mu - \frac{1}{2}\sigma^2\right)(t_{i+1} - t_i) + \sigma[W(t_{i+1}) - W(t_i)] + \sum_{j=N(t_i)}^{N(t_{i+1})} \log Y_j$$

$$(12.26)$$

where $s(t) = \log S(t)$ is simulated and in addition we have assumed that Y_j is a Poisson $(\lambda(t_{i+1} - t_i))$ process, with λ being the size or intensity of the jump.

12.6 APPLICATION OF THE EULER METHOD
TO SOLVE SDES

As the SDE in (12.7) has no analytical solution, simulation is required. The Euler discretization method consists in defining a set of times $t_0 < t_1 < \ldots < t_n$ and replacing (12.7) by (12.8). This will introduce some discretization bias. However, the bias can be reduced by increasing the number of time steps. This strategy reduces the efficiency since it increases the computational effort. In general, the choice of the time steps in the Euler method is an important issue. To achieve convergence of the simulated price to the true price, the number of time steps is generally set proportional to the square root of the number of simulations. However, the constant of proportionality is rather difficult to determine a priori.[3]

---

[3] Broadie and Kaya (2004), for example, suggest using the coefficient of proportionality that minimizes the difference between standard errors and bias. In this way no error will overcome the other and correct convergence is guaranteed.

12.7   EXACT SIMULATION UNDER SV

The stochastic differential equations in (12.9) or (12.25), due to discretization bias, do not yield exact solutions. Broadie and Kaya (2004) use a square root diffusion model as the one in (12.7) and based on the result in Cox *et al.* (1985) suggest a method for the exact simulation of stock prices and variance under the Heston model. To understand the approach, let us rewrite equations (12.9) and (12.10) in their integral forms:

$$S(t) = S(s) \exp \left[r(t - s) - \frac{1}{2} \int_s^t V(s)ds + \rho \int_s^t \sqrt{V(s)}dW_1(s) \right.$$

$$\left. + \sqrt{1 - \rho^2} \int_s^t \sqrt{V(s)}dW_2(s) \right] \qquad (12.27)$$

$$V(t) = V(s) + k\theta(t - s) - k \int_s^t V(s)ds + \sigma_V \int_s^t \sqrt{V(s)}dW_1(s) \quad (12.28)$$

with $s < t$.

The method suggested in Broadie and Kaya (2004) is described by the following steps:

(a) Simulate $V(t)$ given $V(s)$ from Equation (12.28).
(b) Simulate $\int_s^t V(s)ds$, given $V(t)$ and $V(s)$.
(c) Recover $\int_s^t \sqrt{V(s)}dW_1(s)$ from (d) given $V(t)$, $V(s)$ and $\int_s^t V(s)ds$.
(d) Simulate $S(t)$ given $\int_s^t \sqrt{V(s)}dW_1(s)$ and $\int_s^t V(s)ds$.

Step (a) is rather simple. All we need is to simulate a noncentral chi-square distribution with $d = 4\theta k/\sigma_v^2$ degrees of freedom:

$$V(t) = \frac{\sigma_v^2(1 - e^{-k(t-s)})}{4k} \chi_d^2 \left[\frac{4ke^{-k(t-s)}}{\sigma_v^2(1 - e^{-k(t-s)})} V(s) \right] \qquad (12.29)$$

and the noncentrality parameter:

$$\lambda = \frac{4ke^{-k(t-s)}}{\sigma_v^2(1 - e^{-k(t-s)})} V(s)$$

Step (b) is the key one and is rather demanding. In fact, the simulation of $\int_s^t V(s)ds$, given $V(t)$ and $V(s)$, uses Fourier inversion methods to invert the characteristic function:[4]

$$\phi(s) = E\left[\exp(ia\int_s^t V(s)ds)|V(s), V(t)\right] \tag{12.30}$$

where $V(s)$ is the variance process at the time s and $a > 0$.

One can use the scheme above to simulate $S(t)$ and compute the option prices or Greeks. For example, the price of a plain vanilla European option can be obtained as

$$E\left[BS\left(S_0\xi, \bar{\sigma}\sqrt{1-\rho^2}|\int_s^T V(s)ds, \int_s^T \sqrt{V(s)}dW_1(s)\right)\right] \tag{12.31}$$

where BS is the Black and Scholes formula

$$\bar{\sigma} \equiv \sqrt{\frac{1}{T}\int_s^T V(s)ds}$$

and the expectation operator outside the bracket indicates that the BS price is obtained conditionally on $\int_s^T V(s)ds$ and $\int_s^T \sqrt{V(s)}dW_1(s)$.

A delta can also be computed, using

$$E\left[\Delta S_0\left(\xi, \bar{\sigma}\sqrt{1-\rho^2}|\int_S^T V(S)ds, \int_S^T \sqrt{V(S)}dW_1(S)\xi\right)\right] \tag{12.32}$$

Practically, Equation (12.32) can be used to accommodate jumps.

This approach overcomes the different drawbacks of the Euler method. In fact, the method simulates the process at T rather than t_i. Also, the estimation of the Greeks in this case gives rise to an exact simulation (in the sense that the distribution of the estimator of the delta at T is the same as the distribution of the simulated path).

One major drawback with this approach is that it becomes very time consuming in many interesting ways (for example computing Greeks for exotics under stochastic volatility). In fact, this case will require the inversion of the characteristic function, not only at T but instead at each possible time step. In this case, the method will no longer be superior to a simple Euler scheme. We shall see in the next section how this methodology can be extended to overcome this.

---

[4] We do not write the characteristic function in an explicit form here. Refer to the paper by Brodie and Kaya (2004) for the explicit functional equation representing the characteristic function in (12.30).

12.8   EXACT SIMULATION OF GREEKS UNDER SV

Likelihood ratio methods can be used to compute Greeks for exotic options when the stock price follows the process in (12.27) and (12.28). We follow Broadie and Kaya (2004). Suppose that $f(S)$ is the payoff of an option. In the stochastic volatility case, the payoff of the option is determined conditional on the variance path V. Thus, the expected payoff of the option is

$$E[(f(S)] = E[E(f(S))/V] \qquad (12.33)$$

The process in (12.33) can be obtained using the steps (a) and (b) described above.

Suppose in this case that s, t are two steps.[5] Once $\int_s^t V(s)ds$ has been simulated, then

$$\sigma \equiv \sqrt{(1 - \rho^2)\frac{1}{t-s}\int_s^t V(s)ds}$$

can be computed. Now, define the following function:

$$\xi_t = \left[\exp -\frac{\rho^2}{2}\int_s^t V(s)ds + \rho \int_s^t \sqrt{V(s)}dW(s) \right] \qquad (12.34)$$

It follows that the process for the stock price $S(t)$ can now be written as a sequence of lognormal variables:

$$S(t) = S(s)\left[\xi_t \exp r - \frac{\bar{\sigma}_t}{2}(t-s) + \sigma(t)\sqrt{t-s}Z \right] \qquad (12.35)$$

Given $S(t)$, one could use a pathways estimator to estimate the sensitivity parameter of interest. Otherwise, a likelihood ratio estimator can also be used. In the case of a plain vanilla European option, under (12.27) and (12.28), we know the transition density at T and therefore we can use it to simulate paths for the stock price. We define the following density related to the stock price process in (12.35):

$$g(s) = \frac{\phi(d(s))}{s\sigma\sqrt{T}} \qquad (12.36)$$

where

$$d(s) = \frac{\ln(S(T)/S(0)\xi) - (r - 0.5\bar{\sigma}^2)T}{\bar{\sigma} - \sqrt{T}}$$

---

[5] Note we are considering only two steps for simplicity here. In the case of exotics, however, there would be more than just two steps.

Differentiating the density in (12.36) with respect to the parameter of interest (i.e. $S(0)$ for the delta) we obtain the following likelihood ratio estimators for the delta and gamma:

$$\Delta = e^{-rT}(S(T) - K)\left(\frac{d}{S(0)\bar{\sigma}\sqrt{T}}\right) \tag{12.37}$$

The gamma is then given by

$$\Gamma = e^{-rT}(S(T) - K)\left(\frac{d^2 - d\bar{\sigma} - \sqrt{T} - 1}{S^2(0)\bar{\sigma}^2 T}\right) \tag{12.37a}$$

Exercise 12.1

Given the probability density in (12.36), derive the delta estimator of the option in (12.37).

In the case of exotic options (for example an arithmetic average option) the stock price $S(t)$ will depend on the entire evolution of the variance process over $0 < t_1 < t_2, \ldots < T$. In this case, we need to simulate the entire evolution of the variance process and compute (12.36) at each possible step. For an Asian option, for example, the delta estimator in (12.37) is given by the following:

$$\Delta = e^{-rT}(\bar{S} - K)^+\left(\frac{d_1}{S_0\bar{\sigma}_1\sqrt{\Delta t_1}}\right) \tag{12.38}$$

and the gamma by

$$\Gamma = e^{-rT}(\bar{S} - K)^+\left(\frac{d_1^2 - d_1\bar{\sigma}_1\sqrt{\Delta t_1} - 1}{S^2(0)\bar{\sigma}_1^2 \Delta r_1}\right) \tag{12.38a}$$

where $\Delta t_i = t_i - t_{i-1}$,

$$d_i = \frac{\ln(S_i/S_{i-1}\xi_i) - (r - 0.5\bar{\sigma}_i^2)\Delta t_i}{\bar{\sigma}_i\sqrt{\Delta t_i}}$$

and $\bar{\sigma}_i^2$ is the variance between t_{i-1}, t_i. Note that if S_i is generated from S_{i-1} using the normal random variable Z_i (see (12.35)), then $d_i = Z_i$.

APPENDIX A12.1   STOCHASTIC VOLATILITY USING THE HESTON MODEL

In this appendix we show an application of the Euler scheme presented in Chapter 12. With very little effort, this methodology can also be extended to jump processes. The function 'GenVoll' generates stock price paths under stochastic volatility. This code can be easily extended to price a put option (European or American).

```
%Stochastic volatility model. Generates paths for
stock prices SPaths under
%stochastic volatility; %k is the rate of mean reversion;
phi is the long run variance;sigma=Vo is the spot
variance (i.e. sigma^2);
%rho is the correlation coefficient; phi is the long run
mean variance;
%sigma1 is the volatility of variance or volatility of
volatility.; r is the drift parameter;q=dividend yield;
%Note T must be expressed in days (i.e. 30/365,60/365,
75/365,etc...);
function [SPaths,Vt]=GenVol1(so,r,q,rho,sigma, sigma1,
k,phi,T,NSteps,Rep)
dt=T/NSteps;Vo=sigma;
y=k*sigma1; k1=k+y; phi1=(k*phi)/(k+y);      %we have
assumed the same specification as in CERRATO
(2009).
RandMat1=rand(Rep,NSteps);
RandMat2=rand(Rep,NSteps);
RandMat1=norminv(RandMat1);
RandMat2=norminv(RandMat2);
RandMat3=rho*RandMat1+sqrt(1-rho*rho)*RandMat2;
              for i=1:Rep
          for j=2:(NSteps+1)
              V(i,1)=Vo;
              SPP(i,1)=so;
          end
      end
      for i=1:Rep                   %Euler schemes
          for j=2:(NSteps+1)
      V(i,j)=V(i,(j-1))+k1*(phi1-V(i,(j-1)))*dt+(sigma1*
(sqrt(V(i,(j-1))))*sqrt(dt)*RandMat1(i,(j-1)));
      V1=abs(V); %prevents negative volatilities
      %SP(i,j)=SP(i,(j-1))+((r+q).*SP(i,(j-1))*dt+(sqrt
(V1(i,(j-1))))*SP(i,(j-1))*sqrt(dt)*RandMat3(i,(j-1)));
          SPP(i,j)=SPP(i,(j-1))+((r+q).*SPP(i,(j-1))
*dt+(sqrt(V1(i,(j-1))))*SPP(i,(j-1))*sqrt(dt)*(RandMat3
(i,(j-1))));
          j=j+1;
      end
```

Table A12.1 Pricing European call option under stochastic volatility

$V = 0.0625$		$V = 0.25$	
$\xi = 0.9$	$\xi = 0.45$	$\xi = 0.9$	$\xi = 0.45$
$k = 5$	$k = 2.5$	$k = 5$	$k = 2.5$
AE 0.0679	0.0284	0.0108	0.0263

European options under stochastic volatility. V is the variance process, k is the rate of reversion and epsilon is the volatility of variance (see Chapter 11.3). AE is the absolute error.

```
end
SPaths=SPP;
Vt=V1;
```

We show an application of this code when pricing European and American options under stochastic volatility. The example is taken from Cerrato (2009).

We consider put options with the following specifications: strike equal to $10, initial stock price $9, the risk-free rate of interest is 10% p.a., the long-run mean variance is 0.16, the correlation coefficient is equal to 0.1 and the expiry date is three months.

We use simple exponential basis functions (the first three) for the stock price, one exponential basis for the variance process and the cross-product of the first basis for the stock price and the variance process. Option prices have been computed using 50 time steps and 3000 simulations. Table A12.1 shows the empirical results.

As shown in Table A12.1, the methodology presented above produces very accurate option prices (see the absolute errors (AE)). This function 'GenVoll' can be combined with an extension of the function 'LSmb2' in Chapter 7, Appendix A7.1 to price American options under stochastic volatility.

13

Implied Volatility Models

13.1 INTRODUCTION

Implied volatility (IV) modelling is very common among practitioners. The idea is to estimate, using observed market prices, market volatilities that can then be used to price derivatives. Although implied volatility can be obtained from any (invertible) pricing function, practitioners generally use the well-known Black and Scholes (1973) model. Given the option strike K, time to maturity T and a price function, it is simple to obtain an estimate of the underlying risk. We showed earlier that, generally, IV is obtained from the Black and Scholes model as the unique value of volatility that makes the theoretical option price (i.e. the Black and Scholes price) equal to the observed market price:

$$\sigma_t^{BS}(K, T) > 0$$
$$V_{BS}(S_t, K, \sigma_t^{BS}(K, T)) = V_{OB}(K, T)$$

where σ_t^{BS} is the volatility at time t obtained from the Black and Scholes model, V_{BS} is the theoretical option price and V_{OB} is the observed option price.

As opposed to historical volatility, which is computed from historical stock returns, IV is essentially forward looking as it is backed out from observed market option prices. Since the value of an option depends on the estimate of the future realized price volatility, unlike historical volatility, IV reflects market expectations of volatility up to time T.

As discussed in Gatheral (2006), option prices hold information about the risk-neutral density (RND)[1] and as a result IV models tend to be popular among practitioners and academics as benchmarks not just to evaluate in- and out-of-sample option prices but also to extract RNDs.

Figure 13.1 shows the typical set of implied volatilities for the FTSE-100 index option European style exercise (ESX). Figure 13.1 plots implied volatilities across different strikes and maturities. Note that since for options, practically, there is a finite number of strikes and maturities available, to obtain the volatility surface in Figure 13.1 we need to interpolate between different maturities and strikes (we shall discuss this in the next section). Furthermore, in contradiction with the strongest assumption of a constant volatility (see Black and Scholes) we note that IVs are nonlinear in strike and time to maturity. The skew is more

---

[1] Taleb (2011) notes from the work of Kairys and Valerio (1997) that option traders employed sophisticated pricing methods.

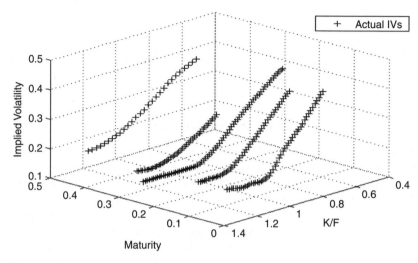

Figure 13.1   Implied volatility surface

evident for short maturity options. The IV skew for these options has at least three explanations:

(i) the non-Gaussian nature of equity returns and the fear of short-term declines;
(ii) the demand/supply hypothesis where hedgers are prepared to pay put premiums exceeding their expected payoff to transfer risk from equity owners;
(iii) volatility of an individual equity is expected to increase as the value of the company's equity declines (leverage effect).

13.2   MODELLING IMPLIED VOLATILITY

Practically, the number of traded options available to obtain a surface (or the RND) is limited and, as a consequence, we need to use parametric methods or interpolation in order to generate the surface. The procedure is rather standard if the objective is to compute the surface for option pricing: use the smoothed volatility estimate for a given (K, T) together with the Black–Scholes equation to produce the model price. Gatheral (2006) refers to this approach as the practitioner's Black–Scholes (PBS). As the IV surface (see Figure 13.1) is time dependent calibration should be done at least daily.

There are different methods for fitting the IV surface to the actual IVs. Parametric methods usually employ a quadratic polynomial as a function of strike and time to determine the parameters. However, these methods may produce a large bias due to the complicated functional form of the observed IV. The most popular method was proposed by Dumas (1998). Interpolation methods are very popular and have been increasingly used in the literature. For interpolation methods to work one requires that the pricing function used should have a second-order derivative (this is required to ensure smoothness).

While IV can be used to calculate the RND from European options, this methodology fails when exotic options are used. This is due to the path dependency nature of these options. Local volatility models (LV) – see Dupire (1994), Derman and Kani (1994) and Rubinstein (1994) – are alternative methods that can be used in this case. In an LV model, volatility is a deterministic function of spot price and time to maturity, and therefore one can consider IVs as 'averages' of expected future volatilities.

13.3   EXAMPLES

As pointed out earlier, due to the scarcity of strikes and maturities, we have to use computational methods to obtain the missing values necessary to construct the surface in Figure 13.1. In what follows, we provide a simple example using polynomial interpolation. Consider the following implied volatility function:

$$IV(K) = b_0 + b_1 \cdot K + b_2 \cdot K^2 \tag{13.1}$$

Fitting this model to the observed implied volatilities σ_{OB} is rather simple: (i) calculate the implied volatilities for each data point $C(K)$ and for a given maturity; (ii) regress the implied volatilities on a quadratic polynomial as a function of strike to determine the ordinary least squares (OLS) coefficients of (13.1):

$$b_{OLS} = \arg\min_b \left(\frac{1}{n} \sum_j (\sigma(K_j) - \sigma_j^{OB})^2 \right) = (\mathbf{A}'\mathbf{A})^{-1}\mathbf{A}'\sigma^{OB}$$

where $\mathbf{A}$ is the matrix that holds the data $[1, K, K^2]$. The MATLAB code for this calculation is given in Exhibit 13.1. Note that this approach may fail to capture more complex functional forms of the observed implied volatilities since we are using a simple quadratic equation.

Gatheral (2006) proposes an arbitrage-free stochastic volatility (SVI) parameterization of the implied volatility. In this model, at each expiry date, the implied variance is given by

$$\sigma_{BS}^2(k) = a + b \left\{ \rho(k - m) + \sqrt{(k - m)^2 + \sigma^2} \right\}$$

where the coefficients a, b, ρ, σ and m all depend on the option's expiry date and the parameter k is equal to $\log(K/S)$. Therefore, the variance is always

```
% Pure Quadratic with dependence to strike level K
% IV(K) = b0 + b1*K + b2*K^2
K  = data(:,1); % Strikes
IV = data(:,2); % Market IV's
beta = [ones(11,1) K K.^2]\IV; % Estimate parameters
% Stats = regstats(IV,K,'purequadratic'); % Using matlab's regstats
% beta = Stats.beta;
Exhibit 1
function DWF_IV
% import your data
K  = data(:,1); % strike
IV = data(:,2); % IV
T  = data(:,3); % Maturities
%
start = [0.25, -1, 0.17, 0.10,0.5,.5,.5,.5]; % starting values
options = optimset('Display','iter','TolFun',eps);
[pars feval] = lsqnonlin(@(pars)get_ivDum(pars,K,T,IV),start,[],[],options);
% inline
pars; % output
function y = get_ivDum(pars,X,T,IV)
% DWF general model
sigma = pars(1) + pars(2).*X + pars(3).*X.^2 + pars(4).*T + pars(5).*X.*T;
y = sigma - IV; % error magnitude
```

Exhibit 13.1

positive and increases linearly with k. To determine the parameters we should minimize the nonlinear least squares equation (NLS) given by

$$\min_\vartheta \sum_j (\sigma_j(\theta) - \sigma_j^{OB})^2$$

with θ containing the parameter set $\{a, b, \rho, \sigma, m\}$.

Figure 13.2 compares the two different fits obtained using quadratic volatility and SVI parameterization.

An alternative approach consists in using a quadratic polynomial as in (13.1) but the polynomial now is a function of the strike price level and time to maturity. This method is very popular and it is known as the 'practitioner's Black–Scholes (PBS) model' (Dumas, 1998).

In the PBS we calibrate daily the parameters of the model and use them for pricing or hedging purposes. Application of the PBS takes place in three steps: (i) invert the Black–Scholes (1973) equation for the available data points and obtain the implied volatilities $\sigma_{IV}(K, T)$; (ii) the implied volatilities are

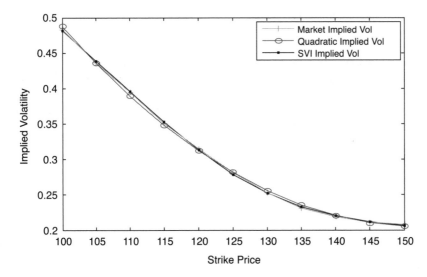

Figure 13.2 Quadratic and SVI implied volatilities

regressed against a quadratic polynomial; (iii) the fitted implied volatilities are
then plugged back into the Black–Scholes equation to get the practitioner's
option price. To use the model for out-of-sample pricing one then uses the
smoothed implied volatility surface for a given time to maturity and price
accordingly.

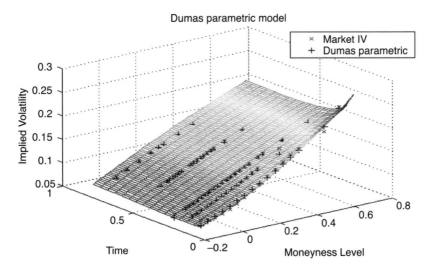

Figure 13.3 Dumas and market IV

Consider the following model:

$$\sigma(K, T) = b_0 + b_1 \cdot K + b_2 \cdot K^2 + b_3 \cdot T + b_4 \cdot KT \qquad (13.2)$$

The estimation of the parameters in (13.2) can be done by simple OLS. Christoffersen (2004) shows that the estimation of (13.2) using nonlinear LS outperforms the SVI method for in- and out-of-sample pricing. Exhibit 13.1 shows the MATLAB procedure for this case. Figure 13.3 plots the smoothed IV surface based on the Dumas (1998) model.

14
Local Volatility Models

14.1 AN OVERVIEW

As discussed earlier, the market implied volatilities of equity index options vary with both strike and maturity and this is not consistent with what the Black and Scholes model would predict. There are several possible reasons for the observed option's smile (skew): market prices have fatter tails (i.e. not consistent with geometric Brownian motion); news events could cause jumps; investors' preferences could affect supply and demand of options. Different approaches have been suggested in the literature to explain the smile, for example introducing jump processes or even stochastic volatility models or even both.

Stochastic volatility models are rather popular and model the variance as an unobservable random variable and use the stochastic differential equation (SDE) with correlated Brownian motions. This approach is computationally challenging, and leads to incomplete markets.

Local volatility models (see, for example, Dupire, 1994) use an alternative approach and assume a simple deterministic relationship between volatility, asset price and time. Define by $\bar{\sigma}$ the Black and Scholes implied volatility. This is a kind of estimated average of future volatility over the option's life and, as mentioned, it depends on the strike and time to expiry of the option. If implied volatility varies with the maturity of the option, it is also reasonable to assume that it varies locally. If we define by σ_1 the local volatility, we see a relationship between $\bar{\sigma}$ and σ_1. This relationship plays an important role in financial derivatives. In fact, if we assume that options prices are efficient, we can include them in a model that relaxes the assumption that future volatilities will remain constant and we retrieve the market's consensus of future local volatility as depending on the future stock price and time.

This result is very important. In fact, in this way, as we shall discuss, we can price options consistently with a risk-neutral valuation. Local volatility models assume three important concepts for the volatility process:[1]

- $\sigma(S, t, \cdot)$ is the instantaneous volatility, which measures the instantaneous standard deviation of the return process. It depends on the current level of the spot price and any other possible stochastic state variables.

---

[1] Fengler (2005).

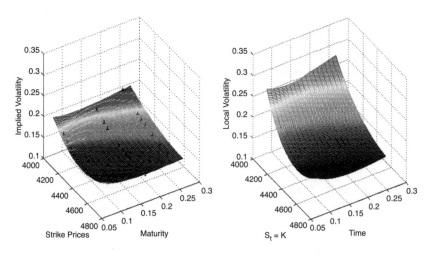

Figure 14.1 Implied (left) and local (right) volatility functions. Note that on the *x* axis of the IV plot we have maturities whereas in the LV plot we have time; the *y* axis holds strike prices on the IV plot and spot levels on the LV plot. In the main text we have described how to link the two surfaces for information on the future evolution of IV and for pricing

- $\bar{\sigma}(K, T)$ is the volatility implied by the Black and Scholes (1973) equation for a particular level of strike (K) and maturity (T). In these models the implied volatilities are 'averages' of future expected volatilities between today and expiration.
- $\sigma_{K,T}(S_t, t)$ is instead the local volatility. This is the expected instantaneous volatility on a particular level of the asset price $S(T) = K$ at $t = T$. When the instantaneous volatility is a deterministic function in spot price and time, we may then rewrite it as $\sigma(S, t) = \sigma(K, T)$.

Therefore, when the instantaneous volatility is deterministic in spot price and time, the two concepts of instantaneous and local are the same.

To better understand the difference between implied and local volatility, Figure 14.1 shows the implied volatility (left-hand-side panel) and the corresponding local volatility (right-hand-side panel) plots. If you can obtain estimates of dividend yield and growth rate, you can use the local volatility surface in Figure 14.1 to simulate the evolution of the stock (index).

Note how implied volatility changes with maturity and strike. The local volatility surface shows the 'fair' value of local volatility at future times and market levels. It is important to note that the local volatility decreases as the stock level increases. Also, local volatility varies with the stock level about twice as rapidly as implied volatility varies with strike.

14.2   THE MODEL

Consider the following stochastic differential equation (SDE) for the asset price process:

$$\frac{dS(t)}{S(t)} = \mu(S(t), t)dt + \sigma_{KT}(S(t), t)dW(t) \tag{14.1}$$

where $S(t)$ is the asset price at time t, $\mu(.)$ is the drift, σ_{KT} is the local volatility process and $W(t)$ is a Brownian motion on the real probability measure.

Thus, the local volatility process in Equation (14.1) is modelled as a deterministic function of its arguments. The most important feature of these models is that the smile changes with the spot price; that is σ_{KT} in Equation (14.1) depends both on the spot price and strike rather than the moneyness S/K alone. This has important implications for hedging.

The simple concept of local volatility becomes very useful in many practical cases, for example in the case of exotic options when computing the probability density at each time $t \in T$. Indeed, in this case, Dupire (1994) and Derman and Kani (1994) show that one can retrieve the unique risk-neutral diffusion from which these distributions come. The unique diffusion process, which is risk-neutral, has a unique functional form given by the local volatility in (14.1).

Derman and Kani (1994), Dupire (1994) and Rubinstein (1994) show that European option prices can be consistently priced using the implied volatility smile and a one-factor diffusion process as in Equation (14.1), but with deterministic volatility. The estimation of the local volatility (LV) surface allows one to obtain smile-consistent prices. Rubinstein (1994) creates a backward inductive implied tree that uses as inputs options with the same maturity. As a result the volatility has a skew structure only. On the other hand, Derman and Kani (1994) also allow for skew/term structure of the volatility. The construction of the implied tree is rather simple. Dupire (1994) proves, for continuous time processes, that if implied volatility (of plain vanilla options) were available for all strikes and maturities the local volatility function would be uniquely defined. Thus the local volatility and the risk-neutral process are determined by complete knowledge of the arbitrage-free prices of European calls.

Consider Equation (14.1) above. A simple application of Ito's lemma (and risk neutrality) gives the following PDE for the option C:

$$\frac{\partial C(t, S(t))}{\partial T} = \frac{\sigma_{KT}^2 K^2}{2} \frac{\partial^2 C}{\partial K^2} + (r(T) - D(T)) \left(C - K \frac{\partial C}{\partial K} \right)$$

where $r(t)$ is the risk-free rate and $D(t)$ is the dividend yield. After inverting the PDE above we obtain

$$\sigma_{KT}^2(K, T, S_0) = \frac{\dfrac{\partial C}{\partial T} + (r(t) - D(t)) \left(-K \dfrac{\partial C}{\partial K} \right)}{\dfrac{1}{2} K^2 \dfrac{\partial^2 C}{\partial K^2}}$$

where S_0 is the initial stock price, $r(t)$ the interest rate at time t and $D(t)$ the dividend yield at time t. Therefore, given today's price of a plain vanilla option (the right-hand side of the equation above), the variance is the local volatility that will prevail at time $t = T$ when the future spot price is equal to $K (S(t) = K)$. Therefore, once we have a set of European options with different strikes and maturities, local volatilities can be obtained uniquely using the equation above.

On the other hand, if we quote options as a function of their forward price $F(t) = S_0 \exp(\int_0^T \mu(t) dt)$, the equation above becomes

$$\sigma_{KT}^2(K, T, S_0) = \frac{\partial C / \partial T}{\frac{1}{2} K^2 (\partial^2 C / \partial K^2)} \tag{14.2}$$

Since prices of European options are also quoted in terms of their Black–Scholes implied volatilities, Gatheral (2006) provides an alternative approach to derive the local volatility function of Dupire in terms of the corresponding IV. In particular, if we define the Black–Scholes total variance $w(S_0, K, T) = \sigma_{BS}^2(S_0 K, T)$ and the log-strike $y = \log(K / F_T)$, we can obtain the expression for the local variance (v_L) given by

$$v_L = \frac{\dfrac{\partial w}{\partial T}}{1 - \dfrac{y}{w} \dfrac{\partial w}{\partial y} + \dfrac{1}{4} \left(-\dfrac{1}{4} - \dfrac{1}{w} + \dfrac{y^2}{w^2} \right) \left(\dfrac{\partial w}{\partial y} \right)^2 + \dfrac{1}{2} \dfrac{\partial^2 w}{\partial y^2}}$$

A very important result in Dupire (1994) and Derman and Kani (1998) is the link between local variance and instantaneous variance. To see this, consider Equation (14.1) and write it in terms of the forward price $F(t, T)$:

$$dF(t, T) = \sigma F(t, T) dW(t)$$

Note that $F(t, T)$ is a martingale and that $dF(t, T) = dS(T)$. The value of a European option with strike K and time to expiry T is given by

$$C(S, K, T) = E[S(T) - K]^+$$

If we differentiate twice with respect to the strike we get $\partial C / \partial K$ and $\partial^2 C / \partial K^2$. Applying Ito's lemma to the payoff above gives

$$d(S(T) - K)^+ = \frac{\partial C}{\partial K}(S(T) - K) dS(T) + \frac{1}{2} \sigma S^2 \frac{\partial^2 C}{\partial K^2}(S(T) - K) dT$$

After using the martingale condition and taking the expectations on each side, the equation can be rewritten as

$$dE(S(T) - K)^+ = \frac{1}{2} E \left[\sigma S^2 \frac{\partial^2 C}{\partial K^2}(S(T) - K) \right] dT$$

We can now write the right-hand side of the equation above as

$$E\left[\sigma_{KT}|S(T) = K\right] \frac{1}{2}K^2 E\left[\frac{\partial^2 C}{\partial K^2}(S(T) - K)\right]$$

$$E\left[\sigma_{KT}|S(T) = K\right] \frac{1}{2}K^2 \frac{\partial^2 C}{\partial K^2}$$

Finally, we obtain the following equation:

$$\frac{\partial C}{\partial T} = E\left[\sigma|S(T) = K\right] \frac{1}{2}K^2 \frac{\partial^2 C}{\partial K^2} \tag{14.3}$$

If we compare Equations (14.2) and (14.3), we see that

$$\sigma_{KT} = E\left[\sigma|S(T) = K\right]$$

where the expectation is taken with respect to the risk-neutral measure. Thus, the local variance is the risk-neutral expectation of the instantaneous variance conditional on $S(t) = K$. In other words, as the instantaneous volatility is deterministic in spot and time it evolves along the local volatility function.

It is straightforward to compute the right-hand side of the above local variance equations if one knows option prices/implied volatilities. However, note that option prices in the market are only quoted for a finite number of strikes and maturities, but for a stable numerical differentiation we require a continuum of option prices/implied volatilities. As a result interpolation is generally used to either interpolate between option prices or implied volatilities.

14.3   NUMERICAL METHODS

As interpolation of option prices requires many conditions in order to avoid price arbitrage, it is much more straightforward to interpolate through implied volatilities and convert them into option prices using the Black–Scholes equation.[2] Obviously the resulting LV surface will depend on the method chosen to construct the IV surface. Apart from this choice there is a trade-off between accurately fitting the quoted option prices and smoothness of the resulting IV surface.

In contrast to other methods such as stochastic volatility and jump-diffusion models, which introduce an extra degree of randomness, local volatility models can replicate the Black–Scholes market and hence form a complete market. Market completeness is essential for arbitrage pricing and hedging. As we pointed out earlier, under risk neutrality the diffusion of (14.1) will satisfy the

---

[2] Practitioners tend to prefer this method of getting a complete mapping of option prices across (K, T).

following partial differential equation (PDE):

$$\frac{\partial C(t, S(t))}{\partial T} = \frac{\sigma_{KT}^2 K^2}{2} \frac{\partial^2 C}{\partial K^2} + (r(T) - D(T)) \left(C - K \frac{\partial C}{\partial K} \right)$$

Since $\sigma_{KT}^2(S(t), t) = \sigma^2(K, T)$, we can obtain the estimated LV from the Dupire equation using a numerical method (for example the finite difference method). The finite difference method is a good choice in this case since it is straightforward to adjust the algorithm to account for the local volatility function.[3]

Given that the Dupire equation involves computation of first- and second-order partial derivatives, this implies that for accurate calculation the complete mapping of option prices across strike prices and maturities is required. Any structural break will cause inaccurate computation, especially of the second-order derivatives. As a result, if we are to create a complete mapping of option prices our resulting LV surface will be very sensitive to the interpolation method employed for the missing option prices. As discussed in the previous section, and given that our instantaneous volatility is a deterministic function of spot price and time, an alternative is to consider local volatility estimation by the family of inverse problems. Thus, we infer the local volatility surface directly from the observed option prices. A salient feature of the inverse problem is the so-called ill-posedness (see Rebonato, 1998, for information on this issue).

Lagnado and Osher (1997) infer the instantaneous volatility function[4] on a finite difference grid directly from option prices. Under this method every point in the finite difference grid is a local volatility, so every option price on the finite difference grid is a function of the instantaneous volatility at each point $\sigma(S, t)$. Thus, we can write the option price as $C_j(\sigma(S, t)) = C_j(S_0; \sigma(S, t), K_j, T_j)$ and, using a least squares approach:

$$\min_{\sigma(S_t, t) \in H} \sum_{\forall} (C_j(\sigma(S(t), t) - \bar{C}_j))^2$$

where $\bar{C}$ is the observed option price.

Lagnado and Osher (1997) are able to meet the well-posedness condition using the well-known Tikhonov regularization (for more details see Lagnado and Osher, 1997, and Crêpey, 2003). Regularization consists of finding the smoothest function possible that minimizes the sum of squared errors (SSE) sacrificing accuracy in matching option prices. The method while effective is computationally challenging. Trying to infer the instantaneous volatilities at every point of the finite difference grid, on the other hand, results in having

---

[3] We can also employ Monte Carlo simulation and use the corresponding LV value for the spot value.

[4] Remember that when the local volatility function is deterministic in spot and time then instantaneous and local are the same.

a discrete representation of the instantaneous volatility with a small array of nodes in space and time.

The method suggested by Lagnado and Osher is not very useful when we have too few input data and require the estimation of a large number of unknowns (the local volatilities at the grid points). Jackson *et al.* (1998) and Coleman *et al.* (2003) suggest representing the instantaneous volatility function using a spline functional. Let $\{C_j\}$, $j = 1, 2, \ldots, m$, denote the observed market option prices. A spline-based representation of the local volatility function has p knots in $\{(S_k, t_k)\}_{k=1}^{p}$, with $p \leq m$, over a finite grid with corresponding local volatilities $\sigma_{KT1}(S_k, t_k)$. The interpolating cubic spline $\varsigma(S, t)$ will completely determine the local volatility function once we set the final condition $\varsigma(S_k, t_k) = \sigma_{KTk}$.

We can formalize this problem as

$$\min f(\bar{\sigma})_{\bar{\sigma} \in R^p} = \frac{1}{2} \sum_{j=1}^{m} \omega_j (C_j(\bar{\sigma}) - \bar{C}_j)^2$$

subject to

$$lb_k \leq \sigma_k \leq ub_k$$

where $C(.)$ are the given option prices while lb and ub are the lower and upper bounds respectively. To estimate the function $f(.)$ above we need to calculate $C_j(.)$ for each pair of strike and time to maturity of the options. This can be done by solving the Black and Scholes PDE:

$$\frac{\partial C}{\partial t} + \frac{1}{2}\sigma(S, t)^2 S^2 \frac{\partial^2 C}{\partial S^2} + (r - D)S \frac{\partial C}{\partial S} - rC = 0$$

subject to the usual conditions:

$$\lim_{S \to \infty} \frac{\partial C(S, t)}{\partial S} = \exp(-D(T - t)), t \in [0, T]$$
$$C(S = 0, t) = 0, t \in [0, T]$$
$$C(S, T) = \max(S - K, 0)$$

This approach is computationally intensive since it requires solving the PDE above (jointly with the terminal conditions) m times at each iteration. An alternative (and more efficient) approach is to replace the above PDE with the forward equation, as shown earlier.

The idea behind using a smooth spline functional lies in the fact that splines possess features that allow for complicated functional forms. Furthermore, given that the Dupire equation sees the local volatility equation as the product of the first- and second-order derivatives, it is reasonable to use splines that consider smoothness (Coleman *et al.*, 2003).

Andersen and Andreasen (2001) propose jump diffusions coupled with an LV function. The introduction of the jump part aims to address the steep short-term skew in IVs. However, given that there is a large combination of jump parameters that will yield an appropriate distribution to capture the steep short-term skew in the IV, the problem is ill-posed as no unique solution exists. Coleman *et al.* (2003) find that, although jump parameter estimation is ill-posed, calibration of the local volatility surface tends to be unique.

As a general rule, we can say that if the horizon is short then LV models will perform well up to a given extent. Practically, we must be cautious with LV models. Several authors (Dumas *et al.*, 1998, and Rebonato, 1998) argue that, on a longer horizon, it would be wiser to look at stochastic volatility models. However, on the other hand, the latter are computationally challenging and the estimation of the parameters is not trivial. Extensions to improve the LV models are the so-called local stochastic volatility models, which consider the stochastic evolution of the local volatility surface rather than of the spot volatility. This research builds on the results of Ren *et al.* (2007) and Alexander and Nogueira (2007), based on Gyongy's lemma (Gyongy, 1986).

APPENDIX A14.1

We now provide an example to compute local volatilities using the Dupire (1994) model. We use options on the FTSE-100 (ESX). Due to data limitation, we use interpolations to obtain the complete set of option prices. For this purpose we choose to interpolate on the market IVs using the parametric model of Dumas (1998) and use the estimated surface to compute the Black–Scholes prices (see Exhibit 14.1).

```
% Euronext FSTE-100 ESX Index Options @ 18-Sep-2003
data = load('ESX_data');              % load your data
CP = data(:,1); T = data(:,2); K = data(:,3); % Call/Put, Maturity & Strikes
P = data(:,4); S = data(1,5); IV = data(:,6);  % Price, Spot & IV
r = data(1,7); q = data(:,8);          % risk free (rf), & dividend
% part 1
mn = log(F./K)./sqrt(T);  % moneyness

start = [0.25, -1, 0.17, 0.10,0.5,.5,.5,.5];      % starting values
options = optimset('Display','iter','TolFun',eps);
[pars feval] = lsqnonlin(@(pars)get_ivDum(pars,mn, T,IV),start,[],[],
options); % inline
```

```
dK = 5; Ki = min(K):dK:max(K);              % create a grid of K
dt = 0.01; Ti = min(0.90*T):dt:max(1.10*T);   % create a grid of T
[Tm,Km] = meshgrid(Ti,Ki);                  % create array for K,T
MNm = log(F./Km)./sqrt(Tm);                 % moneyness (array)
IVm = IV_ff(pars, MNm, Tm);                 % create IV surface (array)
%
mesh(Km,Tm,IVm); grid on;                   % plot IV surface
zlabel('Implied Volatility';);
% part 2
[Tu,Iu] = unique(T);
qi = interp1(Tu,q(Iu),Ti,'linear','extrap');   % interpolate rf – dividend
mm = repmat(r-qi,length(Ki),1);             % create array
C = bls(IVm,S,Km,Tm,r,q,1);                 % compute IV surface BS-calls
%
% Dupire Equation
d_CT = (C(:,3:end)-C(:,1:end-2))/(2*dt);        % 1st deriv wrt T
d_CK = (C(3:end,:)-C(1:end-2,:))/(2*dK);        % 1st deriv wrt K
d_C2K = (C(3: end,:) -2*C(2:end -1,:) + C(1:end -2,:))/dK^2; % 2nd
deriv wrt K  % local volatility function
LV1 = d_CT(2:end-1,:) + mm(2:end-1,2:end-1).*...
        (- Km(2:end-1,2:end-1).*d_CK(:,2:end-1));
LV2 = (0.5*Km(2:end-1,2:end -1).^2.*d_C2K(:,2:end-1));
LV = LV1./LV2;                              % Local Variance
LV = sqrt(LV);                              % Local Volatility

figure, mesh(Km(2:end-1,2:end-1),Tm(2:end-1,2:end-1),LV)    % LV plot
zlabel('Local Volatility');
% aux functions
function y = get_ivDum(pars,X,T,IV)               % DWF general model
sigma = IV_ff(pars,X,T);                          % IV parametric function
y = sigma - IV;                                   % error magnitude

function y = IV_ff(pars,X,T)                       % choice of parametric fn
y = pars(1) + pars(2).*X + pars(3).*X.^2 + pars(4).*T + pars(5).*X.*T;
```

Exhibit A14.1 MATLAB code to compute the local volatility function using Dupire's equation.

The first line of the code imports the data and computes the parameters of the model. We then create a continuum of strikes and maturities and compute the IV surface. Using the computed IV surface we can then calculate Black–Scholes option prices from which we can differentiate straightforwardly to obtain the LV function. It is important to note that although IV surfaces share stylized facts with LVs such as time homogeneity, the resulting LV surface cannot tell us if the resulting IV smile is going to be sticky/floating. The code fits the market IVs to the parametric model to generate a mapping of the IV surface over a 'continuum' of K strikes and T maturities, resulting in an $N_K \times N_T$ matrix of implied volatilities.

We now discuss how to compute the Dupire equation. Since we are working with a rectangular grid and our computations involve first- and second-order derivatives, it is wise to stick with it. Before we proceed, as we now have created a continuum of maturities, we need to find the assumed dividend rate for these maturities. We shall do this by linearly interpolating the dividend (q) across all maturities (the result would be $q(t \in T)$ of size $1 \times N_T$). Since we want to work with matrices we need to transform the quantity $(r - q)$ used in the Dupire model into a matrix of size $N_K \times N_T$ (we use the command repmat). We then compute the local volatility. The resulting local volatility function will be of size $(N_K - 2) \times (N_T - 2)$, due to the computations of the first- and second-order derivative computation.

15

An Introduction to Interest
Rate Modelling

15.1 A GENERAL FRAMEWORK

We start with a general framework to model interest rate dynamics and obtain an interest rate term structure. Here the focus is on modelling the short-term rate.[1] We assume that the short-term interest rate process $r(t)$ is driven by the following SDE:

$$dr(t) = u(r, t)dt + \sigma(r, t)dW(t) \qquad (15.1)$$

where $u(r, t)$ is the instantaneous drift process, $\sigma^2(r, t)$ is the volatility of the spot rate and W is a standard Brownian motion process under the physical measure.

Interest rates are not observable in the market place but prices of bonds are. Suppose that $B(r, t)$ is the price of a bond at time t that depends on the interest rate r. The dynamics for $B(r, t)$ using the Ito lemma is given by

$$dB = \frac{\partial B}{\partial r}dr + \frac{\partial B}{\partial t}dt + \frac{1}{2}\frac{\partial^2 B}{\partial r^2}dr^2 \qquad (15.2)$$

Substituting Equation (15.1) into Equation (15.2), we obtain

$$dB = \frac{\partial B}{\partial r}\left[u(r, t)dt + \sigma(r, t)dW\right] + \frac{\partial B}{\partial t}dt$$
$$+ \frac{1}{2}\frac{\partial^2 B}{\partial r^2}\left[u^2(r, t)dt^2 + \sigma^2(r, t)dW^2\right]dr^2 \qquad (15.3)$$

$$dB = \frac{\partial B}{\partial r}u(r, t)dt + \frac{\partial B}{\partial r}\sigma(r, t)dW + \frac{\partial B}{\partial t}dt + \frac{1}{2}\frac{\partial^2 B}{\partial r^2}\sigma^2(r, t)dW^2$$

$$dB = \frac{\partial B}{\partial r}u(r, t)dt + \frac{\partial B}{\partial r}\sigma(r, t)dW + \frac{\partial B}{\partial t}dt + \frac{1}{2}\frac{\partial^2 B}{\partial r^2}\sigma^2(r, t)dt \qquad (15.4)$$

If we replace $u(r, t)$ and $\sigma(r, t)$ by (u, σ) and collect the terms together we have

$$dB = \left(\frac{\partial B}{\partial t} + \frac{\partial B}{\partial r}u + \frac{1}{2}\frac{\partial^2 B}{\partial r^2}\sigma^2\right)dt + \frac{\partial B}{\partial r}\sigma dW \qquad (15.5)$$

---

[1] These models assume a perfect correlation for the forward rate dynamics as described in the previous chapter (i.e. $\rho_{i,j} = 1$).

in which we define

$$\mu = \left(\frac{\partial B}{\partial t} + \frac{\partial B}{\partial r}u + \frac{1}{2}\frac{\partial^2 B}{\partial r^2}\sigma^2 \right)$$

This is the drift process. We define the volatility process as

$$\delta = \frac{\partial B}{\partial r}\sigma$$

Now denote by V the value of a portfolio containing two bonds with different times to maturity, say T_1 and T_2, in a proportion equal to $(\beta_{T_1}, \beta_{T_2})$. Thus,

$$V = V_1 \beta_{T_1} V_2 \beta_{T_2}$$

The change in the portfolio value over time dt is

$$\beta_{T_1}dV_1 = \beta_{T_1}\mu_1 dt + \beta_{T_1}\delta_1 dz$$
$$\beta_{T_2}dV_2 = \beta_{T_2}\mu_2 dt + \beta_{T_2}\delta_2 dz$$

and

$$dV = (\mu_1 \beta_{T_1} + \mu_2 \beta_{T_2})dt + (\delta_1 \beta_{T_1} + \delta_2 \beta_{T_2})dW \qquad (15.6)$$

If we impose

$$\beta_{T_1} + \beta_{T_2} = 1 \qquad (15.7)$$

and further the condition of a riskless portfolio, given by the following relationship:

$$\delta_1 \beta_{T_1} + \delta_2 \beta_{T_2} = 0 \qquad (15.8)$$

Equation (15.6) can now be rewritten as

$$dV = (\mu_1 \beta_{T_1} + \mu_2 \beta_{T_2})dt \qquad (15.9)$$

This shows that the value of the portfolio is deterministic.

Solving the system in (15.7) and (15.8) for β_{T_1} and β_{T_2}, we obtain

$$\beta_{T_2} = -\frac{\delta_1}{\delta_2 - \delta_1} \text{ and } \beta_{T_1} = \frac{\delta_2}{\delta_2 - \delta_1} \qquad (15.10)$$

If we substitute the above result into Equation (15.9) and perform some algebraic manipulation, we obtain

$$\frac{(\mu_1 - r)}{\delta_1} = \frac{(\mu_2 - r)}{\delta_2} \qquad (15.11)$$

Remark 15.1

Note that neither side of Equation (15.11) depends on the maturity of the bonds. Thus, Equation (15.11) holds for any bonds with any maturity. This is an important result.

Assumption 15.1

If the market is arbitrage free, the following theorem is true.

Theorem 15.1

Under Assumption 15.1, the market price of risk υ can be written as

$$\upsilon(.) = \frac{\mu - r}{\delta} \tag{15.12}$$

If we now substitute (μ, δ) into Equation (15.12), we have

$$\frac{\partial B}{\partial r}u\upsilon = \frac{\partial B}{\partial t} + \frac{\partial B}{\partial r}u + \frac{1}{2}\frac{\partial^2 B}{\partial r^2}\sigma^2 - r$$

and also

$$\frac{\partial B}{\partial t} + \frac{1}{2}\frac{\partial^2 B}{\partial r^2}\sigma^2 + \frac{\partial B}{\partial r}(u - \sigma v) - r = 0 \tag{15.13}$$

with the final condition that $B(T, T) = 1$.

Proposition 15.1

In an arbitrage-free market the price of the bond $B(r, t)$ satisfies the term structure partial difference equation (PDE) given by Equation (15.13).

15.2   AFFINE MODELS (AMs)

This section introduces the so-called affine models and discusses the reason why these models are popular. We introduce the following proposition.

Proposition 15.2

If, under the term structure in Equation (15.13), the bond price $B(r, t)$ is $B(r, t) = F(t, r(t); T)$, where $F(t, r; T) = e^{A(t,T)-\beta(t,T)r}$ with A, β deterministic terms, then the model for the interest rate is said to have an affine term structure (ATS).

Remark 15.2

Proposition 15.2 is very important. In fact, if we can show that an interest rate model has an ATS, since A, β are deterministic functions, the algebra involved to find a solution to the model is highly simplified. There is also a computational advantage. In fact, since A, β are not stochastic, we will have fewer factors to simulate. This is one of the cases in which binomial models can be implemented with minimum effort.

Consider the SDE in Equation (15.1) and suppose that it shows an ATS structure. How should the functional form for u and σ be specified in this case? In addition, can we also obtain functional forms for A, β? We shall try to address these questions in the following sections.

If we consider Proposition 15.2 and the functional form for $F(.)$, we can compute all the partial derivatives:

$$\frac{\partial B}{\partial t} = e^{(\cdot)}(A_t - \beta_r r) = (-A_t + \beta_t r)F(.)$$

$$\frac{\partial B}{\partial r} = e^{(\cdot)}(-\beta(.)) = F(.)(-\beta(.))$$

$$\frac{\partial^2 B}{\partial r^2} = e^{(\cdot)}\beta^2(.) = F(.)\beta^2(.)$$

where β_t and β_r indicate the partial derivatives with respect to t and r respectively. The term structure dynamics are defined in Equation (15.13) given by

$$\frac{\partial B}{\partial t} + \frac{1}{2}\frac{\partial^2 B}{\partial r^2}\sigma^2 + \frac{\partial B}{\partial r}(u - \sigma v) - r = 0$$

Thus, after substituting the partial derivatives above in the term structure equation we have

$$-(A_t + \beta_t r)B(.) + [u - B(.)\beta(.)] + \frac{1}{2}[\sigma^2 - B(.)\beta^2(.)] - rB(.) = 0$$

(15.14)

$$-A_t + \beta_t r - u\beta(.) + 1/2\sigma^2\beta^2(.) - r = 0 \qquad (15.15)$$

and

$$-A_t + r(\beta_t - 1) - u\beta(.) + 1/2\sigma^2\beta^2(.) = 0 \qquad (15.16)$$

Suppose now that the drift u and the volatility σ take the following form:

$$u = a_0 r + a_1 \text{ and } \sigma = \sqrt{c_0 r + c_1}$$

It follows that Equation (15.16) can be rewritten as

$$-A_t + r(\beta_t - 1) - (a_0 r + a_1)\beta(.) + 1/2\beta^2(.)[c_0 r + c_1] = 0 \qquad (15.17)$$

Rearranging Equation (15.17), we obtain

$$-A_t + r(\beta_t - 1) - a_0\beta(.)r - a_1\beta(.) + \frac{1}{2}\beta^2(.)c_0 r + \frac{1}{2}\beta^2(.)c_1 = 0$$

and hence

$$- A_t - a_1\beta(.) + \frac{1}{2}\beta^2(.)c_1 - r[-\beta_t + 1 + a_0\beta(.) - \frac{1}{2}\beta^2(.)c_0] = 0 \quad (15.18)$$

Equation (15.18) holds for all values[2] of r and t. We can set the coefficient of r to zero and write the following relationship:

$$- \beta_t + a_0\beta(.) - \frac{1}{2}\beta^2(.)c_0 = -1 \quad (15.19)$$

We are now in the position of stating a second important result:

$$- A_t - a_1\beta(.) + \frac{1}{2}\beta^2(.)c_1 = 0 \quad (15.20)$$

The main result is stated in Lemma 15.1 below.

Lemma 15.1

If the drift and the volatility parameters u, σ are of the form $u = a_0 r + a_1$ and $\sigma = \sqrt{c_0 r + c_1}$, then the term structure equation is an ATS, with A, β being of the following form:

$$-\beta_t + a_0\beta(.) - 1/2\beta^2(.)c_0 = -1 \quad (15.21)$$
$$-A_t - a_1\beta(.) + 1/2\beta^2(.)c_1 = 0 \quad (15.22)$$

Also, the final conditions are $A = 0$, $\beta = 0$. These conditions also imply that $B(T, T) = 1$.

The differential equations (15.21) and (15.22) can be solved using integration. This model is the basis of some of the most important interest rate models, some of which we introduce in the following sections.

15.3   THE VASICEK MODEL

In this model the dynamics of the spot interest rate under the risk-neutral measure is given by a mean reverting diffusion process:

$$dr = a(\gamma - r)dt + \sigma dW \quad (15.23)$$

where a represents the strength of mean reversion and γ the long-run mean of the process.

---

[2] We assume here that T is fixed and therefore we consider it a parameter of the model.

If the interest rate deviates from its long-run average, the process will be pushed back to equilibrium at a speed that is measured by a. The reason for this approach is justified by the economic observation that interest rates, in general, appear to be pulled back to equilibrium.

Using the same approach as we did above, one can show that the dynamics of the term structure in this case are given by the following relationship (this proof is left as an exercise):

$$\frac{\partial B}{\partial t} + \frac{\delta^2}{2} \frac{\partial^2 B}{\partial r^2} + [a(\gamma - r) - v\sigma] \frac{\partial B}{\partial r} - rB = 0 \qquad (15.24)$$

In this case, Equations (15.21) and (15.22) can be written as

$$\beta_t - a\beta(.) = -1 \qquad (15.25)$$

$$A_t = -\gamma B(.) - \frac{1}{2}\sigma^2 B^2(.) \qquad (15.26)$$

which can be solved to obtain the solutions for β and A:

$$B(t, T) = \frac{1}{a}\left[1 - e^{-a(T-t)}\right] \qquad (15.27)$$

$$A(t, T) = \frac{[B(t, T) - T + t]\left(a\gamma - 1/2\sigma^2\right)}{a^2} - \frac{\sigma^2 B^2(t, T)}{4a} \qquad (15.28)$$

Remark 15.3

Note that if we integrate (15.23) for each $s \leq t$ and compute the first two moments of the distribution we have

$$E(r(t)/F_s) = r(s)e^{-k(t-s)} + \gamma\left(1 - e^{-k(t-s)}\right) \quad \text{and}$$

$$\text{Var}(r(t)/F_s) = \frac{\sigma^2}{2k}\left[1 - e^{-2k(t-s)}\right]$$

If, on the one hand, working with a Gaussian density may be analytically convenient (see also the discussion above), on the other hand interest rates can now be negative.

The model can also be specified under the objective measure

$$dr = [a\gamma - (a + \lambda\sigma)r]\,dt + \sigma dW^p$$

with λ indicating the market price of risk. This can be obtained using the change of measure introduced in Chapter 4 (see Equation (4.5)):

$$\frac{dQ(W)}{dP(W^p)} = \exp\left[\int_0^t \lambda dP^p - \frac{1}{2}\int_0^t \lambda^2 ds\right]$$

with $s < t$.

Note that the two models under the two measures have the same diffusion coefficient.

Whether or not this model is analytically tractable depends on the specification of the market price of risk. For example, in Brigo and Mercurio (2007) it is assumed to have the functional form $\lambda(t) = \lambda r(t)$. Under this parameterization, the model becomes analytically tractable. This offers some advantages since one may, at this point, estimate σ using historical data and the maximum likelihood, and calibrate the remaining parameters to market data.

15.4   THE COX, INGERSOLL AND ROSS (CIR) MODEL

The stochastic process driving the short-term rate under the risk-neutral measure is given by

$$dr = a(\gamma - r)dt + \sigma\sqrt{r}dW \qquad (15.29)$$

With an initial positive interest rate, the interest rate will never become negative in this model.[3] The process described by Equation (15.29) belongs to the class of square root diffusion processes discussed previously.

If we define the density of the process for the interest rate in Equation (15.29) at time T, conditional on its value at time s, with $s < T$ and $G(r(T), r(s))$, the CIR (1985) model shows that

$$G(.) = de^{-u-v}\left(\frac{v}{u}\right)^{q/2} I_q\left(2(uv)^{1/2}\right) \qquad (15.30)$$

where $\quad d = 2a/\delta^2\left[1 - e^{-a(T-s)}\right], \quad u = dr(t)e^{-a(T-s)}, \quad v = dr(T),$ $q = 2a\gamma/\delta^2 - 1$ and I_q is a modified Bessel function.

The CIR (1985) model shows that the process in (15.30) follows a noncentral χ^2 distribution. As we did in the case of stochastic volatility models, this property can be exploited for simulation purposes. As with the Vasicek model, and using the same approach as described in the previous section, this model can also be formulated under the objective measure.

Using Lemma 15.1, the solution of the model is of the following form:

$$A_t - a\gamma A\beta = 0 \qquad (15.31)$$

$$\beta_t - (a + \lambda\delta)\beta - \frac{1}{2}\delta^2\beta^2 + 1 = 0 \qquad (15.32)$$

We assume that λ is a constant and the market price of risk is given by $\lambda\sqrt{r}$. If we now assume the following term structure:

$$F(t, r) = A_0(T - s)e^{-\beta(T-s)r} \qquad (15.33)$$

---

[3] This is not necessarily true in the case of the Vasicek model.

and solve for A_0 and β, we obtain

$$\beta = \frac{2(e^\psi - 1)}{(\gamma + a)(e^\psi - 1) + 2\psi} \qquad (15.34)$$

and

$$A_0 = \left[\frac{2\psi e^{(a+\psi)1/2}}{(\psi + a)(e^\psi - 1) + 2\psi} \right]^{2a\gamma/\delta^2} \qquad (15.35)$$

Hence, closed-form solutions to price European style options on zero coupon bonds[4] can be easily obtained.

15.5   THE HULL AND WHITE (HW) MODEL

Hull and White (1990) consider the same stochastic process as in the previous section to model interest rate dynamics. It is an extension of the Vasicek model. However, the parameter describing the long-run equilibrium is now made time dependent. Furthermore, under certain assumptions for the function $\gamma(t)$, the SDE below can now be solved explicitly:

$$dr = a(\gamma(t) - r)dt + \sigma\sqrt{r}dW \qquad (15.36)$$

The value of a zero coupon bond is given by

$$B(t, r; T) = e^{A(t,T) - \beta(t,T)r} \qquad (15.37)$$

The model belongs to the class of affine models and satisfies the ATS given above. The parameters A_t and β_t are given by

$$\beta_t = a\beta(.) - 1 \qquad (15.38)$$

$$A_t = \lambda(t)\beta(.) - \frac{1}{2}\sigma^2\beta^2(.) \qquad (15.39)$$

Following Hull and White, we define the forward rate as

$$f(0, T) = \beta_T(t, T)r_0 - A_T(t, T) \qquad (15.40)$$

Also, note that, from Equation (15.37), the yield $y(t, T)$ is equal to

$$y(t, T) = \frac{\beta_T(t, T)}{T - t}r_t - \frac{A_T(t, T)}{T - t} \qquad (15.41)$$

Suppose there are bonds in the market with different maturities and we observe $B^*(0, T)$ and the forward rate $f^*(0, T)$. Hull and White show that we can

---

[4] Since the Vasicek and the CIR models are affine models, one can also obtain analytical expressions for the volatility of the instantaneous forward rates. This result is very useful for calibration purposes (see Brigo and Mercurio, 2001, for a detailed discussion).

calibrate the model (with $f^*(0, T) = f(0, T)$) if we choose:

$$\gamma(T) = af^*(0, T) + f_T^*(0, T) + \sigma^2\beta(0, T)(e^{-aT} + 1/2aB(0, T)) \qquad (15.42)$$

The price of a zero coupon bond $B(0, T)$ can then be obtained:

$$B(0, T) = \frac{B^*(0, T)}{B^*(0, t)}$$

$$\times \exp\left[\beta(t, T)f^*(0, t) - \frac{\delta^2}{4a}\beta^2(t, T)(1 - e^{-2at}) - \beta(t, T)r\right]_t$$

$$(15.43)$$

The model can also be used to price options on bonds.

15.6   THE BLACK FORMULA AND BOND OPTIONS

Bond options were initially priced using the Black and Scholes formula (5.11) and by replacing the stock price with the price of a bond. However, very soon this approach showed its limitations. Indeed, the interest rate in the model was assumed to be constant. This was inconsistent with the primary objective of an interest rate model (i.e. modelling interest rate dynamics). Furthermore, the bond volatility in the model was assumed to be constant. This assumption, obviously, is not consistent with the fact that a bond's volatility should go to zero as $t \rightarrow T$.

The Black model assumes that the bond price at T (i.e. the time when the option expires) is lognormal. The formula is obtained using the same method as in Chapter 5 using the Black and Scholes formula after a change of numeraire. In fact, the model uses the forward numeraire $B(t, T)$ rather than the bank account numeraire. Under this change of measure the option's price at time t, with expiry at time T, for a zero coupon bond with maturity S, with $S > T$, is given by the following:

$$BF(t, T, S, K) = B(t, T)[B(t, T, S)N(d_1) - KN(d_2)]$$

$$d_1 = \frac{\log(P(t, T, S)/K) + \sigma_F^2/2}{\sigma_F} \quad \text{and} \quad d_2 = d_1 - \sigma_F\sqrt{T}$$

where σ_F is the forward volatility that is to be estimated using market data or obtained from other contracts.

16

Interest Rate Modelling

16.1 SOME PRELIMINARY DEFINITIONS

The following sections are based on the main concepts introduced in Chapter 5 (including Appendices A5.1 to A5.3). Suppose we deposit $1 in a bank account at time t (we assume that today $t = 0$). What is the fair amount of money we can expect at time $t = T$? This value depends on the short rate $r(t)$[1] and is uncertain since the short rate is stochastic. Suppose now that, given $1 at time $t = T$, we want to calculate its present value at time $t = 0$. This is given by $1/\beta(T)$. Denote by $P(0, T)$ the price of a zero coupon bond at $t = 0$, with maturity $t = T$. Also, suppose that $P(0, T) = 1/\beta(T) = \$1$. Thus, this quantity is no longer stochastic. However, note that $P(t, T)$ is still stochastic at time $t = 0$. In fact, this depends on the expectations of the short rate.[2] We can also ask, what is the value of $1 at time t, invested at time $t = 0$, for the period $0 \leq t \leq T$? In the same way as before, this is given by $\beta(t)/\beta(T)$.

Definition 16.1

The stochastic discount factor between two dates (t, T) is defined as

$$D(t, T) = \frac{\beta(t)}{\beta(T)} = \exp\left(\int_t^T r(s)ds\right) \qquad (16.1)$$

From Equation (16.1) we see that if the interest rate is deterministic $P(t, T)$ and $D(t, T)$ are equal. On the other hand, if the interest rate is stochastic, $D(t, T)$ is also stochastic. However, $P(t, T)$ can still be inferred from the market price of zero coupon bonds.

Definition 16.2

The market LIBOR rate at time t, with maturity T, is given by

$$L(t, T) = \frac{1 - P(t, T)}{\delta(T - t)P(t, T)}$$

---

[1] See Chapter 5, Appendix A5.2 for further details.
[2] What is the difference between $r(t)$ and $P(t, T)$? The former is not observable while the latter is.

Therefore, LIBOR rates are linked to zero coupon bonds and in general markets use some conventions for the day count $\delta(T - t)$. Thus, it follows that

$$P(t, T) = \frac{1}{1 + L(t, T)\delta(T - t)}$$

Definition 16.3

A forward rate (at time t) with maturity S, on a contract with expiry time T, with $t \leq T \leq S$, is given by

$$F(t; T, S) = \frac{1}{\delta(S - T)} \left(\frac{P(t, T)}{P(t, S)} - 1 \right)$$

Thus, the forward rate can be seen as an estimate of the future spot rate $L(T, S)$.

Definition 16.4

The instantaneous forward rate is defined as

$$f(t, T) = \lim_{S \to T} F(t; T, S) = \frac{\partial \ln P(t, T)}{\partial T}$$

It is often very useful when modelling interest rate derivatives to use as a numeraire the price of a zero coupon bond with the same maturity as the expiry date of the derivative security we are considering, particularly if the expiry date of the derivative security is at time S. For example, we know that $P(S, S) = \$1$. The expected payoff of the derivative is now divided by one. The expectation taken under this new numeraire is called *forward measure* and is often represented by Q^S. Under this new measure, the expected payoff of the derivatives can be written as

$$V(T) = P(T, S)E^S [V(S/F_T)]$$

We know already from Chapter 5 (Appendix A5.2) that this process is a positive martingale.

Definition 16.5

Even for forward rates we can state that a forward rate with maturity S is a martingale under the measure Q^S and in particular it can be written as a Q^S expectation of the LIBOR rate given by $E^S(L(T, S)/F_t) = F(t; T, S)$.

16.2   INTEREST RATE CAPLETS AND FLOORLETS

Consider a set of dates $(T_0, T_1, \ldots, T_M)$ and the expiry maturity dates for the forward rates (T_{i-1}, T_i), with $i > 0$. We assume that $T_{-1} = 0$ and also that

$(\delta_0, \ldots, \delta_M)$ are the year fractions for the maturities identified. Note that for a generic forward rate with maturity at time $T_k, k = 1, 2, \ldots, M$, we can simply write $F_k(t) = F(t; T_{i-k}, T_k)$.[3]

Consider now an interest rate derivative which pays a fixed amount A at time T_i if the forward rate $F_i(T_{i-1})$ is above a strike K:

$$A\delta_i \, (F_i(T_{i-1}) - K)^+ \tag{16.2}$$

We know that the forward rate at time T_{i-1} coincides with the LIBOR rate $L_i(T_{i-1})$; therefore the payoff above can also be written in terms of LIBOR rates as

$$A\delta_i \, (L_i(T_{i-1}) - K)^+ \tag{16.3}$$

A contingent claim with a payoff given by (16.3) is called a caplet. A caplet is an interest rate call option having the LIBOR rate as the underlying rate. A floorlet is an interest rate put option on LIBOR rates and is similarly defined. Note that the payoff of a caplet is made at time T_i but the LIBOR rate is known at time T_{i-1}. Therefore the payoff is made at some later time than when the LIBOR rate is known.

The payoff of the caplet at time T_{i-1} can be written as $P(T_{i-1}, T_i)(L_i(T_{i-1}) - K)^+$. In what follows, for simplicity, we set $A = \$1$. Using the result in Definition 16.2, we can write it as

$$\frac{1}{\delta_i} P(T_{i-1}, T_i) \left(\left(\frac{1}{P(T_{i-1}, P_i)} - 1 \right) - K \right)^+$$

$$\text{or} \quad \frac{1}{\delta_i} (1 - (1 + K\delta_i)P(T_{i-1}, T_i))^+$$

However, this is the payoff of an option at time T_{i-1}. Note that this payoff can also be written as $K^* - P(T_{i-1}, T_i)^+$ and this is the payoff of $(1 + K\delta)/\delta$ options with a strike[4] $K^* \equiv 1/(1 + K\delta)$. Thus, a caplet is a put option on a zero coupon bond.

Caps are a linear combination of caplets at specified dates. Therefore, these can be priced by adding together the price of each individual caplet. When the sequence of dates is such that the payoff of the first caplet is known on the date the cap is entered into, the convention is to disregard the first caplet. Floors, on the other hand, are linear combinations of floorlets.

Prices of caps and floors are generally quoted in the market in terms of Black's implied volatility and therefore they also display variation with skew and smiles.

---

[3] Note that using Definition 16.4, at time T_{k-1} the forward rate coincides with the LIBOR rate, $F_k(T_{k-1}) = L(T_{k-1}, T_k)$.

[4] You can see this by replacing K^* in the payoff formula.

16.3   FORWARD RATES AND NUMERAIRE

In the previous sections, we pointed out that the forward rate is a martingale process under an appropriate numeraire (measure). We now need to clarify this statement. We follow Brigo and Mercurio (2001).

Consider the (lognormal) forward rate F_k and the measure Q^k:

$$dF_k(t) = \sigma_k(t)F_k(t)\,dW^k(t) \tag{16.4}$$

where σ is the forward rate volatility and W is a Brownian motion under the measure specified above with instantaneous covariance ρ, such that $dW_t^k dW_t^{k'} = \rho dt$.

Proposition 12.1

$$dF_k(t) = \sigma_k(t)F_k(t)\sum_{j=i+1}^{k}\frac{\rho_{k,j}\delta_j\sigma_j(t)F_j(t)}{1+\pi_j F_j(t)}dt + \sigma_k(t)F_k(t)dW_k(t);$$
$$i < k, t \le T_i \tag{16.5}$$

$$dF_k(t) = \sigma_k(t)F_k(t)\,dW^k(t); \qquad i = k, t \le T_{k-1} \tag{16.6}$$

$$dF_k(t) = -\sigma_k(t)F_k(t)\sum_{j=i+1}^{k}\frac{\rho_{k,j}\delta_j\sigma_j(t)F_j(t)}{1+\pi_j F_j(t)}dt + \sigma_k(t)F_k(t)\,dW_k(t);$$
$$i > k, t \le T_{k-1} \tag{16.7}$$

In (16.5) we are using as a numeraire a bond with a maturity (T_i) shorter than the forward rate maturity (T_k), while in (16.6) the maturity of the numeraire bond and forward rate coincide. We know that, in this case, the forward rate is a martingale. It is not the case with Equations (16.5) and (16.7). Note that it is also required that $\sigma_k(t)$ is bounded. However, one can still use Equations (16.5) and (16.7). In fact, one can prove that (16.5) and (16.7) admit a unique strong solution if the coefficients $\sigma(.)$ are bounded (see Brigo and Mercurio, 2001).

The model in (16.6) is often used to obtain analytical formulae for interest rate derivatives. Consider the example in (16.3) above. With a stochastic interest rate, the payoff for a caplet is given by

$$A\delta_i E^Q\left[e^{-\int_t^{T_i} r_s ds}(L_i(T_{i-1}) - K)|F_t^+\right] \tag{16.8}$$

Using the numeraire $P(t, T_i)$ and under the lognormal assumption for the forward rate, we can write (16.8) as

$$A\delta_i P(t, T_i)E^i\left[(F_i(T_{i-1}) - K)^+|F_t\right] \tag{16.9}$$

From (16.9) Black's formula for the caplet can then be derived:[5]

$$Caplet = \delta_i P(t, T_i)[F_i(t)N(d_1) - KN(d_2)]$$

with

$$d_1 = \frac{1}{v_i\sqrt{T_{i-1}}} \log\left(\frac{F_i(t)}{K}\right) + \frac{1}{2}\int_t^{T_{i-1}} \sigma_i^2(s)ds$$

$$d_2 = d_1 - v_i\sqrt{T_{i-1}}$$

where $N(.)$ is the cumulative normal distribution function and $v_i = \sigma_i\sqrt{T_{i-1}}$, with σ_i obtained from market quotes.

Practitioners use Black's formula above to price caplets and floorlets. Prices for caps and floors are given by

$$Cap = \sum Caplets \quad \text{and} \quad Floor = \sum Floorlets$$

This is possible since each caplet or floorlet only depends on one single forward rate.[6]

Black's model described above is widely used in practice to compute implied volatilities for caps and floors with different strikes and maturities. It represents the market standard model.

16.4   LIBOR FUTURES CONTRACTS

Three-month LIBOR futures contracts are contracts traded in all the major currencies (EUR, AUD, CAD, JPN, etc.). These are very actively traded in the market and the bid-ask spread is generally very small. In the US three-month LIBOR futures contracts trade with maturities out of ten years. The delivery (settlement) price for these contracts is set at 100 minus the three-month LIBOR (in percentages).

Denote by T_1 the future contract maturity. If the LIBOR rate at T_1 is $L(T_1, T_1, T_2)$, the payoff of the contract is $100(1 - L(T_1, T_1, T_2))$. Differently from forward contracts, future contracts are daily marked to market by the exchange. For example, suppose you buy a future contract on 8 February when its market price is 97.21. Suppose that at the end of the trading day its closing price is 97.33. An amount equal to $97.33 - 97.21 = 0.12$ is paid into your account. This mark-to-market procedure continues until maturity (i.e. T_1).

We aim to derive a theoretical formula for the value of a three-month LIBOR future contract at time t, with $t < T_1$. In what follows we suppose that the

---

[5] Here we set $A = 1$.

[6] This does not apply to swaptions, for example. In fact, with these derivatives the decomposition used for caps and floors is no longer true.

theoretical value of the contract is given by $G(t, T_1, T_2)$. Therefore, the delivery price is given by

$$G(t, T_1, T_2) = 100(1 - L(T_1, T_1, T_2))$$

$$= 100 \left(1 - \frac{1}{\delta} \left(\frac{1}{P(T_1, T_2)} - 1 \right) \right) \qquad (16.10)$$

Note that $G(t, T_1, T_2)$ depends both on $P(t, T_1)$ and $P(t, T_2)$. Therefore

$$G(t) \equiv G(t, T_1, T_2) \equiv G(t, P(t, T_1), P(t, T_2))$$

Suppose that the dynamics of the price $P(t, T)$ under the real world measure is given by

$$\frac{dP(t, T_i)}{P(t, T_i)} = \mu_i(t)dt + \sigma_P(t, T_i)dW_i(t)$$

where i is 1 or 2, μ is the drift and σ the volatility. Applying the multidimensional Ito lemma and writing $P(t, T_1) \equiv P_1$ and $P(t, T_2) \equiv P_2$, we obtain

$$dG(t) = \frac{\partial G(t)}{\partial t} dt$$

$$+ \frac{\partial G(t)}{\partial P_1} (\mu_1 dt + \sigma_P(t, T_1)dW_1(t))P_1$$

$$+ \frac{\partial G(t)}{\partial P_2} (\mu_2 dt + \sigma_P(t, T_2)dW_2(t)) P_2$$

$$+ \left(\frac{1}{2} \frac{\partial^2 G(t)}{\partial P_1^2} \sigma_P^2(t, T_1)P_1^2 + \frac{1}{2} \frac{\partial^2 G(t)}{\partial P_2^2} \sigma_P^2(t, T_2)P_2^2 \right.$$

$$\left. + \rho_{12} \frac{\partial^2 G(t)}{\partial P_1 \partial P_2} \sigma_P(t, T_1)\sigma_P(t, T_2)P_1 P_2 \right) dt$$

where ρ_{12} is the deterministic instantaneous correlation between dW_1 and dW_2.

Consider a self-financing strategy at time t consisting of a long-position on a future contract, a short-position on $\partial G(t)/\partial P_1$ bonds with maturity T_1 and a short-position on $\partial G(t)/\partial P_2$ with maturity T_2. The portfolio has a zero net aggregate investment at any time and its value is given by

$$0 - \frac{\partial G(t)}{\partial P_1} P_1 - \frac{\partial G(t)}{\partial P_2} P_2 = 0 \qquad (16.11)$$

where zero on the right-hand side of the equation accounts for the fact that there is no up-front cost to buy (sell) a future contract.

In order to satisfy Equation (16.10), $\partial G(t)/\partial P_1$ and $\partial G(t)/\partial P_2$ must have a different sign. The change in the value of this portfolio between t and $t + dt$ is given by

$$dG(t) \quad -\frac{\partial G(t)}{\partial P_1}dP_1 - \frac{\partial G(t)}{\partial P_2}dP_2 = \frac{\partial G(t)}{\partial t}dt$$

$$+ \left(\frac{1}{2}\frac{\partial^2 G(t)}{\partial P_1^2}\sigma_P^2(t, T_1)P_1^2 + \frac{1}{2}\frac{\partial^2 G(t)}{\partial P_2^2}\sigma_P^2(t, T_2)P_2^2 \right.$$

$$\left. + \rho_{12}\frac{\partial^2 G(t)}{\partial P_1 \partial P_2}\sigma_P^2(t, T_1)\sigma_P(t, T_2)P_1 P_2 \right) dt$$

This is now a portfolio holding a zero aggregate investment. Therefore, in the absence of arbitrage it must earn exactly zero for all t:

$$dG(t) - \frac{\partial G(t)}{\partial P_1}dP_1 - \frac{\partial G(t)}{\partial P_2}dP_2 = 0$$

Therefore, it follows that

$$dG(t) + \left(\frac{1}{2}\frac{\partial^2 G(t)}{\partial P_1^2}\sigma_P^2(t, T_1)P_1^2 + \frac{1}{2}\frac{\partial^2 G(t)}{\partial P_2^2}\sigma_P^2(t, T_2)P_2^2 \right.$$

$$\left. + \rho_{12}\frac{\partial^2 G(t)}{\partial P_1 \partial P_2}\sigma_P^2(t, T_1)\sigma_P(t, T_2)P_1 P_2 \right) = 0$$

After solving the PDE above with the conditions in Equations (16.10) and (16.11), we obtain

$$Y(t) = \int\limits_{t}^{T_1} \left(\sigma_P^2(s, T_2) - \rho_{12}\sigma_P(s, T_1)\sigma_P(s, T_2) \right) ds$$

$Y(t)$ can be easily computed once we know $\sigma_P(s, T_1)$ and $\sigma_P(s, T_2)$; therefore the solution is

$$G(t, T_1, T_2) = 100 \left(1 - \frac{1}{\delta}\left(\frac{P(t, T_1)}{P(t, T_2)}\exp(Y(t, T_1, T_2)) - 1 \right) \right) \qquad (16.12)$$

16.5 MARTINGALE MEASURE

In this section we show that $G(t, T_1, T_2)$ is a martingale under the risk equivalent measure and also discuss the implications for this result. Define $H(t, T_1, T_2) \equiv H(t, T_1, T_2)$:

$$H(t, T_1, T_2) = \frac{P(t, T_1)}{P(t, T_2)}\exp(Y(t, T_1, T_2))$$

Suppose the zero coupon bond price, under the risk-neutral equivalent measure, has the following dynamics. Here we consider only two periods and therefore

$i = 1,2$:

$$\frac{dP(t, T_i)}{dP(t, T_i)} = r(t)dt + \sigma_P(t, T_i)dW_i(t)$$

Using Ito's lemma, the dynamics of $H(t)$ are

$$\frac{dH(t)}{H(t)} = \sigma_P(t, T_1)dW_1(t) - \sigma_P(t, T_2)dW_2(t)$$

Thus, $H(t)$ is a martingale under the risk-neutral measure and as a consequence $G(t, T_1, T_2)$ is also a martingale. Note that in a deterministic interest rate environment, we would expect $G(t, T_1, T_2) = 100(1 - L(t, T_1, T_2))$. However, with stochastic interest rates we expect $Y(t)$ to be positive since bond prices of different maturity will be positively correlated. Therefore, it follows that $G(t, T_1, T_2) < 100(1 - L(t, T_1, T_2))$ (see Equation (16.12)). This implies that when pricing futures contracts a convexity adjustment will have to be considered.

Remark 16.1

The convexity bias is an important issue, especially for long dated futures. One can use the theoretical futures value formula obtained above and its quoted price to build the yield curve.[7] In the past financial institutions have lost money when failing to adjust for convexity and assuming $Y(t, T_1, T_2) = 0$.

---

[7] Therefore it is important to account for the convexity adjustment when we build the yield curve; otherwise one would misprice a variety of interest rate derivatives.

Binomial and Finite Difference Methods

17.1 THE BINOMIAL MODEL

To introduce the model, we consider the Black and Scholes economy and the Black and Scholes model described in Chapters 4 and 5. In addition, we assume that the time to expiry of the option (T) is constant and choose a time step Δt such that $i\Delta t, i = 0, 1, 2, \ldots, T/\Delta t$.

Let us start with a simple example and consider the same portfolio as the one discussed in Chapter 5 (Section 5.2):

$$P(0) = C(0) - nS(0)$$

Suppose that there are two possible scenarios for the stock price at Δt:

$$P_u = C_u - nS_u$$
$$P_d = C_d - nS_d$$

where the subscripts u, d indicate an up or down move in the stock price respectively. This portfolio will be arbitrage free if and only if

$$P_u = P_d = n = \frac{C_u - C_d}{S(0)(u - d)} \tag{17.1}$$

Thus, one can write

$$C(0) = e^{-r\Delta t}[p_r C_u + (1 - p_r)C_d]$$

where

$$p_r = \frac{e^{-r\Delta t} - d}{u - d}$$

and r is the risk-free rate of interest.

Remark 17.1

Note that $0 \le p_r \le 1$, which can be considered the probability of a stock price move over the interval Δt. As the formula above shows, this does not play any role in this context. It can be considered as a risk-neutral probability.

17.2   EXPECTED VALUE AND VARIANCE IN THE BLACK AND SCHOLES AND BINOMIAL MODELS

We know that in the Black and Scholes lognormal model, introduced in Chapter 5, the conditional expectation of $S(t + \Delta t)/S(t)$ is given by

$$E^Q[S(t + \Delta t)/S(t)] = S(t)e^{r\Delta t} \tag{17.2}$$

while the variance is given by

$$\text{Var}[S(t + \Delta t)/S(t)] = S^2(t)e^{2r\Delta t}(e^{\sigma^2\Delta t} - 1) \tag{17.3}$$

Consider now the binomial model introduced above. The conditional expectation in this case is given by

$$E^P[S(t + \Delta t)/S(t)] = S(t)[p_r u + (1 - p_r)d] \tag{17.4}$$

while the variance is

$$\begin{aligned}\text{Var}[S(t + \Delta t)/S(t)] = {}& p_r[S(t)u]^2 + (1 - p_r)[S(t)d]^2 \\ & -S(t)^2[p_r u + (1 - p_r)d]^2\end{aligned} \tag{17.5}$$

One can show convergence of the conditional expectation and variance of both the Black and Scholes and binomial models. After some algebra we obtain the following interesting results:

$$p_r u + (1 - p_r)d = e^{r\Delta t}$$
$$p_r u^2 + (1 - p_r)d^2 = e^{2r\Delta t + \sigma^2 \Delta t}$$

Remark 17.2

Note that $p_r \sim Q$ and that, without loss of generality, as a consequence of the two results above, we can write $E^P[e^{i\lambda \ln S(\Delta t)}] = E^Q[e^{i\lambda \ln S(T)}]$. The binomial price converges, in distribution, to the Black and Scholes price as $i \to \infty$. One can obtain a similar result for the delta.

Remark 17.3

Note that the system of two equations above contains three unknowns. Generally, one has to assume a solution for u. Standard practice in the industry is to assume $u = 1/d$. This leads to the well-known Cox–Ross–Rubinstein (CRR) model (1979). Otherwise, one can set $p_r = 1 - p_r = 1/2$, which leads to the Jarrow–Rudd (1983) model. Note that the CRR model is rather convenient since it implies that an up move followed by a down move is equivalent to a down move followed by an up move ($S(0)ud = S(0)du = S(0)$). The lattice is recombining and thus we avoid the case where there is an explosion in the number of nodes in the tree (see Figure 17.1).

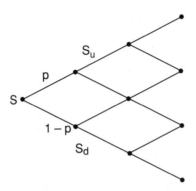

Figure 17.1 Recombining binomial tree

17.3   THE COX–ROSS–RUBINSTEIN MODEL

We know that the solution of the Black and Scholes geometric Brownian motion
is given by

$$S(t) = S(0)e^{(r-d)t+\sigma W(t)}$$

where d is the dividend paid by the stock. Replace this solution by the following:

$$S(i \Delta t + 1) = S(i \Delta t)e^{\varepsilon \sigma \sqrt{\Delta t}} \tag{17.6}$$

where $\varepsilon = 1$ with probability p_r and $\varepsilon = -1$ with probability $(1 - p_r)$ such
that

$$E[e^{-(r-d)\Delta t} S(i + 1)/S(i)] = S(i)$$

Now use (17.6) to simulate the stock prices along the tree, as in Figure 17.1. The price of a European put option, for example, satisfies
$E^{P_r}[e^{-r\Delta t} p(i + 1)/p(i)] = p(i)$, while the price of an American option satisfies $p(i) = (f, E^{P_r}[e^{-r\Delta t} p(i + 1)/p(i)])$, where f is the payoff of the option
following at immediate exercise.[1]

Remark 17.4

A binomial method can also be used to price American options; this was the
main methodology used in this context in the industry. At this point there
are a few issues that we should clarify. As shown in Chapter 6, the rate of
convergence of the typical Monte Carlo estimator of the option is $1/\sqrt{M}$,
where M is the number of replications. Similarly, the rate of convergence of

---

[1] Given the backwards nature of the binomial tree, the dynamic programming problem described
in Chapter 7 can be solved.

a binomial estimator can be shown to be $1/\sqrt[d]{N}$, where d is the dimension of the problem we want to solve. For $d = 1$, there is therefore no competitive advantage in using Monte Carlo over binomial methods. However, in the case of multidimensional problems, while the Monte Carlo estimator preserves its typical rate of convergence, the rate of convergence of the binomial estimator declines substantially. Hence, while binomial methods are suitable when $d = 3$, Monte Carlo methods can also be used in cases where $d > 3$.

To implement the CRR above one needs functional forms for u and d. In the typical CRR model, these can be shown to be equal to $u = e^{\sigma\sqrt{\Delta t}}$ and $d = 1/u$.

17.4   FINITE DIFFERENCE METHODS

This methodology focuses on solving directly the differential equation (5.6) in Chapter 5 subject to some boundaries, depending on the option we want to price. The methodology replaces the differential equation by a set of difference equations. To achieve this goal, it is necessary to define a discrete time interval over the maturity (T) of the option. This can be done in the same way as in the case of the binomial model introduced above. In addition, we need to specify a price $S(\max)$ for the stock price, which is unlikely to be achieved by $S(t)$. Note that $S = 0, \Delta S, 2\Delta S \ldots M\Delta S = S(\max)$.

The goal is to obtain an approximation of the derivatives in Equation (5.6). If we consider a Taylor approximation of general functions $f_{i,j} = f(i\Delta t, j\Delta S)$ and drop all the terms of the order Δt^2 and higher, we can write the first derivative as follows:

$$\text{(Backward difference)} \quad \frac{\partial f}{\partial S} = \frac{f_{i,j+1} - f_{ij}}{\Delta S}$$

or

$$\text{(forward difference)} \quad \frac{\partial f}{\partial S} = \frac{f_{i,} - f_{i,j+1}}{\Delta S} \tag{17.7}$$

Using these two equations, we can also make the approximation more precise and write the following central difference approximation:

$$\frac{\partial f}{\partial S} = \frac{f_{i,j+1} - f_{i,j-1}}{2\Delta S} \tag{17.8}$$

The second-order derivative can be obtained by subtracting the backward difference approximation from the forward difference approximation. Finally, the time derivative is obtained by backward induction. If we replace the terms in (5.6) with equations, after some algebra we obtain the difference equation we need in order to price the option. Subsequently, the difference equation is to be solved at each specified node.

For a typical put option, for example, we specify the terminal conditions $f_{i,M} = 0$, $f_{i,0} = K$ and $f_{N,j} = \max(K - j\Delta S)^+$.

APPENDIX A17.1   THE BINOMIAL METHOD

This appendix shows an application of the methodology presented in Section 14.3 to price American options.

```
function [B_Call] = Binomial(so, X, r, Div, T, sigma,
NSteps)
% Computes the Cox, Ross & Rubinstein (1979) Binomial
Tree for American
% on the following inputs:
% Call = call price
% so = the initial stock price
% X = strike
% r = risk free of interest
% Div = Dividend Yield of Underlying
% T = time to Maturity
% sigma = Volatility of the Underlying
% NSteps = Number of Time Steps.

dt = T/NSteps;

RR = exp(r * dt);
Up = exp(sigma * sqrt(dt));
Down = 1 / Up;
P_up = (exp((r - Div) * dt) - Down) / (Up - Down);
P_down = 1 - P_up;
Df = exp(-r * dt);

% Sets up the asset movements on the binomial tree
for i = 0:NSteps
    State = i + 1;
    St = so * Up ^ i * Down ^ (NSteps - i);
    Value(State) = max(0, (St - X));
end

% Works backwards recursively to determine
the price of the option
for TT = (NSteps - 1):-1:0
    for i = 0:TT
        State = i + 1;
        Value(State) = max((((so * Up ^ i * Down ^
(abs(i - TT)) - X)), (P_up * Value(State + 1) + P_down
* Value(State)) * Df);
```

```
        end
end

B_Call = Value(1);
```

We show an application of the function 'Binomial' to price an at-the-money American option with strike $100, an annual free rate of interest equal to 4%, the stock pays an annual dividend equal to 2%, the stock price volatility is assumed to be 10% and the option expiry date is one year. We use 10 000 time steps. After calling the function above we have the following: B_Call = 4.9175.

Appendix 1
An Introduction to MATLAB

A1.1 WHAT IS MATLAB?

MATLAB stands for 'Matrix Laboratory' and is a powerful package that allows people to do both simple operations (i.e. operations that can normally be done using a calculator) and programming. There are many MATLAB toolboxes, but the main one is a powerful package containing a library to solve a variety of numerical problems such as root-findings, numerical integration and more. The main uses include:

• Maths and computation
• Modelling and simulations
• Data analysis and visualization
• Graphical uses

In this appendix we provide a short introduction to both numerical applications in MATLAB and programming. A short introduction to the main MATLAB toolbox will end the chapter.

A1.2 STARTING MATLAB

Once you have started MATLAB, you should see a window coming up containing information such as:

• The Command Window
• The Current Directory
• The Command History
• The Editor Window

An example is presented in Figure A1.1.

When the screen looks like the one shown in Figure A1.1, you can start using it for simple calculations or programming. We start with simple calculations and solve simple problems using matrices. We shall discuss MATLAB functions and programming in the second part of this appendix.

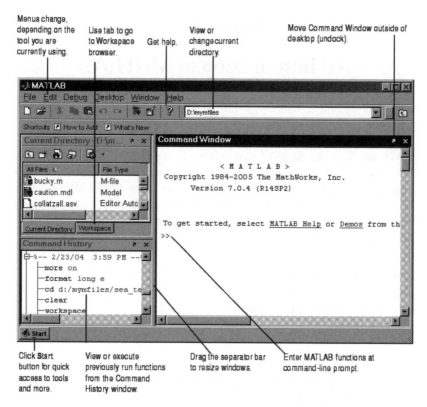

Figure A1.1   The MATLAB workspace

A1.3   MAIN OPERATIONS IN MATLAB

Basic arithmetic operations are easy to compute in MATLAB. As with a normal calculator we could, for example, compute simple summations or products:

$$5 + 6 \text{ ans} = 11 \quad 5*3 \text{ ans} = 15$$

However, we could also compute more complex operations, such as:

$$5^{\wedge}2*3 \text{ ans} = 75$$

A1.4   VECTORS AND MATRICES

You can enter matrices in MATLAB in many different ways. For example, you can enter a list of elements, import an external file containing a matrix or create a matrix using an M-file. Although in MATLAB matrices or vectors can be any list of objects, in this section we assume that the objects are numbers. Numbers in the row vectors are stored horizontally while those in the column vectors are stored vertically. An example is shown below. The example shows ways to build a vector row and column containing some given numbers:

$$z = [1, 0, 2, 3, 4, 5] \text{ ans } z = 1 \quad 0 \quad 2 \quad 3 \quad 4 \quad 5$$
$$z = [1; 0; 2; 3; 4; 5] \text{ ans}$$
$$z =$$
$$1$$
$$0$$
$$2$$
$$3$$
$$4$$
$$5$$

We can also allocate a value to each element of the vector z or even compute the transpose of z in a simple way:

$$z(1) = z(2) + 3*z(1)*10$$
$$z = 30 \quad 0 \quad 2 \quad 3 \quad 4 \quad 5$$
$$z = z'$$
$$z =$$
$$1$$
$$0$$
$$2$$
$$3$$
$$4$$
$$5$$

Matrices can be obtained in the same way. Consider the example below:

$$z = [2 \ 2; 0 \ 4; 3 \ 4] \text{ ans}$$
$$z = 2 \quad 2$$
$$0 \quad 4$$
$$3 \quad 4$$

Given the matrix above we might only be interested in some values contained in the matrix, for example some elements of a single row or column:

$$z(2,2) \text{ ans} = 4 \quad z(2, :) \text{ ans} = 0 \quad 4$$
$$z(:, 1) \text{ ans} = 2$$
$$0$$
$$3$$

Computational methods make a large use of special matrices. These matrices can be easily obtained in MATLAB. Consider the examples below:

$$m = 2; \quad n = 2;$$
$$z = \text{zeros}(m, n) \qquad z = \text{ones}(m, n)$$
$$z = 0 \quad 0 \qquad\qquad z = 1 \quad 1$$
$$\quad\; 0 \quad 0 \qquad\qquad\quad\; 1 \quad 1$$

Identity and diagonal matrices can also be created:

$$z = \text{eye}(n) \qquad z = [4 \quad 5 \quad 6];$$
$$z = 1 \quad 0 \qquad \text{diagonal} = \text{diag}(z)$$
$$\quad\; 0 \quad 1 \qquad \text{diagonal} = 4 \quad 0 \quad 0$$
$$\qquad\qquad\qquad\qquad\qquad 0 \quad 5 \quad 0$$
$$\qquad\qquad\qquad\qquad\qquad 0 \quad 0 \quad 6$$

Upper and lower triangular matrices can be obtained using the commands 'triu' and 'tril':

$$z = [1\ 2\ 3; 3\ 4\ 6; 1\ 3\ 4];$$
$$\text{upper} = \text{triu}(z) \qquad \text{lower} = \text{tril}(z)$$
$$\text{upper} = 1 \quad 2 \quad 3 \qquad \text{lower} = 1 \quad 0 \quad 0$$
$$\qquad\quad\;\; 0 \quad 4 \quad 6 \qquad\qquad\quad\;\; 3 \quad 4 \quad 0$$
$$\qquad\quad\;\; 0 \quad 0 \quad 4 \qquad\qquad\quad\;\; 1 \quad 3 \quad 4$$

A1.5 BASIC MATRIX OPERATIONS

Define the following matrices:

$$z1 = [1\ 2\ 3; 4\ 5\ 6] \qquad z2 = [3\ 4; 0\ 1] \qquad z3 = [2\ 1; 0\ 1]$$
$$z1 = 1 \quad 2 \quad 3 \qquad\quad z2 = 3 \quad 4 \qquad\quad z3 = 2 \quad 1$$
$$\quad\;\; 4 \quad 5 \quad 6 \qquad\qquad\quad\; 0 \quad 1 \qquad\qquad\quad\; 0 \quad 1$$

A simple summation of z2+z3 or a matrix product is given by

$$z = z2 + z3 \qquad z = z2*z1$$
$$z = 5 \quad 5 \qquad\quad z = 19 \quad 26 \quad 3$$
$$\quad\;\; 0 \quad 2 \qquad\qquad\quad\; 4 \quad 5 \quad 6$$

MATLAB provides different alternatives to the one discussed above to generate matrices. For example, the command 'rand' generates a matrix containing uniformly distributed random numbers while the command 'randn' generates normally distributed random numbers. Consider the examples below:

$$m = 3; n = 3; \quad \text{uniform} = \text{rand}(m, n)$$
$$\text{uniform} = 0.8147 \quad 0.9134 \quad 0.2785$$
$$\qquad\qquad\;\; 0.9058 \quad 0.6324 \quad 0.5469$$
$$\qquad\qquad\;\; 0.1270 \quad 0.0975 \quad 0.9575$$

This is a 3×3 matrix containing uniform random numbers. A 3×3 matrix of normal random numbers can be obtained in the same way:

> normal = randn(m, n)
> normal = −0.4326   0.2877   1.1892
> −1.6656   − 1.1465   − 0.0376
> 0.1253   1.1909   0.3273

A1.6   LINEAR ALGEBRA

Finally, linear algebra methods can be easily implemented in MATLAB. Let us start with a simple example where, given a matrix and its transpose, we add to the initial matrix its transpose to obtain a symmetric matrix:

> m = 2; n = 2;
> z = randn(m, n)

> z = 0.1746   0.7258
> − 0.1867   − 0.5883
> transpose_z = z′
> transpose_z = 0.1746   − 0.1867
> 0.7258   − 0.5883
> symmetric = z + transpose_z
> symmetric = 0.3493   0.5391
> 0.5391   − 1.1766

The second example involves solving a linear algebra system of the form:

$$Ax = b$$

where A is a nonsingular matrix and b is a vector. The system can be easily solved for x as follows:

> A = [1 2 3; 2 − 1 3; 3 5 − 2];
> b = [2; 3; −4];
> x = A\b
> x = −0.0962
> − 0.3654
> 0.9423

The determinant and the rank of a matrix can also be computed using the commands 'det' and 'rank':

> det(A) ans = 52
> rank(A) ans = 3

A1.7   BASICS OF POLYNOMIAL EVALUATIONS

MATLAB is a very flexible tool for polynomial evaluation. For example, consider the following function:

$$y(x) = 2x^2 + 4x - 2$$

One can find the root of the polynomial $y(x)$ by using the command 'roots(y)'. For example:

$$
\begin{aligned}
&y = [2\ 4\ -2]; \\
&\text{root} = \text{roots(y)} \\
&\text{root} = -2.4142 \\
&\qquad\qquad 0.4142
\end{aligned}
$$

We can use the command 'polyval' to evaluate a polynomial at a fixed point (fixedp). For example, we can evaluate the polynomial above at a fixed point $x = 2$:

$$
\begin{aligned}
&y = [2\ 4\ -2]; \\
&\text{fixedp} = \text{polyval(y, 2)} \\
&\text{fixedp} = 14
\end{aligned}
$$

Finally, eigenvalues and eigenvectors of a matrix A can also be obtained:

$$
\begin{aligned}
&A = [1\ 2\ 3;\ 2\ -1\ 3;\ 3\ 5\ -2]; \\
&[U, D] = \text{eig(A)} \\
&U = -0.6400 \quad -0.7795 \quad -0.2535 \\
&\qquad\ -0.4859 \quad\ \ 0.4860 \quad -0.4531 \\
&\qquad\ -0.5952 \quad\ \ 0.3952 \quad\ \ 0.8547
\end{aligned}
$$

$$
\begin{aligned}
&D = 5.3084 \quad 0 \quad 0 \\
&\qquad\ \ 0 \quad -1.7681 \quad 0 \\
&\qquad\ \ 0 \quad 0 \quad -5.5403
\end{aligned}
$$

where U is a matrix containing columns as eigenvectors and D is a diagonal matrix with eigenvalues on the diagonal.

A1.8   GRAPHING IN MATLAB

MATLAB can produce different types of plots (i.e. two-dimensional as well as multidimensional). A simple command for a plot is 'plot'. For example, consider the following example:

$$a = 1;\ c = 3;\ b = 0.1;\ x = a : b : c;\ y = \exp(x) + 2;$$

where 'c' is the lower bound (upper) of an interval and 'b' is the width. Using the command 'plot', find plot(x,y), as shown in Figure A1.2.

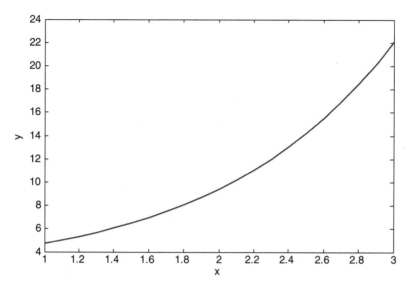

Figure A1.2   Plot of the function $y = f(x)$

For a three-dimensional graph, consider the following example:

a = 1; c = 3; b = 0.1; x = a : b : c; y = x; [X, Y] = meshgrid(x, y);
Z = −2*X + Y; mesh(X, Y, Z)

where a and c are lower (upper) values of the interval and b is the width. We have created a meshgrid for the x and y axes and computed the function Z. The graph is shown in Figure A1.3.

A1.9   SEVERAL GRAPHS ON ONE PLOT

Suppose we want to compute graphs of the following functions:

$$y1 = \exp(x) + 3; \quad y2 = \exp(x) - 3; \quad y3 = \exp(x)$$

We can use the command 'plot' followed by 'grid' to obtain the plot shown in Figure A1.4:

a = 1; c = 3; b = 0.1; x = a : b : c; y1 = exp(x) + 3; y2 = exp(x) − 3;
y3 = exp(x); plot(x, y1, x, y2, x, y3); grid; shg

Grids have been added to the graph using the commands 'grid' and 'shg'.

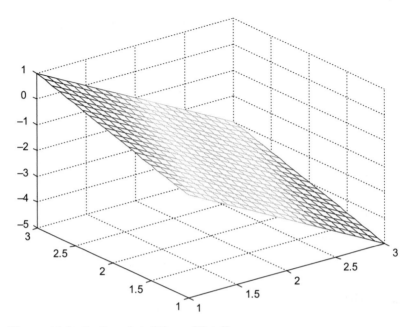

Figure A1.3   Surface plot of $Z = -2X + Y$

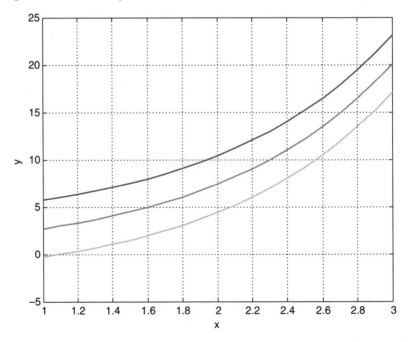

Figure A1.4   Plot of the functions $y1 = \exp(x) + 3$; $y2 = \exp(x) - 3$; $y3 = \exp(x)$

A1.10   PROGRAMMING IN MATLAB: BASIC LOOPS

We now discuss the structure of MATLAB programs. MATLAB programs work in an integrated environment and each variable is returned by MATLAB in the form of matrices. The main commands for programs in MATLAB are the commands 'if', 'while' and 'for'. We start with a demonstration of the so-called 'for loop'. Consider the example where we want to construct a 100 entry array using the function $x(y) = \frac{y}{\cos(y)}$. We can use the following loop:

```
x = zeros(1, 100);
fory = 1 : 100
x(y) = y./ cos(y);
end
```

The loop above returns a 100 entry array (i.e. x) containing the results of the function $x(y)$. The semicolon terminating the inner statement avoids repeated printing. There are also alternative ways to achieve the same goal. For example, in the above code we have first initialized the reserve vector x by filling it with zeros. However, this is not always necessary.

In many applications in finance, we deal with solving equations using trial and error methods. The command 'while' allows the programmer to do this. The command allows the number of times the loop is executed to depend on the result. For example, suppose we want to run a loop as many times as possible until the value of a variable, say x, is greater than 0.02. We can specify the following loop:

```
x = 1;
while x > 0.02
x = x./2;
disp(x)
end
```

We initialize the variable x and use the command 'disp' to display the output:

```
x = 0.5000
    0.2500
    0.1250
    0.0625
    0.0313
    0.0156
```

Finally, we introduce the command[1] 'if'. This command is very useful if we want to take different actions depending on the value of a specified variable. Consider the following example containing a logic statement where the variable

---

[1] Note that the commands we have introduced in this section can also be used in the same loop.

z takes the value $z = 0$ if the product x*y is greater than one; otherwise it takes the value zero:

```
x = 1; y = 3;
if x >= 1
z = 0
else
z = x*y
end
z = 0
```

A1.11   M-FILE FUNCTIONS

MATLAB will let the programmer define functions. A function takes some input parameters, which are then passed to MATLAB commands. These are then executed and an output is generated. Note that with functions, the name of the M-file and of the function should be the same.

The first line of a function takes the following form:

Functionoutput = filename(input)

An example is provided below:

```
function z=discounting(t,N,r);
z=zeros(N,1);
yo=10;dt=t/N;
d=exp(-r*dt*(1:N));
for i=1:N
y(i)=yo;
end
z=y.*d;
z =  9.9005    9.8020    9.7045    9.6079    9.5123
     9.4176    9.3239    9.2312    9.1393    9.0484
```

The code generates N cash flows (starting from \$10) at equal intervals given by dt and uses the discount factor d to discount them. The cash flows are given by the function y and their discounted values by z. The necessary input values to run this code are t (time), N (interval) and r (interest rate), which should be specified by the programmer. We have specified t = 1 (year), N = 10 and the annual interest rate r = 10%.

A1.12   MATLAB APPLICATIONS IN RISK MANAGEMENT

In this section we provide a few examples of programming in MATLAB that are closely related to many problems generally analysed in finance. For example, bootstrapping methods are widely used in risk management to compute value at risk (VaR). An example of resampling from a given vector is the following:

```
T=5;
ehatb=ehat(ceil(max(T)*rand(max(T),B)));
```

Here it is an example of a resampling scheme given a vector 'ehat' whose dimension is 5 × 1. Given 'ehat', we draw (randomly) B (we set B = 2) bootstrap samples from it to obtain:

$$
\begin{aligned}
&T = 5; \ \text{ehat} = \text{randn(T, 1)} \\
&\text{ehat} = -0.2584 \\
&\qquad\quad 0.4933 \\
&\qquad\quad -0.8027 \\
&\qquad\quad -0.0083 \\
&\qquad\quad 0.6276 \\
&\text{ehatb} = \text{ehat(ceil(max(T)*rand(max(T), 2)))} \\
&\text{ehatb} = -0.0083 \qquad 0.6276 \\
&\qquad\quad\ \ -0.2584 \quad -0.0083 \\
&\qquad\quad\ \ -0.2584 \qquad 0.4933 \\
&\qquad\qquad\ \ 0.4933 \qquad 0.4933 \\
&\qquad\quad\ \ -0.8027 \qquad 0.6276
\end{aligned}
$$

We can also extend the methodology shown above to the case where we want to generate bootstrap samples for the variables (x,y) according to an autoregressive process (AR(1)). Consider, for example, the function 'arbootstrap' below:

```
%Bootstrap for ar(1) process
function [yt,ylag]=arbootstrap(rho,ehat);
T=size(ehat);
r=rho;
ehatb=ehat(ceil(max(T)*rand(max(T),2)));
y=zeros(T+1,1);
y0=0;      %initialize the process at y0=0
y(1)= y0;
for i=2:(T+1)
    y(i)=(1-rho)+rho*y((i-1))+ehatb(i-1);
    i=i+1;
end;
yt=y(2:(T+1));
ylag=yt(1:T);
```

The function uses as an input the root of the process[2] (rho) and a given vector 'ehat' whose size is $T \times 1$. Data for y are generated using the bootstrap methodology described earlier and according to an AR(1) process of the following type:

$$y_t = \rho y_{t-1} + \varepsilon_t$$

where ρ is the autoregressive parameter and the innovations ε_t are drawn from the bootstrap vector 'ehatb'.

An application of the function above is presented below. The vector 'ehat' is randomly drawn from a normal distribution:

rho = 1; ehat = randn(10, 1);
[yt, ylag] = arbootstrap(rho, ehat);

yt =	ylag =
0.8262	
0.7219	0
0.6176	0.8262
0.2308	0.7219
0.1265	0.6176
−0.4673	0.2308
−1.1749	0.1265
0.0679	− 0.4673
−0.3188	− 1.1749
−0.7056	0.0679

A1.13   MATLAB PROGRAMMING: APPLICATION IN FINANCIAL ECONOMICS

We now turn to the second example. Modelling financial time series using vector autoregressive processes (VARs) is rather appealing for several reasons. For example, VAR models have very little serial correlation in residuals. We can also use VAR models to investigate complex relationships among financial variables (for example the relationship between the cash market and the option market). Consider, for simplicity, only two variables y and x. A VAR can be written as

$$y_t = \alpha_0 + \alpha_1 y_{t-1} + \beta_1 x_{t-1} + \varepsilon_t$$
$$x_t = \beta_0 + \beta_2 x_{t-1} + \alpha_2 y_{t-1} + z_t$$

where $[\alpha, \beta]$ are parameters to be estimated and $[\varepsilon, z]$ are such that $E\varepsilon_t = 0$, $Ez_t = 0$, $\mathrm{Var}(\varepsilon_t) = \sigma_\varepsilon^2 = \mathrm{cons\,tan}\,t$, $\mathrm{Var}(z_t) = \sigma_z^2 = \mathrm{cons\,tan}\,t$ and

---

[2] If we specify rho = 1, we generate a nonstationary process, while rho = 0.6, for example, would generate a stationary process.

$Cov(\varepsilon_t, z_t) = 0$. In simple matrix notation:

$$\begin{bmatrix} y_t \\ x_t \end{bmatrix} = \begin{bmatrix} a_0 \\ \beta_0 \end{bmatrix} + \begin{bmatrix} a_1\beta_1 \\ \beta_2 a_2 \end{bmatrix} \begin{bmatrix} y_{t-1} \\ x_{t-1} \end{bmatrix} + \begin{bmatrix} \varepsilon_t \\ z_t \end{bmatrix}$$

The example below shows an application of the ordinary least squares (OLS) estimator to estimate a VAR model. The variable y_t in the code is a $T \times k$ matrix containing the dependent variables. T is the time and k is the lag order (lag) of the VAR. The code takes y_t and a lag as inputs. Using OLS it generates the parameter estimates of the VAR (beta) and the residuals (resid):

```
function [beta,resid] = VarOLS(y,lag)
% n = size of raw data;
[n,k] = size(y);

% store lag variables into matrix lagdata
lagdata = ones(n,lag*k+1);
for i=1:lag
    lagdata(i+1:n,(i-1)*k+2:i*k+1) = y(1:n-i,:);
end

% define matrix lagdata as x = explanatory variables
adjusted for lags
x = lagdata(lag+1:n,1:lag*k+1);

% adjust original data for lags
yy = y(lag+1:n,:);
beta = x\yy;        % VAR OLS estimates of beta
yhat = x*beta;      % compute fitted y's
resid = yy - yhat;  % save residuals
```

The lagged variables are stored in the matrix 'lagdata', the original data are adjusted for lag in the matrix 'yy' and finally the OLS is used to compute the estimates (see 'beta'). An example is presented below. We consider the two-variable VAR above and two lags to estimate the parameters $[a_0, \beta_0, a_1, \beta_1, a_2, \beta_2]$:

$$y = (y); \quad lag = 1;$$
$$[beta, resid] = VarOLS(y, lag);$$
$$beta = -0.0495 \quad -0.0683$$
$$0.0644 \quad 0.2217$$
$$0.0567 \quad -0.0334$$

Appendix 2
Mortgage Backed Securities

A2.1 INTRODUCTION

Mortgage backed securities (MBS) are securities collateralized by residential mortgage loans. The MBS market has grown to become the largest fixed income market in the United States. Probably one of the reasons for the large growth of these assets was the higher return paid by these securities and the perception that most of them carried a lower risk than other fixed income securities.[1] However, although the market for MBS was very dynamic and many studies have focused on pricing these financial instruments (see, for example, Longstaff, 2004, and Chen, 2004), there are still issues concerning their interest rate risk management.

Because of the borrowers' pre-payment option in the underlying mortgage loans, mortgage backed securities have characteristics similar to those of a callable bond. Unlike callable bonds for which the issuers' refinancing strategies are assumed to be close to optimal, mortgage borrowers may be slow to refinance when it would be financially favourable and sometimes pre-pay when it is financially unfavourable.

Investors in mortgage backed securities hold long-positions in noncallable bonds and short-positions in call (prepayment) options. The noncallable bond is effectively a portfolio of zero coupon bonds and the call option gives the borrower the right to pre-pay the mortgage at any time prior to the maturity of the loan. Therefore, the value of the MBS is given by the difference between the value of the noncallable bond and the value of the call (pre-payment) option. In the market place, dealers generally price the mortgage by pricing these two components separately.

To evaluate the call option, the option adjusted spread (OAS) methodology uses option pricing techniques. When the option component is quantified and taken away from the total yield spread, the yield to maturity of a nonbenchmark bond can be compared to a risk free of a benchmark security.[2]

---

[1] The market turbulence in the last few years shows that this is not the case. In this appendix we only consider pass-through MBS and assume that these are guaranteed by the US Treasury. Therefore, we do not consider credit and liquidity risk but instead focus on managing interest rate risk.

[2] See the option adjusted spread application in this appendix.

The academic literature in this area has mainly focused on modelling OAS dynamics in a way that the embedded mortgage call option price can be estimated and consequently the mortgage priced (see, for example, Dunn and Spatt, 1986, Liu and Xu, 1998, Schwartz and Torous, 1992, amongst others). However, the main drawback with these models is that they are not used in practice since, generally, they are unable to fit the observed market prices. Academics and practitioners have instead used econometric models to estimate the parameters of interest and calibrate the reduced form models (see, for example, Chen, 2004).[3] Thus these models have become widely used to price MBS. The main drawback is that they are generally proprietary models and their functional form is not published to the public. Also, as already mentioned earlier, these models might be incorrectly specified since they assume a constant option adjusted spread over the lifetime of the mortgage.

In this appendix we show a novel approach based on what we call a 'dynamic option adjusted spread' (DOAS), which, as we shall see, accounts for volatility shifts in the interest rate term structure. Also, we show that the DOAS can also be used as a hedging tool by investors in this market.

A2.2   THE MORTGAGE INDUSTRY

The mortgage industry is mainly characterized by four groups: mortgage originators, mortgage services, mortgage insurers and investors. The mortgage originator is the original lender of the mortgage (commercial banks, mortgage lenders, etc.). The mortgage service organizes the collection of all mortgage payments made by the borrowers, reminding them when payments are overdue, and forwards the proceeds to the owner of the mortgage. Mortgage insurers protect the lender against a default by the borrower. In the US these are mainly Government Agencies. Figure A2.1 shows how the mortgage industry works in the United States.

There are several mortgage products with different payment features. For example, in a fixed rate fully amortized mortgage, the borrower pays (periodically) a fixed interest rate and part of the principal in equal installments. Therefore, by the end of the lifetime of the mortgage it is fully amortized.

In the case of the adjustable rate mortgages, instead, at each reset time, rates are adjusted according to a reference benchmark (LIBOR, US Treasury securities, etc.). Generally, borrowers in this market are offered initially lower interest rates than the market rate to encourage them to accept them. At each

---

[3] Obviously practitioners have been able to develop reduced-form models since, generally, they also dispose of proprietary data needed to calibrate the model.

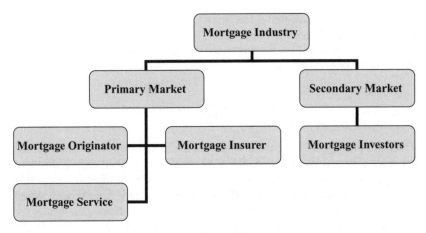

Figure A2.1 The mortgage industry in the US

reset time caps and floors (i.e. maximum increase and fall) for the interest rates are set. Because of these features, pricing these mortgages is rather complex.[4]

Balloon mortgages are exotic mortgages where the lender and the borrower agree to renegotiate the main features of the mortgage at a specific date in the future. The large majority of these mortgages have a lifetime of thirty years, carry a fixed rate and require a balloon payment of the principal at the end of the fifth year. However, there are also a variety of more exotic mortgages that allow the borrower to enter into a new mortgage to finance the existing mortgage at a rate that is capped.

Thus, there are a variety of different mortgages offered in the market having more or less exotic features. In the next section we will assume that the underlying of the MBS is a pool of homogeneous mortgages, with each of the mortgages falling within the category of fixed rate fully amortized mortgages.

A2.3 THE MORTGAGE BACKED SECURITY (MBS) MODEL

Consider the following probability space (Ω, F, P) and the process $p(t, D, C, z)$ adapted to the filtration F. The price process depends on the risk-neutral vector of discounted bond prices $D(t) 0 < t < T$, with Q being the risk-neutral probability measure; z is a state variable that will be defined shortly and $C(t)$ is the cash flow paid by the mortgage at t. In this model z could

---

[4] There are also other possible variations of this mortgage that we will not discuss in this appendix.

represent the option adjusted spread used to match the theoretical and the market prices of the MBS.

Define the price process for a mortgage at time t as the expected value of the discounted future cash flows:

$$p(t) = E^Q \left[\sum_{t=0}^{T} C(t)D(t) \right] \tag{A2.1}$$

The main problem with Equation (A2.1) is that the borrower can at each time consider a pre-payment action. We have already described earlier different ways of modelling the pre-payment option for MBSs. In the analysis in this section we follow Chen (2004) and implement a reduced form model. When pricing an MBS one has to generate the mortgage cash flows $C(t)$ using, for example, a reduced form model. Once the cash flows have been generated, the value of the mortgage can be obtained by discounting the simulated cash flows and summing them up.

Using Monte Carlo to generate m paths for $C(t)|m|$, we have that

$$E^Q(p) = \frac{1}{m} \sum_{t_i=0}^{T} \left[\sum_{m=1}^{M} C(t)D(t) \right], \lim_{m \to \infty} C(t)|m| \to C$$

and therefore the simulated price, say p^*, will converge to the true price p. Using Equation (A2.1) one can also estimate the option adjusted spread z. Suppose that p is the observed market price of a mortgage. As we do when we want to retrieve implied volatilities from plain vanilla options, we can compute z using a root finding method to solve

$$P(t_0, C, D, z) = p \tag{A2.2}$$

A2.4 THE TERM STRUCTURE MODEL

However, in order to solve Equation (A2.2) one has to simulate the term structure of interest rates out of the maturity of the mortgage. We use a two-factor Heath, Jarrow and Morton (1992) model (HJM). In the HJM model one needs to specify the initial forward rates and volatilities. In what follows, we will explain how we have done that.

The HJM model is a model that is consistent with the observed term structure. The state variable in this model is the forward rate at time t for instantaneous borrowing at $T > t$, $F(t, T)$. In differential form the model can be written as

$$dF(t, T) = m(t, T) \, dt + \sum_{k=1}^{N} \sigma_k(t, T) dW_k(t) \qquad \text{for} \quad 0 \le t \le T \tag{A2.3}$$

or also in integral form

$$F(t, T) = F(0, T) + \int_0^t m(v, T)dv + \int_0^t \sum_{k=1}^N \sigma_k(v, T)\,dW_k(t) \qquad \text{(A2.4)}$$

Here $F(0, T)$ is the fixed initial forward rate curve, $m(t, T)$ is the instantaneous forward rate drift, $\sigma_k(t, T)$ is the instantaneous volatility process of the forward rate curve and $W_k(t)$ is a standard Brownian motion process defined on the physical measure. This model is very general and encompasses all the short rate models such as, for example, the Hull and White (1993) model, which we discussed in Chapter 12.

The drift process is specified as

$$m(t, T) = \sum_{k=1}^N \sigma_k(t, T) \int_t^T \sigma(t, s)ds \qquad \text{(A2.5)}$$

When using the HJM approach to simulate $F(t, T)$, we have the problem that the model is specified in terms of instantaneous forward rates and these are not observable. To overcome this problem one could specify a deterministic specification for the volatilities:

$$\sigma_k(t, T) = \bar{\sigma}_k(t, T - t)$$

Therefore, the new model will now be a Gaussian model. If we set $\tau = T - t$, it follows that

$$d\bar{F}(t, \tau) = \bar{m}(t, \tau)\,dt + \bar{\sigma}(t, \tau)dW(t) \qquad \text{(A2.6)}$$

where the drift takes the following form:

$$\bar{m}(t, \tau) = \bar{\sigma}(t, \tau) \int_0^\tau \bar{\sigma}(t, s)ds + \frac{\partial}{\partial \tau}\bar{F}(t, \tau) \qquad \text{(A2.7)}$$

We use the model above to simulate the forward rates. The spot rate $r(t)$ used to discount the cash flows can be determined from (A2.6) as follows:

$$r(t) \equiv \lim_{\tau \to t} \bar{F}(t, \tau)$$

Finally, we need to specify the initial forward rates and volatilities. In our empirical application we use Bloomberg to obtain the forward rates necessary to initiate the process and the implied volatilities on interest rate caps necessary for the calibration of the model. Two volatilities are used in this case. The first is set fixed for all the maturities and is equal to the implied volatility of a thirty-year interest rate cap option. The second refers to the implied volatility of interest rate caps with maturities between 1 and 30 years. A Euler discretization scheme, with 360 time steps and 5000 simulations, is used.

A2.5   PRELIMINARY NUMERICAL EXAMPLE

In this section we provide a preliminary numerical example and describe how the option adjusted spread (OAS) is computed. The MBS price can be obtained by simulating the mortgage's cash flows (i.e. $C(t)$) over the lifetime of the mortgage using a pre-payment model. The pre-payment model used in this study is described at the end of the appendix. Furthermore, one also needs to simulate the term structure dynamics over the relevant horizon. We use the model described earlier. Finally, Equation (A2.1) gives us the bond's price. The simulated MBS price, with its standard error in parentheses, is 102.1786 (0.063124).

The value of the mortgage is equal to 102.1786%. Suppose the size of the underlying mortgage pool is $1 000 000.00; the price of a mortgage backed security issued from the underlying pool will thus be $1 021 786.00. For simplicity, we assume that the observed market price is 100% of the par value. Since all the elements of Equation (A2.1) are known and the market price of the mortgage (or a similar one) can be observed, one can now compute, using Equation (A2.2) and a root finding method, the option adjusted spread. The option adjusted spread in this example is 46 basis points.

Figure A2.2 shows the simulated paths of the monthly cash flows of the mortgage. As the bond approaches maturity the value of the pre-payment option decreases and consequently the mortgage cash flow becomes less uncertain.

A2.6   DYNAMIC OPTION ADJUSTED SPREAD

The option adjusted spread (OAS) can be viewed as a measure of the yield spread and is constant over the benchmark yield curve. It is named 'option

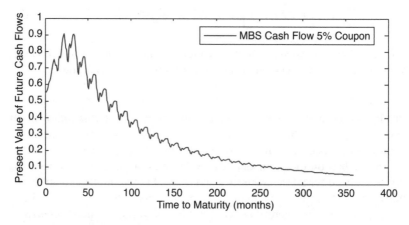

Figure A2.2   MBS cash flow

adjusted' because the cash flows of the underlying security are adjusted to reflect the embedded option. Most market participants find it more convenient to think about yield spread than price differences. One issue with the option spread is that it assumes that the yield spread stays unchanged over the maturity of the bond so that, even if future interest rates become volatile, the OAS stays unchanged. Clearly this is wrong. Also, with OAS, traders will have to compute the spread and recalibrate the model frequently. This may carry an additional cost in terms of time necessary for the recalibration. We discuss a modification of the OAS that we call dynamic option adjusted spread (DOAS). The DOAS allows one to capture pre-payment risks as well as changes in the yield curve. Furthermore, a potential investor holding a mortgage can also use it as a hedging tool. From an investor point of view the DOAS can be viewed as an investment.[5] The value of this portfolio can be positive or negative depending on the spread adjustment. A bond having a positive OAS has a positive portfolio value. On the other hand, a bond with a negative OAS will have a negative portfolio value.[6]

To compute the dynamic option adjusted spread, we use the following procedure. Simulate the cash flows, at each t, over the lifetime of the mortgage. Compute the option adjusted spread (i.e. z) and use it to adjust the cash flows of the bond at each t. In this way we obtain the adjusted cash flows. The difference, at each t, between a plain vanilla bond cash flow (C_p) and the mortgage cash flow is the dynamic option adjusted spread in t. The summation of these up to t_0 is the portfolio value

$$PV_0 = E^Q \sum_{t=0}^{T} \left[(C_p) - (C) \right]_t \qquad (A2.8)$$

Equation (A2.8) describes the way the portfolio value is computed. Thus, the portfolio value is the difference between a noncallable bond and a callable bond. It follows that by buying an MBS and investing in the above portfolio, the investor has indeed created a synthetic noncallable bond but with the difference that he or she is also hedging away interest rate risk.[7]

Figure A2.3 shows the conditional prepayment rate (CPR) function, the refinancing incentive (RI) and the portfolio value (PV). At the beginning of the mortgage there is a positive spread (i.e. the difference between the value of the portfolio and the cash flow of the mortgage). The difference will compensate the investor if the option is exercised by the borrower. The spread is particularly

---

[5] We call this investment a portfolio value (PV).

[6] OAS can be negative when the mortgage coupon is low but interest rate volatility is relatively high. In this case investors in this market might not be very concerned with the MBS optionality, at least not in the short run.

[7] In effect the idea that there is a positive relationship between option adjusted spread and prices of noncallable securities (in this case Treasury securities) was first reported in Brown (1999). He also suggests, in line with our model, that the option adjusted spread is a noisy measure.

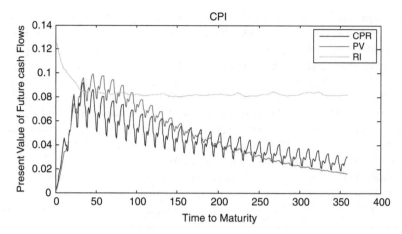

Figure A2.3   Pre-payment model

relevant in the first one hundred months, which, in general, corresponds to the time when the pre-payment risk is higher. As the pre-payment risk becomes less accentuated, the spread decreases.

A2.7   NUMERICAL EXAMPLE

Using Equation (A2.8) we can now compute the portfolio value (with the standard error in parentheses). In this example, the portfolio value is 2.07006% (0.00289) of the par value (see Figure A2.4).

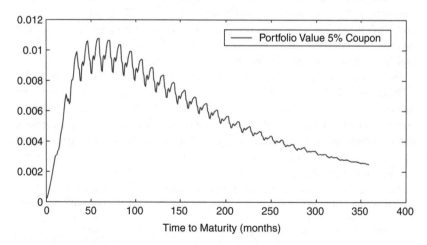

Figure A2.4   Portfolio value

The DOAS in our example is 2.07006% par value. If we assume that the pool size of the mortgage is $1 000 000.00, the portfolio value will be $20 700.60. The investor can buy this option to hedge interest rate risk. The next section shows it using a practical example.

A2.8   PRACTICAL NUMERICAL EXAMPLES

As pointed out earlier, an investor can use the DOAS as a hedging instrument against pre-payment risk and also changes in the yield curve. The examples below show this.

Example A2.1 The 5% coupon rate

Investor A buys at time t_0 a 30-year mortgage backed security with the price of the MBS being 100% of the face value. The investor receives Treasury rate plus 46 basis points (bp) (OAS). We assume that the pool size is $1 000 000.

A second investor, investor B, buys at time t_0 the same mortgage and a DOAS option. The DOAS option is 2.07006% of the par value. Thus, the total value of the investment is 102.07%.

Suppose that at time t_1 the interest rate volatility increases from 13 bp to 26 bp. What is the effect on the MBS price and the investor's portfolio?

At time t_1, the price of the mortgage drops to 99.8534% or $998 534.00. This implies a $1466 loss on the mortgage for investor A. The value of the investment for the investor B is:

Pay-off = bond value at time t_1 − bond value at time t_0
  + (portfolio value at time t_1 − portfolio value at time t_0)

Pay-off = 99.8534 − 100 + (2.08289 − 2.07006) = −0.1337 or $1337

Example A2.2 The 6% coupon rate

In this second example we set a coupon rate at a level, which is higher than the initial interest rate used in the simulation. Thus, the pre-payment risk is more relevant now. Investor A buys at time t_0 the mortgage and receives interest plus 227.70 basis points. Investor B buys the same mortgage but also invests in a DOAS option and its price is 9.9080%, for a total of 109.908%.

Suppose that at time t_1 the interest rate volatility increases from 13 bp to 26 bp. What is the effect on the bond price and on the investor's portfolio? At time t_1 the price of the mortgage drops to 99.9825% or $999 825.00. The loss for investor A is therefore $175.00. As a consequence of the increase in interest rate volatility the value of the DOAS option increases to 9.9275%. The pay-off

Table A2.1   Mortgage backed security values and dynamic option adjusted spreads

Coupon rate%	5.00	5.50	6.00	6.50	7.00
MBS price	102.17	106.28	110.26	114.21	117.58
SE	0.06312	0.06204	0.07211	0.06606	0.05265
OAS bp	46.18	135.66	227.70	321.05	412.33
DOAS%	2.0700	6.0034	9.9080	13.7460	17.0849
SE	0.00289	0.00837	0.01223	0.01690	0.02427

Note. SE are standard errors obtained by 100 trials. OAS bp is the option adjusted spread in basis point.

for the investor B is therefore:

Pay-off $=$ bond value at time t_1 $-$ bond value at time t_0
$+$ (portfolio value at time t_1 $-$ portfolio value at time t_0)

Pay-off $= 99.9825 - 100 + (9.9275 - 9.9080) = 0.0020\%$ or $20.00

A2.9   EMPIRICAL RESULTS

We now use the model described in this appendix to price mortgage backed securities with different coupon rates. Table A2.1 shows the MBS prices and the option adjusted spreads. As expected the price of the mortgage increases as the coupon rate increases.[8] This is due to the refinancing incentive for the borrower when the coupon rate is above the market interest rate.

The highest price is achieved with the bond paying a 7% coupon (117.58). Such a high premium clearly cannot be explained by par plus a number of refinancing points. These high prices are consistent with what generally is observed in the market (see also Longstaff, 2004, for a discussion on this issue).

Conditional on the interest rate level used in our simulation, we see that higher coupon rates will increase the incentive for the borrower to repay the mortgage and this clearly will affect the spread (i.e. what an investor would expect to receive to compensate him or her for the pre-payment risk). Our model suggests a spread over the Treasury curve of more than 400 bp when a 7% coupon is used. We have also computed standard errors from the simulation by using 100 independent trials of the model. These empirical results are in line with theoretical and empirical studies in this area (see, for example, Gabaix *et al.*, 2007).

Table A2.1 also shows the simulated dynamic option adjusted values. We notice that, conditional on the (initial) interest rate level used in the simulation, the value of the option increases as the coupon increases. This is consistent with a higher pre-payment risk implicit with higher coupons. An investor could

---

[8] Note that the initial rate used for the simulation is 5%.

buy this option, pay a higher price for the mortgage, but hedge the pre-payment and interest rate risk implicit with an MBS.

A2.10   THE PRE-PAYMENT MODEL

The model assumes that four factors (i.e. refinancing incentive, burnout, seasoning and seasonality) explain 95% of the variation in pre-payment rates. These factors are then combined into one model to project pre-payments (CPR):

$$CPR_t = RI_t \times AGE_t \times MM_t \times BM_t$$

where RI_t represents the refinancing incentive, AGE_t represents the seasoning multiplier, MM_t represents the monthly multiplier and BM_t represents the burnout multiplier.

Thus, the prepayment model can be written as

$$CPR_t = RI_t \times AGE_t \times MM_t \times BM_t$$

where

$$RI_t = 0.28 + 0.14 \tan^{-1}[-8.571 + 430\,(WAC - r_{10}(t))]$$

$$AGE_t = \min\left(1, \frac{t}{30}\right)$$

$$BM_t = 0.3 + 0.7\left(\frac{B_{t-1}}{B_0}\right)$$

MM_t takes the following values, which start from January and end in December: (0.94, 0.76, 0.74, 0.95, 0.98, 0.92, 0.98, 1.1, 1.18, 1.22, 1.23, 0.98), r_{10} is 10-year Treasury rate and WAC is the weighted average coupon rate.

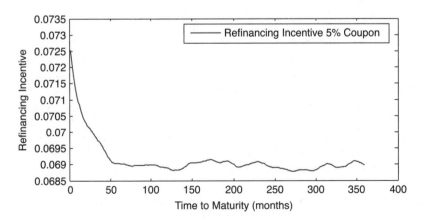

Figure A2.5   Refinancing incentive (5% coupon)

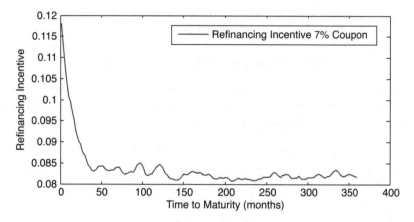

Figure A2.6   Refinancing incentive (7% coupon)

Figures A2.5 and A2.6 show the refinancing incentive function for 5% and 7% coupon rates. Borrowers have a higher incentive to exercise the pre-payment option and refinance the mortgage when the coupon rate is higher than the interest rates. This is shown in Figure A2.6.

Appendix 3
Value at Risk

A3.1 INTRODUCTION

In this appendix we shall discuss the use of value at risk (VaR) in risk management. Today's volatility of financial markets reminds us that risk needs to be carefully quantified and monitored. The purpose of this appendix is to present and discuss the fundamentals of VaR. We shall only discuss a few basic techniques applied to different portfolios.

After the recent financial crisis, measuring risk has become more and more complex, forcing the industry to replace old-fashioned ways with new ways that are more relevant and realistic. The need for new ways of quantifying and managing risk is nowadays clear and essential for the survival of financial institutions in future crises. The financial world has become more uncertain and risky than ever.

The modern era of risk management began in 1973, where trading international portfolios became more complex as the Bretton Woods system of fixed exchange rates collapsed. The years since 1973 have shown a higher volatility in exchange rates as well as in the whole market.

The concept of VaR is recent. It was in the late 1980s when the first financial institutions used VaR as a technique to measure the risk of their trading portfolios. Since then, more and more firms have started to recognize the marked advantages of this technique. In October 1994 the release of 'Risk Metrics' by JP Morgan led to a tremendous growth in the use of 'value at risk'. Since then an increasing number of financial institutions have started using VaR.

However, VaR has been appreciated, as a measure of risk, not just by the industry but also by regulators. For example, in 1995 the US Securities and Exchange Commission proposed rules for corporate disclosure. A more recent example is the implementation of Basel III.

A3.2 VALUE AT RISK (VaR)

VaR is the estimate of the maximum potential loss, at a given confidence level, to be expected over the period under consideration. Consider a portfolio worth $10 000 and suppose the manager is uncertain about changes in the dollar value for this portfolio over the next 10 days. The simplest assumption that is generally made is that the return of the portfolio over the next 10 days is normally distributed with mean zero and constant variance.

Table A3.1   VaR of an equity portfolio

	Equity	Investment	Total VaR	%VaR
Apple	2045	1%	591	3%
IBM	23 567	16%	2 004	9%
Intel Corp.	76 888	51%	9 949	59%
Sun Microsystems	36 476	24%	4 902	27%
Northen Telecom	9 841	7%	849	3%
Hitachi	55	0%	4	0%
Minolta Camera	536	0%	40	0%
Sum of above	149 408		18 338	
Diversification			−2347	
Portfolio	149 408		15 991	

Table A3.1 shows the composition of our portfolio, the VaR for each of the securities in the portfolio. The total value of a security is given by the price of each share multiplied by the number of shares. VaR is therefore the maximum amount an investor could lose. If we specify a 5% confidence level and a 10 day period, the VaR is about $15 991. This is the maximum expected loss over that period for this portfolio.

It is clear from the example above that, to obtain the VaR, we need to specify a time period, a confidence level and identify the market factors that may impact on our portfolio over a given period.

A3.3   THE MAIN PARAMETERS OF A VaR

As mentioned above, to obtain a VaR, we need to specify a set of parameters. In this appendix, we shall discuss them. The first parameter we need is the period (holding period). This is the length of time over which we measure the VaR. Financial institutions, generally, to meet regulatory standard, compute daily VaRs. For example, in the case when the market for a given portfolio is not sufficiently liquid, regulators may oblige financial institutions to compute daily VaRs. Furthermore, for validation purposes, it is generally simpler to find the necessary data when daily VaRs are computed rather than monthly, for example.[1]

A second important element is the choice of the confidence interval. In fact, the VaR is often expressed as the percentile, which corresponds to a given confidence interval. Thus, if the VaR is $100 at a 5% confidence level and a holding period of, say, 5 days, it means that over the next 5 days there is a

---

[1] For example, with daily VaR and a holding period of 1 day to have a sufficiently long time series (say more than 500 observations), one would need 2 years of data.

5% probability that an investor will lose more than $100 (or a 95% probability that he or she will not lose more than $100). Obviously, the VaR for the same portfolio will be different at different confidence levels.[2]

The third element is more complex and is about the choice of the market factors that can impact on our portfolio. We shall discuss it in the next sections.

A3.4   VaR METHODOLOGY

There are various methodologies to compute the VaR: historical simulation, the variance–covariance method and the Monte Carlo method. In this chapter, we shall discuss a few.

A3.4.1   Historical simulations

Historical simulation is a simple nonparametric approach that requires few assumptions about market factors. This methodology uses historical returns to generate cash scenarios for future profits and losses.

The first step requires the identification of the market factors that are related with the portfolio. This is the most challenging part. For example, in the case of a portfolio of options, volatility may well be an important market factor to consider. The second step is to obtain a time series of historical values for the market factors. The calculation of the VaR is obtained by calculating the observed changes in the market factors over the holding period. After the calculation of the historical changes in the market factors, the vector(s) with the hypothetical values of the market factors can be obtained by combining the current values to each of the values in the vector of the observed changes.

The portfolio value is then obtained using the current and hypothetical values for the market factor(s). After using this procedure we obtain many hypothetical mark-to-market profits and losses on the portfolio, which can then be compared to the current mark-to-market values of the portfolio.

The final step involves ordering the profits and losses from the largest profit to the largest loss and choosing a confidence interval (for example 95% would correspond to the 5% percentile worst loss).

Thus, the historical simulation method is very simple to use and implement, especially when historical data on market factors are widely available. It does not make any sort of assumptions about the distribution of returns and therefore it is 'model free'. Historical simulation can be used for any kind of position and risk and therefore it can capture gamma, volatility risk, etc.

---

[2] Generally the choice of the confidence level depends on the objective for which VaR is used (i.e. capital requirements, etc.).

Mahoney (1996) finds that historical simulation yields unbiased estimates of the VaR and it works better than other methods when it comes to forecasting tail probabilities.

However, there are also a number of drawbacks with this methodology. For example, VaR estimates depend completely on the data set used and the assumption that the future will be similar to the past may be too restrictive. Additionally to that, the historical simulation approach requires time series of market factors. This may be rather challenging for some markets such as emerging markets.

A3.4.2   Variance–covariance method

This methodology relies on the estimation of the variance–covariance matrix. The VaR is calculated assuming multivariate normality. Using the variance–covariance matrix, we can produce the mark-to-market portfolio profits and losses and therefore estimate the VaR. The procedure is rather simple.

The variance–covariance matrix is determined on the basis of the so-called 'risk mapping'; that is, financial instruments in the portfolio can be decomposed ('mapped') into simpler ones. Thus, the first step is to identify the market factors and the positions related to the latter and map the assets on to the standardized positions.

The second step relies on assuming that the changes in the market factors follow a multivariate normal distribution. Thus, the variance–covariance matrix measures the variability and co-movements of the market factors.

In the next step, standard deviation and correlation are used to determine deviations and correlations of changes in the standardized positions. Finally, one can calculate the portfolio variance (for two assets):

$$\sigma_P^2 = \varpi_x^2 \sigma_x^2 + \varpi_y^2 \sigma_y^2 + 2\varpi_x \varpi_y \rho_{xy} \sigma_x \sigma_y$$

where σ_P^2 is the portfolio variance, ϖ_x, ϖ_y are portfolio weights and ρ is the correlation coefficient between market factors. Using the properties of the normal distribution that outcomes less than or equal to 1.65, standard deviations below the mean occur only 5% of the time, we can write the VaR as

$$VaR = 1.65\sigma_P \sqrt{\Delta t}$$

where Δ is a small time interval.

There are several advantages with this approach. Firstly, the estimation of the variance–covariance matrix is rather simple if the portfolio contains instruments that are not complex. Under the assumption of normality, VaR is a multiple of the portfolio standard deviation.

Using a normal distribution has the advantage of making VaR informative about all possible confidence levels and holding periods. For example, following up with the example above, one can easily compute the 99% confidence level for the VaR based on the 95% confidence level VaR. For example, given the 95% VaR above, the 99% VaR is given by $(2.33/1.65)VaR_{0.95}$.

However, there are also several drawbacks related to the variance–covariance approach. For example, the assumption that market factors follow a multivariate normal distribution may be too restrictive. In fact, this assumption would imply that fat tails are not considered. Empirical studies (see, for example, Boudoukh *et al.*, 1998) find evidence that financial data exhibit fat tails. This means that losses occur more often than the variance–covariance approach would suggest.

Another drawback of the variance–covariance method is that it is very challenging to implement when instruments with nonlinear payoffs (for example options) are considered.

A3.4.3   Monte Carlo method

The Monte Carlo method is a parametric technique that provides a forward-looking approach to compute the risk of a portfolio. This methodology can be implemented to estimate the VaR for nonlinear portfolios.

The procedure is rather simple. We start with the identification of the market factor(s). Once market factors have been identified, we can simulate future scenarios using a given statistical model. Thus, if $F(i)$ is the empirical distribution for the market factor i over a given time horizon and S is the asset price, we can simulate a large number of scenarios $[S\Delta F_1(i), S\Delta F_2(i), \ldots, S\Delta F_M(i)]'$, given M replications.

Given the hypothetical portfolio values, we can subtract the actual mark-to-market portfolio value of the most recent period in the data to obtain M hypothetical profits and losses. At this point, we order the mark-to-market profits and losses from the largest profit to the smallest loss. Finally, we choose the loss that is equalled or exceeded 5% of the time.

The Monte Carlo method is very attractive as a VaR approach. For example, it can be used in cases when other methodologies are difficult to implement. It can easily cope with a portfolio of nonlinear instruments and allow for a large number of factors affecting our portfolio. Thus, we can incorporate volatility, jump, etc., and handle fat tails.

However, if, on the one hand, the Monte Carlo method has all the advantages pointed out earlier, it also has several drawbacks. For example, it can be very time consuming, especially when multifactors are considered and/or in the case of large portfolios.

Remark A3.1

We have discussed above several different VaR methodologies, but which of these techniques should be preferred practically? To address this issue, we use an example taken from Jordan *et al.* (1996). We consider two portfolios, the first

Table A3.2   VaR refers to the 95% VaR reported in Jordan *et al.* (1996)

	Equity		
	Daily	Weekly	Monthly
Historical simulation	$16 142	$42 902	$76 684
Monte Carlo	$16 268	$30 272	$62 427
Variance–covariance	$15 642	$32 676	$60 500
	Options		
	Daily	Weekly	Monthly
Historical simulation	$214 274	$423 322	$764 504
Monte Carlo	$187 605	$433 536	$865 146
Variance–covariance	$83 500	$178 892	$225 196

containing five shares and the second containing equity options. Given these two portfolios, the 95% VaR is computed using three different methodologies: historical simulation, the Monte Carlo method and the variance–covariance approach. Results are reported in Table A3.2.

It is clear from Table A3.2 that while for an equity portfolio the three approaches generate VaRs that are roughly comparable, with nonlinear portfolios the variance–covariance method generates VaRs that are very different from the results of historical simulation and Monte Carlo.

A3.5   EMPIRICAL APPLICATIONS

This section discusses ways to implement the three VaR methodologies discussed earlier.

The example might be very useful to those students who have never used VaR methods before. We start with historical simulation.

A3.5.1   Historical simulations

The example uses a foreign exchange forward contract initiated by a US investor at a given time. The remaining maturity of the contract is assumed to be 91 days. On the delivery, the US investor will deliver $15 million and receive £10 million. The market factors used in this example are the three-month US Treasury bill rate, the three-month British Treasury rate and the exchange rate ($/£).

The mark-to-market dollar value of the contract can be obtained as

$$\left[ER_{\$/£} \frac{£\,10m}{1 + r_{GBP}(91/360)} \right] - \frac{\$15m}{1 + r_{US}(91/360)}$$

where ER is the exchange rate and m refers to million. We assume 360 days per year. We then collect historical data on the market value (i.e. US and UK interest rates and the exchange rate). Once historical data are collected, we can calculate the changes in the market values, for example $\Delta r_{GBPt} = (r_{GBPt} - r_{GBP_{t-1}})/r_{GBPt-1}$. This can also be expressed in percentages. Thus, we obtain vectors containing changes in the market factors:

$$IV_{USD} = AV_{USD} + (AV_{USD} + \%\Delta r_{USD})$$

where IV is the hypothetical value expressed in US dollars, AV is the actual value of the factor and Δr is the change in the market value (expressed in percentages).[3] The hypothetical market values of the factors are then used to obtain hypothetical mark-to-market portfolio values:

$$\left[IV_{\$/£} \frac{£\,10m}{1 + IV_{GBP}(90/360)} \right] - \left[\frac{\$15m}{1 + IV_{US}(90/360)} \right]$$

By subtracting the actual values from the hypothetical portfolio values, we obtain the hypothetical profits and losses.

A3.5.2 Variance–covariance method

We consider a portfolio with 13 shares. In order to apply the variance–covariance method, we need to obtain the VaRs for each share. The latter is simply given by the initial position on share i, multiplied by the standard deviation: $I\,P_i\sigma_i 1.65$. Once the individual VaRs are obtained we can compute the VaR for our portfolio:

$$[VaR_{BARC}, .., VaR_{WMPY}] \begin{bmatrix} 1 & \sigma_{(BARC)(BT)} & \cdot & \sigma_{(BARC)(WMPY)} \\ \sigma_{(BT)(BARC)} & \cdot & & \cdot\;\; \sigma_{(BT)(WMPY)} \\ \cdot & \cdot & \cdot & \\ \sigma_{(WMPY)(BARC)} & \sigma_{(WMPY)(BT)} & \cdot & 1 \end{bmatrix} \begin{bmatrix} VaR_{BARC} \\ VaR_{BT} \\ \cdot \\ VaR_{WMPY} \end{bmatrix}$$

where BARC, WMPY and BT are some of the shares in the portfolio. The matrix above can be easily computed using MATLAB, Microsoft Excel, etc.

---

[3] One will have to apply these calculations to all the market factors.

Table A3.3   Performance of different VaR models (1000 day horizon)

Confidence level	95%	99%	99.95%
Expected number of VaR violations	50	10	0.5
Average number of realized violations (percentages)			
Variance–covariance	4%	63%	610%
Historical simulation	−14%	−23%	−100%
Tail estimator	−14%	−18%	18%

Source: Danielsson *et al.* (1998)

A3.6   FAT TAILS AND VaR

As pointed out earlier, there is substantial empirical evidence showing that asset prices exhibit fat tails. We have also discussed the implications of this. Danielsson *et al.* (1998) show that when fat tails are not correctly accounted for in a VaR methodology, the distribution of large losses occurs with probability given by

$$P_r(R < -r) = F(-r) \approx ar^{-a} \quad \text{as } r \to \infty$$

where R is the portfolio return, r a given loss and a a parameter.

The tail probability depends on the parameter a. Thus, the smaller the tail index is, the more likely are extreme events and therefore fat tails. Danielsson *et al.* (1998) estimate the parameter a using data on oil prices and predicted that the maximum expected (one day) loss over a period of 15 years is 28%. After comparing this result with a model under the normality assumption, they find that the assumption of normality leads to substantial underestimation.

Danielsson *et al.* (1998) use the same approach as above to estimate a simulated portfolio of US stocks (under fat tails) and compare different VaR methodologies. We report in Table A3.3 the main result of that paper.

Thus, the variance–covariance method performs better at the 95% confidence interval but as the confidence interval increases its performance deteriorates. The tail estimator performs the best at the 99% confidence level. On the other hand, the variance–covariance method appears to do well only at the 95% confidence level.

A3.6.1   Generalized extreme value and the Pareto distribution

An alternative approach to approximate fat tails has been recently suggested by Bali (2007). While the typical VaR approach estimates the maximum likely loss under the assumption of 'normal market conditions', therefore using the distribution of all returns, the VaR method based on extreme value theory uses only the distribution of extreme returns.

Consider a random variable x denoting profits and losses from a distribution $F(x)$ and a sample period that we divide into subsamples. Define the extreme event of a subsample as the minimum value of the return in a given subsample. One can show that as the number of extreme observations m increases, the distribution of the extreme values converges to the generalized extreme value distribution (GEVD), given by

$$H_{\varepsilon GEVD,u,\sigma}(x) = e^{-(1+\varepsilon_{GEVD}(r-u)/\sigma)^{-1/\varepsilon_{GEVD}}} \qquad \text{if } \varepsilon_{GEVD} \neq 0$$
$$H_{\varepsilon GEVD,u,\sigma}(x) = e^{-\exp(r-u)/\sigma} \qquad \text{if } \varepsilon_{GEVD} = 0$$

where u is the unknown location parameter (which is a measure of the central tendency), σ a scale parameter (which is a measure of dispersion) and ε_{GEVD} is the shape parameter providing information about the shape of the tail.

The distribution allows for three possible cases: (1) if $\varepsilon_{GEVD} > 0$, $F(x)$ has a fat tail; (2) if $\varepsilon_{GEVD} = 0$, $F(x)$ has the same kurtosis as the normal distribution; (3) if $\varepsilon_{GEVD} < 0$, $F(x)$ is short-tailed.

The estimation of the parameters of a GEVD (i.e. u, σ, ε) is done by either maximum likelihood or probability weighted moments.

Bali (2007) shows that the methodology introduced above produces better (in-sample) performances than traditional methods under normal distribution. The one-day 1% VaR is found to be 42% greater than other approaches using normal distribution. The out-of-sample results also show that VaRs based on extreme values are more robust and precise than the ones using normal distribution.

An alternative to the methodology introduced above is to consider peaks once a given threshold is assumed. Consider again the random variable x and a threshold τ. As the threshold increases, the distribution of profits and losses will then converge to a known distribution called the 'Pareto distribution'.

Define the loss or profits that exceed the threshold by $y = x - \tau$; the Pareto distribution is given by

$$G_{\varepsilon P,\sigma}(y) = 1 - (1 + \varepsilon_P(y/\sigma))^{-1/\varepsilon_P} \qquad \text{if } \varepsilon_P \neq 0$$
$$G_{\varepsilon P,\sigma}(y) = 1 - \exp(-y/\sigma) \qquad \text{if } \varepsilon_P = 0$$

where the parameter σ is the scale parameter and ε_P is the shape parameter.

We can define three possible cases: (1) if $\varepsilon_p > 0$, the tail of the distribution decays following a power law; (2) if $\varepsilon_p = 0$, the distribution belongs to a class of medium tailed distributions (exponential, gamma, etc.); (3) if $\varepsilon_p < 0$, there is a finite right endpoint.

As already pointed out, the extreme events are defined after choosing a threshold $\tau:\{x_j : x_j > \tau\}$, for $j = 1, \ldots, M$, and sorting them in descending order $x_{(1)} \geq x_{(2)} \geq \ldots \geq x_{(M)}$ to define $y_{(j)} = x_{(j)} - \tau$.

Table A3.4   The asterisk indicates rejecting the model

Left tail probability	VaR estimate	Failure rate (1000 times)
5%	1.79	55
1%	3.15	17*
0.50%	4.01	9
0.10%	7	0
0.01%	15.2	0

This procedure is only defined for the right-hand tail of the distribution. However, one can use the absolute value of the losses if interested in the left-hand tail.

One of the most important tasks for a correct application of the above methodology is the choice of threshold. The usual way is to define a threshold via the 'mean residual life plot':

$$\bar{e}_M = \frac{1}{M} \sum_{j=1}^{M} (x_{(j)} - \tau)$$

This is the sum of values that exceeds the threshold divided by the number of observations. One can plot $\bar{e}$ on the y axis and τ on the x axis for each data set. The value of the threshold is then chosen such that $\bar{e}$ is approximately linear for $x \geq \tau$.

Once the threshold has been defined, the parameters can be estimated using maximum likelihood or probability weighted moments.

Example A3.1

We provide an example based on the Pareto distribution to the Dutch stock market index (AEX) by Goorbergh *et al.* (1999), where the optimal cut-off level is estimated to be 47. The tail index estimate using a Pareto distribution is 2.81, which implies finite first and second moments but unbounded higher moments.

Table A3.4 shows the VaR estimates for the left-hand tail of the distribution and the Kupiec back test for the null hypothesis of a normal distribution model (at the 1% significance level). As we can see, the test rejects the null hypothesis at 1%,[4] thereby showing evidence that consideration of fat tails is important.

---

[4] Note that the test has very little power at the extreme levels.

Bibliography

Aıt-Sahalia, Y.B. (2001) Goodness-of-fit tests for regression using kernel methods. *Journal of Econometrics*, **105**, 363–412.

Aris, S. (1999) *Probability Theory and Statistical Inference*, Cambridge University Press.

Ash, C. (1996) *The Probability Tutoring Book: An Intuitive Course for Engineers and Scientists (and Everyone Else!)*, John Wiley & Sons, Ltd.

Banks, E. and Siegel, P. (2007) *The Options Applications Handbook: Hedging and Speculating Techniques for Professional Investors*, John Wiley & Sons, Inc., New York.

Barone-Adesi, G., Bourgoin F. and Giannopolos, K. (1998) Don't look back. *Risk*, 100–103.

Boyle, P. (1977) Options: a Monte Carlo approach. *The Journal of Financial Economics*, **4**, 323–338.

Boyle, P., Broadie, M. and Glasserman, P. (1997) Monte Carlo methods for security pricing. *Journal of Economic Dynamics and Control*, **21**, 1267–1321.

Brace, A., Gatarek, D. and Musiela, M. (1997) The market model of interest rate dynamics. *Mathematical Finance*, **7**, 127–155.

Brandimarte, P. (2002) *Numerical Methods in Finance*, John Wiley & Sons, Inc.

Breeden, D.T. and Litzenberger, R.H. (1978) Prices of state-contingent claims implicit in option prices. *Journal of Business*, **51** (4).

Broadie, M. and Glasserman, P. (2004) A stochastic mesh method for pricing high-dimensional options. *Journal of Computational Finance*, **7**, 35–72.

Cairns, A.J.G. (2004) *Interest Rate Models – An Introduction*, Princeton University Press.

Cartea A. C. (2002) *Probability and Distribution Theory*, Birkbeck College, London.

Chourdakis, K. (2008) Financial engineering: a brief introduction using the Matlab system. Retrieved from http://love.theponytail.net/.

Crosby, J. (2011) *Lecture Notes on Interest Rates Modelling*, University of Glasgow.

Davidson, R. and MacKinnon, J.G. (1993) *Estimation and Inference in Econometrics*, Oxford University Press, Oxford.

Glasserman, P., Heidelberger, P. and Shahabuddin, P. (1999) Asymptotically optimal importance sampling and stratification for pricing path dependent options. *Mathematical Finance*, **9**, 117–152.

Haug, E.G. (2007) Option pricing and hedging from theory to practice, in *Derivatives: Models on Models*, John Wiley & Sons, Ltd.

Haugh, M. and Kogan, L. (2004) Pricing American options: a duality approach. *Operations Research*, **52**, 258–270.

Houcque, D. (2005) *Introduction to MatLab for Engineering Students*, Northwestern University. Mimeo.

Hull, C.J. (1997) *Options, Futures, and Other Derivatives*, Prentice-Hall, New Jersey.

Hull, C.J. (2009) *Options, Futures, and Other Derivatives*, 7th edition, Pearson Education International.

James, J. and Webber, N. (2000) *Interest Rate Modelling*, Wiley Finance, John Wiley & Sons, Ltd.

Kac, M. (1949) On distribution of certain Wiener functionals. *Transactions of the American Mathematical Society*, **65**, 1–13.

Kemna, A.G.Z. and Vorst, A.C.F. (1990) A pricing method for options based on average asset values. *Journal of Banking and Finance*, **14**, 113–129.

Kerk, K. and Patrick, C. (1998) *Data Analysis with Microsoft Excel*, Brooks/Cole Publishing Company, US.

Kyprianou, A.E., Schoutens, W. and Wilmott, P. (2005) *Exotic Option Pricing and Advanced Levy Models*, John Wiley & Sons, Inc., Hoboken, New Jersey.

Marshall, C. and Siegel, M. (1996) *Value at Risk: Implementing a Risk Measurement Standard*, Working Paper, Harvard Business School.

Rebonato, R. (2002) *Modern Pricing of Interest-Rate Derivatives*, Princeton University Press.

Stanton, R. and Wallace, N. (1998) Mortgage choice: what's the point? *Real Estate Economics*, **26**, 173–205.

Wilmott, P. (2006) *On Quantitative Finance*, 2nd edition, John Wiley & Sons, Ltd.

Zangari, P. (1996) How accurate is the delta–gamma methodology? *Risk Metrics Monitor*, Third Quarter 1996, 12-29.43.

References

Alexander, C. and Nogueira, L.M. (2007) Model-free hedge ratios and scale-invariant models. *Journal of Banking and Finance*, **31** (6), June, 1839–1861.

Andersen, L. and Andreasen, J. (2001) Factor dependence of Bermudan swaptions: fact or fiction? *Journal of Financial Economics*, **62**, 3–37.

Bali, T.G. (2007) A generalized extreme value approach to financial risk measurement. *Journal of Money Credit and Banking*, **39**, 1613–1649.

Barone-Adesi, G. and Whaley, R.E. (1987) Efficient analytic approximation of American option values. *The Journal of Finance*, **42**, 301–320.

Black, F. and Scholes, M. (1973) The pricing of options and corporate liabilities. *Journal of Political Economy*, **81** (3), 637–654.

Boudoukh, J., Richardson, M. and Whitelaw, R. (1998) The best of both worlds. *Risk*, May, 64–67.

Brandimarte, P. (2006) *Numerical Methods in Finance*, 2nd edition, John Wiley & Sons, Inc.

Brigo, D. and Mercurio, F. (2001) *Interest Rate Models – Theory and Practice with Smile, Inflation and Credit*, 2nd edition, 2006, Springer-Verlag.

Broadie, M. and Glasserman, P. (1996) Estimating security price derivatives using simulation. *Management Science*, **42**, 269–285.

Broadie, M. and Glasserman, P. (1997) *A Stochastic Mesh Method for Pricing High Dimensional American Options*, Columbia University, Working Paper.

Broadie, M. and Kaya, O. (2004) Exact simulation of options Greeks under stochastic volatility and jump diffusion models, in *Proceedings of the 2004 Winter Simulation Conference,* The Society for Computer Simulation, pp. 1607–1615.

Broadie, M., Detemple, J., Ghysels, E. and Torres, O. (2000) Nonparametric estimation of American option exercise boundaries and call price. *Journal of Economic Dynamics and Control*, **24**, 1829–1857.

Brown, D. (1999) The determinants of expected returns on mortgage-backed securities: an empirical analysis of option-adjusted spreads. *Journal of Fixed Income*, **9**, 8–18.

Carr, P. and Chou, A. (1997) Breaking barriers. *Risk*, 139–145.

Cerrato, M. (2008) *Valuing American Style Derivatives by Least Squares Methods*, Department of Economics, Glasgow University, Discussion Paper Series in Economics.

Cerrato, M. (2009) *Valuing American Derivatives by Least Squares Methods*, Department of Economics, University of Glasgow, Discussion Paper 2008-12.

Cerrato, M. and Abbasyan, A. (2009) *Optimal Martingales and American Option Pricing*, Department of Economics, University of Glasgow, Discussion Paper 2009-27, Working Paper Series.

Chen, J. (2004) Simulation based pricing of mortgage backed securities, in *Proceedings of the 2004 Winter Simulation Conference*.

Chen, N. and Glasserman, P. (2007) Additive and Multiplicative Duals for American Option Pricing. *Finance and Stochastics*, **11**, 153–179.

Christoffersen, P.A. (2004) The importance of the loss function in option valuation. *Journal of Financial Economics*, **72**, 291–318.

Clement, E., Lamberton, D. and Protter, P. (2002) An analysis of a least squares regression method for American option pricing. *Finance Stochastics*, **6**, 449–471.

Crépey, S. (2003) Calibration of the local volatility in a generalized Black–Scholes model using Tikhonov regularization. *SIAM Journal on Mathematical Analysis*, **34**(5), 1183–1206.

Coleman, T., Kim, Y., Li, Y. and Verma, A. (2003) *Dynamic Hedging in a Volatile Market*, Cornell University, Technical Report.

Cox, J.S., Ross, A. and Rubinstein, M. (1979) Option pricing: a simplified approach. *Journal of Financial Economics*, **7**, 229–263.

Cox, J.C., Ingersoll, J.E. and Ross, S.A. (1985) A theory of the term structure of interest rates. *Econometrica*, **53**, 385–407. DOI:10.2307/1911242.

Danielsson, J., Hartmann, P. and de Vries, G.C. (1998) *The Cost of Conservatism: Extreme Returns, Value at Risk, and the Basle Multiplication Factor*, LSE Financial Markets Group Special Paper Series.

Davidson, R. and MacKinnon, G. (2001) *Bootstrap Tests: How Many Bootstraps?*, Department of Economics, Queen's University, Working Paper 1036.

Davis, M. (2007) *Lecture Notes*, Imperial College, London.

Derman, E. and Kani, I. (1994) Riding on a smile, *Risk*, **7** (2).

Derman, E. and Kani, I. (1998) Stochastic implied trees: arbitrage pricing with stochastic term and strike structure of volatility. *International Journal of Theoretical and Applied Finance*, **1**, 61–110.

Dumas, B.F. (1998). Implied volatility functions: empirical tests. *Journal of Finance*, (53), 2059–2106.

Dunn, K.B. and Spatt, C.S. (1986) *The Effect of Refinancing Costs and Market Imperfections on the Optimal Call Strategy and the Pricing of Debt Contracts*, Carnegie-Mellon University, Working Paper.

Dupire, B. (1994) Pricing with a smile. *Risk*, January, 18–20.

Elliot, R.J. and Kopp, P.E. (1999) *Mathematics of Financial Markets*, Springer, New York.

Etheridge, A. (2002) *A Course in Financial Calculus*, Cambridge University Press.

Feller, W. (1951) Diffusion processes in genetics, in *Berkeley Symposium on Mathematics, Statistics and Probability*, pp. 227–246.

Fengler, M. R. (2005) *Semiparametric Modeling of Implied Volatility*, Springer Finance.

Gabaix, X., Arvind, K. and Vigneron, O. (2007) Limits of arbitrage: theory and evidence from the mortgage backed securities market. *Journal of Finance*, **62**, 557–595.

Gatheral, J. (2006). *The Volatility Surface: A Practitioner's Guide*, John Wiley & Sons, Ltd.

Geman, H. and Yor, M. (1992). Quelques relations entre processus de Bessel, options Asiatiques, et fonctions confluences hypergeometriques. *Comptes Rendus de l'Académie des Sciences de Paris*, Série I, 471–474.

Geman, H. and Yor, M. (1993) Bessel processes, Asian options, and perpetuities. *Mathematical Finance*, **3**, 349–375.

Glasserman, P. (2003) *Monte Carlo Methods in Financial Engineering*, Springer-Verlag, New York.

Glasserman, P. (2004) *Monte Carlo Methods in Financial Engineering*, Springer.

Glasserman, P. and Staum, J. (2001) Conditioning on one-step survival for barrier option simulations. *Operations Research*, **49**, 923–937.

Glasserman, P. and Yu, B. (2004a) Number of paths versus number of basis functions in American option pricing. *Annals of Applied Probability*, **14**, 2090–2119.

Glasserman, P. and Yu, B. (2004b) Simulation for American options: regression now or regression later?, in *Monte Carlo and Quasi Monti Carlo Methods* (ed. H. Niederreiter).

Goorbergh, R.V.d. and Peter, V. (1999) *Value at Risk Analysis of Stock Returns – Historical Simulation, Variance Techniques or Tail Index Estimation?*, Econometric Research and Special Studies Department, De Nederlandsche Bank.

Gyongy, I. (1986) Mimicking the one-dimensional marginal distributions of processes having an Ito differential. *Probability Theory and Related Fields*, **71**, 501–516.

Heath, D., Jarrow, R.A. and Morton, A. (1992) Bond pricing and the term structure of interest rates: a new methodology for contingent claims valuation. *Econometrica*, **60**(1), 77–105.

Heston, S. (1993) A closed-form solution for options with stochastic volatility with applications to bond and currency options. *Review of Financial Studies*, **6**, 327–343.

Hull, J.C. and White, A. (1987) The pricing of options on assets with stochastic volatilities. *Journal of Finance*, **42**, 281–300.

Hull, J. and White, A. (1990) Pricing interest rate derivative securities. *Review of Financial Studies*, **3** (4), 573–592.

Hull, J. and White, A. (1993) One factor interest rate models and the valuation of interest rate derivative securities. *Journal of Financial and Quantitative Analysis*, (28), 235–254.

Jackson, N., Süli, E. and Howison, S. (1998) Computation of deterministic volatility surfaces. *Journal of Computational Finance*, **2** (2), 5–32.

Jamshidian, F. (2003) *Minimax Optimality and Bermudan and American Claims and Their Monto Carlo Upper Bounds Approximation*, NIB Capital.

Jarrow, R. and Rudd, A. (1983) *Option Pricing*, Homewood, Illinois, pp. 183–188.

Jordan, J.V. and Mackay, R.J. (1996) *Assessing Value at Risk for Equity Portfolios: Implementing Alternative Techniques*, Center for Study of Futures and Options Markets, Pamplin College of Business, Virginia Polytechnic, Mimeo.

Kairys, J.P. and Valerio, N. (1997) The market for equity options in the 1870s. *Journal of Finance*, **52**, 1707–1723.

Kemna, A.G.Z. and Vorst, A.C.F. (1990) A pricing method for options based on average asset values. *Journal of Banking and Finance*, **14**, 113–129.

Lagnado, R. and Osher, S. (1997) A technique for calibrating derivative security pricing models: numerical solution of an inverse problem. *Journal of Computational Finance*, **1** (1), 13–25.

Liu, J.G. and Xu, E. (1998) Pricing of mortgage backed securities with option adjusted spread. *Managerial Finance*, **24** (9/10).

Longstaff, F. (2004) *Borrower Credit and the Valuation of Mortgage Backed Securities*, UCLA Anderson School, Working Papers in Finance.

Longstaff, F.A. and Schwartz, E.S. (2001) Valuing American options by simulation: a simple least-squares approach. *Review of Financial Studies*, **14** (1), 113–147.

Lord, R., Koekkoek, R. and van Dijk, R. (2008) A comparison of biased simulation schemes for stochastic volatility models. *Journal of Quantitative Finance*, **12**, 34–48.

Mahoney, J.M. (1996) *Forecast Biases in Value-at-Risk Estimations: Evidence from Foreign Exchange and Global Equity Portfolios*, Federal Reserve Bank of New York, Working Paper.

Merton, R.C. (1976) Option pricing when the underlying stock returns are discontinuous. *Journal of Financial Economics*, **4** (125), 144.

Nielsen, L.T. (1999) *Pricing and Hedging of Derivative Securities*, Oxford University Press.

Rebonato, R. (1998) *Interest-Rate Options Models*, Financial Engineering, John Wiley & Sons, Ltd.

Ren, Y., Madan, D. and Qian, M. (2007) Calibrating and pricing with embedded local volatility models, *Risk Magazine*, September.

Rogers, C.L. (2002) Monte Carlo valuation of American options. *Mathematical Finance*, **12**, 271–286.

Rogers, L.C.G. and Williams, D. (2000) *Diffusion, Markov Processes and Martingales*, volumes 1 and 2, Cambridge University Press.

Rubinstein, M. (1994) Implied binomial trees. *The Journal of Finance*, **49** (3), 771–818.

Schwartz, E.S. and Torous, W.N. (1992) Prepayment, default, and the valuation of mortgage pass-through securities. *Journal of Business*, **65**, 221–239.

Stentoft, L. (2004) Assessing the least squares Monte Carlo approach to American options valuation. *Review of Derivatives Research*, **7**, 129–168.

Taleb, E.G. (2011) Option traders use (very) sophisticated heuristics, never the Black–Scholes–Merton formula. *Journal of Economic Behavior and Organization*, **77** (2).

Vasicek, O. (1977) An equilibrium characterisation of the term structure. *Journal of Financial Economics*, **5** (2), 177–188. DOI:10.1016/0304-405X(77)90016-2.

Index

Index compiled by Terry Halliday